If you wish to learn from the theoretical physicist anything about the methods which he uses, I would give you the following piece of advice: Don't listen to his words, examine his achievements. For to the discoverer in that field, the constructions of his imagination appear so necessary and so natural that he is apt to treat them not as the creations of his thoughts but as given realities.

ALBERT EINSTEIN

by Jay Haley (as author, co-author, editor)

STRATEGIES OF PSYCHOTHERAPY: Second Edition

FAMILY THERAPY AND RESEARCH; A BIBLIOGRAPHY

ADVANCED TECHNIQUES OF HYPNOSIS AND THERAPY; SELECTED PAPERS OF MILTON H. ERICKSON, M.D.

TECHNIQUES OF FAMILY THERAPY

CHANGING FAMILIES: A FAMILY THERAPY READER

UNCOMMON THERAPY: THE PSYCHIATRIC TECHNIQUES OF MILTON H. ERICKSON, M.D.

PROBLEM SOLVING THERAPY: Second Edition

LEAVING HOME

REFLECTIONS ON THERAPY, AND OTHER ESSAYS

CONVERSATIONS WITH MILTON H. ERICKSON, M.D.
Volume 1 CHANGING INDIVIDUALS
Volume 2 CHANGING COUPLES
Volume 3 CHANGING CHILDREN AND FAMILIES

THE FIRST THERAPY SESSION: Audio Program

STRATEGIES OF

PSYCHOTHERAPY

BY

JAY HALEY

THE TRIANGLE PRESS
ROCKVILLE, Md.

ISBN   0-931513-06-5

Manufactured in the United States of America

Published by Triangle Press

Distributed by W. W. Norton & Co., Inc.
500 Fifth Avenue
New York, N. Y. 10110

W.W, Norton & Co., Ltd.
37 Great Russell Street
London, WC1B3NU

Originally published, 1963, by
Grune & Stratton, Inc.
111 Fifth Avenue
New York, New York 10003
Library of Congress Catalog Number 63-16660

CONTENTS

PREFACE TO SECOND EDITION

This book introduced a communication point of view into the field of psychotherapy. It was the product of 10 years work on Gregory Bateson's project on communication, sometimes called the double bind project (1). We studied a variety of kinds of psychotherapy, explored a strategic approach to therapy, and innovated family therapy. This work represents a step from the study of therapy in terms of the individual to therapy as communication between at least two people. Symptoms and other psychological problems are seen as having a function in a relationship. Therapeutic change is defined as a shift in relationship between people. This view proposes that symptoms are not irrational and inappropriate behavior caused by the past. They have a current function and are adaptive behavior to the present social situation. Therefore the social situation needs to be changed if a person is to change. The reactions to this different view continue to be controversial in the therapy field.

For this edition I decided not to change the text by expanding upon it or correcting it. This is a description of therapy from a dyadic point of view, and I have little to add to that way of conceptulizing problems and change. Since then I have described therapy in terms of a triadic unit, which requires a different language of description (2). As I considered whether to add to the text, I was surprised how little I wanted to change. Psychoanalysis was more important at that time than it is today, so I would emphasize that less now, as well as the theory of repression on which psychodynamic theory is based. That is one reason why I am dropping the Epilogue which consists of "The Art of Psychoanalysis." That seems out of date to me now, and the article is available in *THE POWER TACTICS OF JESUS CHRIST* (3) I might expand the section on Milton H. Erickson, but I have described his work at length in *UNCOMMON THERAPY* (4), *ORDEAL THERAPY* (5) ,and in three volumes of conversations with him (5). At the time of this book he was hardly known, and today he has a large following and is the guru of a major approach to therapy.

With a shift to a communication view of therapy rather than a focus on the individual, it was necessary to propose a new theory of motivation. The beginnings of such a theory were proposed here with the idea that people seek to make their worlds more predictable. They stabilize the situations they are in. A symptom not only helps a woman control her husband, but it is also a "method of protecting him from facing his own problems and the other difficulties in their marriage." (pg. 15). This is another way of saying a symptom stabilizes a family, even if it is an unpleasant stability. This positive view of symptoms is related to the positive view recommended for therapists in this work. Rather than assume that a person's motivation is based on inner hostility and conflict, it is better to find the positive aspects of the person and emphasize solutions rather than problems. If one hypothesizes a positive view of an adolescent, such as assuming he is protecting and stabilizing the family, a therapist can more easily join the adolescent and work with him or her toward common goals. Communciation theory leads one toward these kinds of hypotheses.

One change evident since this book was written is the change on the therapy of schizophrenia. At that time a variety of people specialized in therapy with psychotics. Today there is little or no therapy done with this most interesting of all psychological problems. On the possibility that there might be a biological cause of schizophrenia, and evidence for that has been promised for at least a century, the psychiatric world now confines itself to medication and not to therapy. Unfortunately the anti-psychotic medications often do neurological harm. If such medications were abandoned, the current generation of psychiatric residents, and other clinicians as well, would not know how to do talk therapy with these difficult people and their families.

There is another change which developed since this work. A high percentage of therapy cases are now compulsory therapy. This is particularly true of sex abuse, physical abuse and substance abuse cases. The client comes to therapy because the court systems says the choice is that or jail. Although we have had experience with compulsory therapy, such as giving psychotics therapy whether they wished it or not, that has been unusual. At times a spouse or an adolescent has been dragged into therapy. but it was always assumed that therapy is a contract between a person wanting help and a person offering it. Now it is apparent that compulsory therapy is a problem for both client and therapist. The client does not choose to be there, and the therapist does not want to treat someone who does not want to be there. The different schools of therapy were based upon the idea that the therapy was voluntary and the person had an involuntary symptom. Today the therapist is rather like an agent of the state rather than of an individual or a family.

It is a pleasure to look over a book I wrote years ago and be pleased with it. That means either one's judgement is clouded or it is a good book. Prefering to believe the latter, I have not changed the text.

---

(1) Haley, Jay, "Development of a Theory: A History of a Research Project.," in Sluzki, C. (Ed), THE DOUBLE BIND, New York, Norton, 1976
(2) Haley, Jay, PROBLEM SOLVING THERAPY, Second Edition, San Francisco, Jossey-Bass, 1987.
(3) Haley, Jay, THE POWER TACTICS OF JESUS CHRIST, Second Edition, Rockville, Triangle Press, 1986.
(4) Haley, Jay, UNCOMMON THERAPY, New York, W.W, Norton, 1973.
(5) Haley, Jay, ORDEAL THERAPY, San Francisco, Jossey-Bass, 1984.

Preface

THIS IS a book about the strategies of psychotherapists and patients as they maneuver each other in the process of treatment. How a therapist induces a patient to change, and why the patient changes, is described within a framework of interpersonal theory. A variety of methods of psychotherapy are described with the general argument that the cause of psychotherapeutic change resides in the therapeutic paradoxes these methods have in common. Such diverse forms of therapy as psychoanalysis, directive therapy and family therapy appear different when viewed in terms of individual psychology, but the methods can be shown to be formally similar if one examines the peculiar types of relationship established between patients and therapists.

Since this approach focusses upon the relationship between two or more people rather than upon the single individual, the emphasis is upon communicative behavior. When human beings are described in terms of levels of communication, psychiatric problems and their resolution appear in a new perspective.

Much of this book was written while the author was a member of a research project exploring the nature of communication. Beginning in 1952 when Gregory Bateson received a grant from the Rockefeller Foundation to investigate communication from the point of view of Russell and Whitehead's logical types,[57] the project terminated in 1962. Data of various types were used in the research: Hypnosis, ventriloquism, animal training, popular moving pictures, the nature of play, humor, schizophrenia, neurotic communication, psychotherapy, family systems, and family therapy. The emphasis in the research was upon the ways messages qualify, or classify, one another in such a way that paradox of the Russellian type is generated. One aspect of paradox was the concept of the "double-bind" which was applied by the group in 1956 to the etiology of schizophrenia.[5] The research project was directed by Gregory Bateson and, besides the author, the staff consisted of John H. Weakland, Research Associate, Don D. Jackson, M.D., psychiatric consultant, and William F. Fry, M.D., psychiatric consultant. The bibliography at the end of this work contains a list of the publications by staff members on psychotherapy as well as references to articles mentioned in the text. (For a complete bibliography of the research group cf. Ref.[6]) During the years the research was supported by grants from the Rockefeller Foundation, the Macy Foundation, the Foundations Fund for Research in

Psychiatry, and the National Institute of Mental Health. These grants were administered by the Department of Anthropology of Stanford University and by the Palo Alto Medical Research Foundation. Office space and other facilities were provided by the Veterans Administration Hospital in Palo Alto, California.

This book is the result of the author's investigation of methods of psychotherapy from the point of view of the paradoxes posed by psychotherapists, an approach of continuing interest to him since he first presented a paper on paradox and psychotherapy in 1954.[29] The ideas presented in this work are a product of the general theoretical approach of the research group and the particular bias of the author, who assumes responsibility for them as presented here. They were developed in ongoing association with the research staff, and grateful acknowledgement is made to the other staff members for their contributions during the many discussions and debates over the decade of collaboration. The general psychiatric approach to the ways people deal with one another in interpersonal relationships was greatly influenced by Dr. Don D. Jackson, who functioned as supervisor of the therapy of the group. During the years many visitors and consultants also exerted their influence. Alan Watts, in particular, was a source of ideas about paradox. The author is especially indebted to Dr. Milton H. Erickson for many hours of conversation and a new perspective on the nature of psychotherapy.

Parts of this work, in different form, appeared in articles in various professional journals, and thanks for permission to republish portions of the articles are given to: *The American Journal of Clinical Hypnosis, Archives of General Psychiatry, Etc., Family Process, Psychiatry,* and *Progress in Psychotherapy, IV,* Grune & Stratton, 1959.

To
Gregory Bateson

CHAPTER 1

Symptoms as Tactics in Human Relationships

THERE HAVE always been persons in the world who wanted to change their ways of life, their feelings, and their thinking, and other persons willing to change them. In the Eastern world the change was brought about within the framework of a religious experience.[54] In the West, a shift has taken place. Change was once the province of religion, but now religious leaders go to schools of secular specialists to learn how to change their parishioners. The rise of specialists whose profession it is to change people has led to more scientific interest in methods and theories of change.

Western theological explanations of why a person changed a distressing way of life rested on the premise that change took place because of a shift in the person's relationship with a deity. A religious leader often acted as an agent in this process. With the shift to secular therapy, an assumption developed, coincident with ideas of the rational man, that the individual changes when he gains greater understanding of himself. A therapist was considered the agent who brought about that self-awareness, and it was thought that someone who wanted to change could be taught he was arranging his life badly and he would correct himself.

After Sigmund Freud, man was looked upon as a far less rational being, but it was still thought that he could change through self-understanding. Freud accepted the idea that self-awareness causes change, but he added the idea that the distressed individual must become aware of how his present ways of thinking and perceiving are related to his past and to his unconscious ideas. In Freudian theory the therapist was still seen only as an agent who provided a situation to help bring about self-understanding, and it was assumed that when the individual had a "deeper" understanding of himself he could and would undergo change. Later in psychiatry there was a major theoretical shift when the emphasis began to be placed upon the ways the individual relates to other people rather than upon his internal processes. Yet, even though psychiatric problems were seen as more interpersonal in nature, the premise that change was caused by increased self-awareness continued to be accepted. As Sullivan stated, "The principal problem of the therapeutic interview is that of facilitating the accession to awareness of information which will clarify for the patient the more troublesome aspects of his life."[51]

The argument that self-understanding causes change is essentially irrefutable if one wishes to make it so. One can always say that if a person has changed without self-understanding he has not *really* changed, and if a person does not change despite massive amounts of self-understanding one can still say that he has not yet sufficient self-understanding. However, the nature and cause of psychiatric change is of such importance that any and all premises related to it should be rigorously examined without taking for granted ideas which have not or cannot be proved.

Because of the proliferation of different methods of psychotherapy in recent years, many of them not emphasizing self-awareness or a religious experience, we should open wide the question of the cause of therapeutic change. It is possible that change does not occur because of religious conversion or greater self-awareness but because of the procedures by which that conversion and self-awareness are brought about.

A scientific approach to the causes of therapeutic change would involve examining and describing the various contexts which bring about change to discover what they have in common. Experimental methods could then be created to test the hypotheses developed. However, such an investigation requires a rigorous way of describing the interchange between a person who wishes to change and a person who wishes to change him. At this time we lack terminology for such a description, and we lack a model to use as a framework for that terminology. The most we can hope to do is to place a small theoretical wedge into an extraordinarily complex problem. The various methods of psychotherapy described in this book are not presented in full and complete description. Only certain aspects of the interchange between therapist and patient are focussed upon, and no attempt is made to be comprehensive. The broader social context which brought therapist and patient together, and the exploration of subjective processes in the patient, are excluded along with many facets of the therapy situation. The focus is upon the tactics of patient and therapist as they maneuver each other.

It is always an oversimplification to describe psychiatric symptoms as if they could be isolated from the general problems of society. The ills of the individual are not really separable from the ills of the social context he creates and inhabits, and one cannot with good conscience pull out the individual from his cultural milieu and label him as sick or well. Yet despite the misery of many people there seems to be a group of people who have what could be called specific psychiatric symptoms and who seek psychotherapy.

It is becoming more clear that Sigmund Freud developed psychoanalysis as a method of dealing with a specific *class* of people. He was faced with the general inability of the medicine men of his day to relieve that type of person who went from doctor to doctor and consistently failed to undergo a change. At that time there was no systematic method for dealing with this class of difficult people, and Freud developed one. Since then, methods of psychotherapy have bred and fostered until it is an accepted idea that one should sit down and have a conversation with a person who has psychiatric symptoms. Although the benefits of drugs, shock treatment, and brain operations are also applauded, the idea that an individual can undergo major changes as the result of a conversation is generally accepted.

It may seem reasonable now to talk to a patient with psychiatric symptoms, but there is not yet general agreement on what to talk about. In fact, there is not general agreement on what a psychiatric symptom is and, therefore, what a therapist is attempting to change. One therapist may argue that he is attempting to change the philosophic ideology of a patient, and another may argue that he wishes to change the way the patient deals with his wife. A therapist's goal may be to relieve anxiety, or to help a patient succeed in life, or to help a patient become happy, or to adjust the patient to his environment, or to liberate his repressed ideas, or to help him accept his weaknesses, and so on. Inevitably the point of view on what procedure to take with a patient will depend upon one's theory of what there is about the patient that needs to be changed.

Since this book deals with one rather narrow aspect of psychotherapy, psychiatric problems will be conceived from a narrow viewpoint. Particular emphasis will be placed upon what are generally agreed as symptoms, although these symptoms will be seen from a communication rather than an intrapsychic point of view.

In recent years there has been a shift in psychiatry and psychology from an emphasis upon the processes within an individual to an emphasis upon his relationships with other people. It is only when the focus is upon behavior within a relationship that psychotherapy becomes describable, because by definition psychotherapy is a procedure which occurs in a relationship. Yet there is inevitably a lag in both terminology and concepts, and most attempts to describe psychotherapy today are in a language designed to describe the individual person.

Here is a list of common ideas and concepts in psychiatry:

Anxiety	Emotions	Introjection	Repression
Awareness	Fantasy	Learning	Role
Compulsion	Fear	Needs	Suppression
Consciousness	Frustration	Orality	Thoughts
Consolidation	Halucinations	Oedipal Conflict	Transference
Delusions	Ideas	Perception	Trauma
Depression	Insight	Phobias	Unconscious
Drives	Integration	Projection	
Ego	Intelligence	Regression	

If one could imagine the individual confined within his skin, all this terminology describes what is assumed to be going on inside that skin. As a result, the language is inappropriate for describing the behavior of a psychotherapist and patient responding to each other. More important, the transactions between therapist and patient cannot be conceptualized with the theoretical models which are the basis for these terms. Yet at this time there is no adequate substitute for the usual psychiatric concepts. The analogies and terms necessary to describe different ongoing relationships are only beginning to be born. The first major step in this direction was taken by Sullivan who struggled to describe relationships between people with the concepts and theories which had been developed for individual description.[51] Others have continued in this attempt, but it would appear now that human relationships will only be adequately described if the individual-centered ideas are largely discarded. The ultimate description of relationships will be in terms of patterns of communication in a theory of circular systems. A move in that direction will be taken in this book.

A particular merit in examining psychotherapy in terms of behavior rather than intrapsychic processes resides in the fact that interior processes must be inferred. Not one of the psychiatric descriptive terms listed represents something observable; all are inferences drawn from observation of behavior. One cannot observe anxiety, any more than one can observe an ego or the process of learning. The difficulty in creating a more precise system of diagnosis has always been the inferential nature of the terms. A psychiatrist may report that a patient is delusional, is hallucinating, has a compulsion, is disordered in his thinking, and so on, but all of these descriptive terms are of processes which can only be assumed. Only recently have psychiatrists begun to include themselves in their description of a patient. Obviously they base their diagnosis upon how the patient responds to them, yet the report they write will only include inferred processes within the patient. A relevant question is always one like this: What was the psychiatrist doing when the patient behaved in such a way that the psychiatrist inferred he was delusional?

Again, however, there is no adequate terminology available if a psychiatrist wishes to describe his interactive behavior with a patient. He must be anecdotal for lack of a rigorous description of communicative behavior. Yet a slight change in viewpoint can produce profound theoretical differences. To define a symptom as a defense against an idea was once common. With the emphasis upon interpersonal relationships it is now becoming common to define a symptom as a way of dealing with another person. These different definitions actually represent a discontinuous change in the history of psychiatry. With the step from the individual to the two person system, most previous terminology and theory must go by the board. For example, one might consider anxious behavior by a patient as a way he defends himself against repressed ideas which are threatening to intrude into consciousness. One could also observe that same patient and notice that his anxious behavior occurs in an interpersonal context and so describe that behavior as a way of dealing with, perhaps of disarming, another person. These two points of views represent astonishingly different theoretical systems.

When one shifts to the study of the two person system, he is entering the field of communication and must describe the individual in terms which apply to the exchange of communicative behavior between two or more people. From the communication point of view, there are two types of phenomena which must be present for a psychiatric symptom to be a proper symptom; the patient's behavior must be extreme in its influence on someone else and he must indicate in some way that he cannot help behaving as he does. The extreme behavior does not have to be a particular type as long as it is extreme and therefore out of the ordinary. Usually symptoms fall into classes of opposites; for every symptom at one extreme there is a comparable one at another. Those people who cannot touch a doorknob and are called phobic are comparable to those people who must touch a doorknob six times before turning it and are classed as compulsive. Some people cannot leave the house, others cannot stay home but must constantly rush out. Some people cannot take a bath, others cannot stop bathing. Those who cannot touch a drink or have a sexual dalliance are at the opposite extreme of those who cannot stop drinking or dallying with whoever comes along. While many people lose their voices, others cannot stop talking, and there are those who starve themselves and those who gorge beyond the point of assimilation. Some people are incapacitated because they cannot move a limb, and others are similarly incapacitated because they cannot stop a limb from trembling. Some avoid all pills and surgery, others constantly seek pills and the surgeon's knife. The specific symptom is less relevant than the formal patterns patients have in common.

From the communication point of view, symptomatic behavior represents an incongruence between one level of message and a metacommunicative level. The patient does something extreme, or avoids doing something, and indicates that *he* is not doing it because he cannot help himself. More severe problems require a description in terms of many levels, and this will be discussed later under schizophrenia. But most neurotic symptoms represent some type of extreme behavior which is qualified with an indication that the person cannot help it.

Granted that neurotic symptoms can be seen as an incongruence of this type, the tactics of psychotherapy become potentially describable. This is a major purpose in making such a description. The most useful classification of psychiatric problems would be one which explains how a symptom is perpetuated and how change can be produced.

It will be argued here that a patient's symptoms are perpetuated by the way he himself behaves and by the influence of other people intimately involved with him. It follows that psychotherapeutic tactics should be designed to persuade the individual to change his behavior and/or persuade his intimates to change their behavior in relation to him. Insofar as the therapist is an intimate of the patient, both goals can be achieved simultaneously. This book will deal with techniques for influencing the individual to change, and also with techniques for influencing the family system to change so that the individuals within it influence each other differently.

DEFINING A RELATIONSHIP

To say that a person with a symptom is behaving in a way that is out of the ordinary implies that there is an ordinary way to behave. To discuss such a proposition thoroughly would require an analysis of a particular culture and the range of individual deviation permissible within that culture before a person is considered out of the ordinary. Rather than approach the problem in that way, the discussion here will assume the individuals described are within the culture of Western ideology and emphasize a few abstract and formal patterns of behavior. The extreme behavior of a person with symptoms will be contrasted with what is generally considered ordinary behavior in a relationship. This approach requires a general description of the ways people ordinarily form and maintain relationships and a few terms for differentiating different types of relationship.

When any two people meet for the first time and begin to establish a relationship, a wide range of behavior is potentially possible between them. They might exchange compliments or insults or sexual advances or statements that one is superior to the other, and so on. As the two people define their relationship with each other, they work out together what type of communicative behavior is to take place in this relationship. From all the possible messages they select certain kinds and reach agreement that these shall be included. This line they draw which separates what is and what is not to take place in this relationship can be called a mutual definition of the relationship. Every message they interchange by its very existence either reinforces this line or suggests a shift in it to include a new kind of message. In this way the relationship is mutually defined by the presence or absence of messages interchanged between the two people. If a young man places his arm around a girl, he is indicating that amorous behavior is to be included in their relationship. If the girl says, "No, no," and withdraws from him, she is indicating that amorous behavior is to be excluded from the relationship. What kind of relationship they have together, whether amorous or platonic, is defined by what kind of messages they mutually agree shall be acceptable between them. This agreement is never permanently worked out but is constantly in process as one or the other proposes a new kind of message or as the environmental situation changes and provokes changes in their behavior.

If human communication took place at only one level, the working out, or defining, of a relationship would be a simple matter of the presence or absence of messages. In that case there would probably be no difficulties in interpersonal relationships. However, human beings not only communicate, but they communicate about that communication. They not only say something, but they qualify or label what they say. In the example given the young lady says "No, no," and she also withdraws from the young man. Her physical withdrawal qualifies, and is qualified by her verbal statement. Since the qualification of her message affirms the message there is no particular difficulty in this example. She is making it clear that amorous behavior does not belong in their relationship. But suppose she had said, "No, no," and moved closer to the young man. By snuggling up to him she would have qualified incongruently, or denied, her statement, "No, no." When one observes a message qualified incongruently, then a more complex situation becomes apparent than is involved in the simple presence or absence of a message in a relationship.

Any message interchanged between two people does not exist separately from the other messages which accompany and comment upon it. If one says, "I'm glad to see you," his tone of voice qualifies that verbal statement and is qualified by it in turn. Human messages are qualified by (a) the context in which they take place, (b) verbal messages, (c) vocal and linguistic patterns, and (d) bodily movement. A person may make a criticism with a smile or he may make a criticism with a frown. The presence or absence of the smile or frown as much as the presence or absence of the criticism defines the relationship between the two people. An employee may tell his boss what to do, thus defining their relationship as one between equals, but he may qualify his statement with a "self effacing" gesture or a "weak" tone of voice and thereby indicate that he is secondary in their relationship and not an equal. When messages qualify each other incongruently, then incongruent statements are being made about the relationship. If people always qualified what they said in a congruent way, relationships would be defined clearly and simply even though many levels of communication were functioning. However, when a statement is made which by its existence indicates one type of relationship and is qualified by a statement denying this, then difficulties in interpersonal relationships become inevitable.

It is important to emphasize that one cannot *fail* to qualify a message. A person must speak his verbal message in a tone of voice, and even if he does not speak he must present a posture or appear in a context which qualifies his muteness. Although some qualifying messages are obvious, like pounding one's fists on the table when making a statement, subtle qualifications are always present. For example, the slightest upward inflection on a word may define a statement as a question rather than an assertion. A slight smile may classify a statement as ironical rather than serious. A minute body movement backwards qualifies an affectionate statement and indicates it is made with some reservations. The absence of a message may also qualify another message. A hesitation or a pause can qualify a statement and make it a different one than it would be without that pause. In the same way, if a person is silent in a context where he is expected to speak, this silence becomes a qualifying message. The absence of a movement may function in the same way. If a man neglects to kiss his wife goodbye when she expects it, the absence of this movement qualifies his other messages as much, if not more, than the presence of it.

When a message classifies or qualifies another message, it may be congruent and affirm that message, or incongruent and negate it. One can say, "I'm glad to see you," in a tone of voice which indicates that one is really glad to see the person. Or one can make the statement in a tone of voice which indicates he wishes the person were on the other side of the moon. When we deal with people we tend to judge whether they are being sincere or deceitful, whether or not they are serious or joking, and so on, by how they qualify what they say. We also judge what kind of statement they are making about the relationship not only by what they say but by the ways they say it. When we respond with our own definition of the relationship, the response is to the person's multiple levels of message.

CONTROL IN A RELATIONSHIP

When one person communicates a message to the other, he is by that act making a maneuver to define the relationship. By what he says and the way he says it he is indicating, "This is the sort of relationship we have with each other." The other person is thereby posed the problem of either accepting or rejecting that person's maneuver. He has a choice of letting the message stand, and thereby accepting the other person's definition of the relationship, or countering with a maneuver of his own to define it differently. He may also accept the other person's maneuver but qualify his acceptance with a message that indicates he is *letting* the other person get by with the maneuver.

In any interchange between two people they must deal not only with what kind of behavior is to take place between them but how is that behavior to be qualified, or labeled. A young lady may object if a young man places his arm around her, but she may not object to this behavior if she has first invited him to place his arm around her. When she invites it, she is in control of what behavior is to take place, and therefore she is in control of the definition of the relationship. If the young man spontaneously initiates this message, she must either accept it, thereby letting him define the relationship, or oppose it, thereby defining the relationship herself. She may also accept it with the qualification that she is *letting* him place his arm around her. By labeling his message as one permitted by her, she is maintaining control of what kind of relationship they have with each other.

Any two people are posed the mutual problems: (a) what messages, or what kinds of behavior are to take place in this relationship, and (b) who is to control what is to take place in the relationship and thereby control the definition of the relationship. It is hypothesized here that the nature of human communication requires people to deal with these problems and interpersonal relationships can be classified in terms of the different ways they do deal with them.

It must be emphasized that no one can avoid being involved in a struggle over the definition of his relationship with someone else. Everyone is constantly involved in defining his relationship or countering the other person's definition. If a person speaks, he is inevitably indicating what type of relationship he has with the other person. By whatever he says, he is indicating "this is the sort of relationship where this is said." If a person remains mute he is also inevitably indicating what type of relationship he is in with the other person because by not speaking he is qualifying the other person's behavior. Just as one cannot *fail* to qualify a message, he also cannot *fail* to indicate what behavior is to take place in the relationship. If a person wishes to avoid defining his relationship with another and therefore talks only about the weather, he is inevitably indicating that the kind of communication which should take place between them should be neutral, and this defines the relationship.

A basic rule of communications theory demonstrates the point that it is impossible for a person to avoid defining, or taking control of the definition of, his relationship with another. According to this rule, all messages are not only reports but they also influence or command.[4] A statement such as "I feel badly today," is not merely a description of the internal state of the speaker. It also expresses something like "Do something about this," or "Think of me as a person who feels badly." Every message from one person to another tends to define the kind of interchange which is to take place between them. Even if one tries not to influence another person by remaining silent, his silences become an influencing factor in the interchange. It is impossible for a person to hand over to another person the entire initiative on what behavior is to be allowed in the relationship. If he indicates he is doing this, he is thereby controlling what kind of relationship it is to be—one where the other person is to indicate what behavior is to take place. For example, a patient may say to a therapist, "I can't decide anything for myself, I want you to tell me what to do." By saying this, he is telling the therapist to take charge of what behavior is to take place in the relationship and therefore to take control of what kind of relationship it is. But when the patient requests that the therapist tell him what to do, he is thereby telling the therapist what to do. This paradox can arise because two levels are always being communicated: (a) "Tell me what to do," and (b) "Obey my command to tell me what to do." Whenever one tries to avoid controlling the definition of a relationship he must at a more general level be controlling what type of relationship this is to be—one where he is not in control.

It should be emphasized here that "control" does not mean that one takes control of another person as one would a robot. The emphasis here is not on the struggle to control another person but rather on the struggle to control the definition of a relationship. Two people inevitably work out together what kind of relationship they have by mutually indicating what kind of behavior is to take place between them. By behaving in a certain way, they define the relationship as one where that type of behavior is to take place. One may behave in a helpless manner and control whatever behavior is to take place in the relationship, just as one may act authoritarian and insist that the other person behave in circumscribed ways. The helpless behavior may influence the other person's behavior as much, if not more, than the authoritarian behavior. If one acts helpless he may be taken care of by another and in a sense be in the control of the other, but by acting helpless he defines *what kind* of relationship this is to be—the kind where he is taken care of.

If a relationship stabilizes, the two people involved have worked out a mutual agreement about what type of behavior is to take place between them. This agreement is achieved "implicitly" by what they say and how they say it as they respond to each other rather than by explicit discussion. If one is to describe a particular relationship, at least some rudimentary terms are necessary so that one type of relationship can be differentiated from another.

If one took all the possible kinds of communicative behavior which two people might interchange, it could be roughly classified into behavior which defines a relationship as *symmetrical* and behavior which defines a relationship as *complementary*. A symmetrical relationship is one where two people exchange the same type of behavior. Each person will initiate action, criticize the other, offer advice, and so on. This type of relationship tends to be competitive; if one person mentions that he has succeeded in some endeavor, the other person points out that *he* has succeeded in some equally important endeavor. The people in such a relationship emphasize their symmetry with each other.

A complementary relationship is one where the two people are exchanging different types of behaviors. One gives and the other receives, one teaches and the other learns. The two people exchange behavior which complements, or fits together. One is in a "superior" position and the other in a "secondary" in that one offers criticism and the other accepts it, one offers advice, and the other follows it, and so on.

This simple division of relationships into two types is useful for classifying different relationships or different sequences within a particular relationship. No two people will consistently have one of the types in all circumstances; usually there are areas of a relationship worked out as one type or another. Relationships shift in nature either rapidly, as when people take turns teaching each other, or more slowly over time. When a child grows up he progressively shifts from a complementary relationship with his parents toward more symmetry as he becomes an adult.

There are certain kinds of messages which make more of an issue of the type of relationship than other kinds. A professor may lecture and one of his students may ask questions to clarify various points and so they continue in a mutual definition of a complementary relationship. But when the student asks a question in such a way that he implies, "I know as much about this as you do," the nature of the relationship is placed in question. The professor must either respond in such a way that he redefines the relationship as complementary again, or he must accept the student's move toward symmetry. The kind of message that places a relationship in question will be termed here a "maneuver." In the example cited, the student made a symmetrical maneuver, defining the relationship as one between two equals. Such maneuvers are constantly being interchanged in any relationship and tend to be characteristic of unstable relationships where the two people are groping towards a common definition of their relationship.

Maneuvers to define a relationship consist essentially of (a) requests, commands, or suggestions that another person do, say, think, or feel something; and (b) comments on the other person's communicative behavior. Should Mr. A ask Mr. B to do something, the problem is immediately posed whether this is the type of relationship where A has the right to make that request. B is also effected by whether the request was made tentatively or apologetically, or whether it was a rude command. Mr. B may do what he is told and so accept the complementary definition of the relationship, or he may refuse to do it and so be maneuvering toward symmetry. As a third possibility, he may do it but with a qualification that he is "permitting" A to get by with this and therefore doing the action but not agreeing to the definition of the relationship. As an example, if one employee asks another of equal status to empty the wastebasket, this could be labeled a maneuver to define the relationship as complementary. If the other raises his eyebrow, this could be labeled as a countermaneuver to define it as symmetrical. The first employee may respond to that raised eyebrow by saying, "Well, I don't mind doing it myself if you don't want to." In this way he indicates his original request was not a complementary maneuver but really a symmetrical one since it was something one equal would ask of another. The issue about the relationship was raised because the first employee used that class of message termed here a maneuver—he requested that the other person do something. Similarly, if a person comments on another person's behavior, the issue is immediately raised whether or not the relationship is of the kind where this is appropriate.

A complication must be added to this simple scheme of relationships. There are times when one person *lets* another use a particular maneuver. If A behaves helplessly and so provokes B to take care of him, he is arranging a situation where he is in a secondary position since he is taken care of. However, since he arranged it, actually B is doing what he is told and so A is in a superior position. In the same way, one person may teach another to behave as an equal, and so ostensibly be arranging a symmetrical relationship but actually doing this within the framework of a complementary relationship. Whenever one person lets, or forces, another to define a relationship in a certain way, he is at a higher level defining the relationship as complementary. Therefore a third type of relationship must be added to the other two and will be termed a metacomplementary relationship. The person who establishes a metacomplementary relationship with another is controlling the maneuvers of the other and so controlling how the other will define the relationship.

Since everyone faces the problem of what kind of relationship he will have with another person, and also the problem of who is to control what kind of relationship he will have, one can assume there are ordinary means of dealing with these problems. One can also view psychopathology as a particular species of methods of gaining control of a relationship. Psychiatric symptoms will be discussed here in terms of the advantages the patient gains in making his social world more predictable by the use of his symptoms.

The type of therapy which anyone devises will be based upon some implicit or explicit theory of human psychopathology and the processes of change. Therapists who see symptoms as a product of conditioning will seek methods of therapy which emphasize deconditioning. If symptoms are seen as a product of repressed ideation, then the therapy will be geared to bringing into awareness repressed ideas. If symptoms are seen as a method of dealing with other people, the therapist will seek to devise means of preventing the use of symptomatic methods and encouraging the patient to develop other ways of dealing with his relationships.

It is possible to argue that the various methods of psychotherapy, including psychoanalysis, have in common a particular kind of interaction between therapist and patient and it is this interaction which produces therapeutic change rather than awareness or unawareness on the part of the patient. To present this point of view it is necessary to describe patients who experience specific symptoms from the point of view of interpersonal involvements rather than in terms of the patient alone, e.g., defenses against repressed ideas or conditioning.

To illustrate the difference in point of view, we can examine a classic case of handwashing compulsion. A woman sought therapy because she was forced to ritually wash her hands many times a day and compulsively take showers. Although she might feel driven to wash her hands at any time, she particularly did so if she was exposed to any type of poison, even household ammonia. From the intrapsychic point of view her ritual washing could be seen as a defense against various kinds of ideas, including murderous impulses toward her husband, children, and herself. Her productions would support such interpretations as well as notions that her compulsion was related to a primal scene incident because of the way she described sleeping in her parents' bedroom as a child. If her case were written up from the classic point of view, she would be described in terms of her history, her fantasies, her guilts, and so on. If her husband were mentioned, it would probably be only a passing statement that he was understandably unhappy about her compulsion. It is improbable that her husband would be seen by a therapist with a focus upon intrapsychic problems.

However, in this case her husband was brought into the therapy and an examination of the interpersonal context of her handwashing revealed an intense and bitter struggle between the patient and her husband over this compulsion. The couple was of German origin, recently emigrated to the United States, and the husband insisted upon being tyranical about all details of their lives. He demanded his own way, wanting his wife to do what he said and do it promptly. However, he was unable to have his own way about the handwashing and the struggle was constant and distressing. The husband regularly, and benevolently, forbade her to wash her hands; he followed her around to make sure she was not washing them; he timed her showers; he hid the soap and rationed it to her. When he had been away, his greeting included a query about her handwashing. He even pointed out that if she loved him she would stop this washing compulsion, so that when she was angry with him she could express her dislike by washing her hands.

Although the wife objected to her husband's tyranical ways, she was unable to oppose him on any issue—except her handwashing. She could refuse to do as he said in that area because she could point out it was an involuntary compulsion. However, as a result of the handwashing she actually managed to refuse to do almost anything he suggested. If he wanted to go somewhere with her, she could not because she might be exposed to some poison. He insisted on a spotlessly clean house, but she could not clean the house because she was busy washing her hands. He liked the dishes done neatly and promptly, but she had difficulty with dishes because once she placed her hands in water she was compelled to go on washing them. Although her husband insisted upon always having his own way and being master in the house (of course, his wife was supporting him financially), he was dethroned by the simple washing of a pair of hands.

It would be possible to dismiss this interpersonal aspect of the woman's symptom as mere secondary gain and confine therapy to bringing into her awareness her repressed ideas. A person with such an approach would assume that as the woman discovers the genesis of her symptom, her compulsion will lessen, and as she washes her hands less her husband will be happier with her. There are several difficulties with this rather naive point of view. For one thing, when the woman enters therapy she may gain some awareness of what is "behind" her symptom, but she is also going to be intensely involved with a therapist whose goal is to get her over the problem of compulsive washing with all the implications of a lifetime of people trying to do just that. The therapist might insist that he is concerned with the ideas behind the symptom and he is not attempting to prevent her washing her hands, but the context of the relationship is the premise that he is going to help her get over this problem. It is a decidedly open question whether improvement will come to her from ideas coming into her awareness or the fact that she cannot deal with the therapist by way of her symptom as she has with her husband and with others, since the therapist declines to openly oppose the compulsion.

A further difficulty in the intrapsychic focus is the assumption that her husband will be happier if she improves. There is a gathering amount of evidence that when a patient improves, the mate becomes disturbed and begins to behave in ways which negate the improvement. A symptom can be seen not only as a way a patient deals with someone else, but also as part of an arrangement which is worked out in implicit collaboration with other people. In this case the husband and wife had built their relationship around the wife's compulsion, in fact, they were unable to fight about any other issue. Further, they had worked out the agreement that she was the sick one and whatever went wrong in the family it could be blamed upon her and her compulsion. Should this woman receive some "insight" into her internal conflicts about the symptom, she would still be faced with giving up a way of life and a way of dealing with her husband if she were to give up her symptom. Of course, the symptom can be seen not only as a rather desperate way of dealing with her husband, but also as a method of protecting him from facing his own problems and the other difficulties in their marriage.

From the point of view offered here, the crucial aspect of a symptom is the advantage it gives the patient in gaining control of what is to happen in a relationship with someone else. A symptom may represent considerable distress to a patient subjectively, but such distress is preferred by some people to living in an unpredictable world of social relationships over which they have little control. A patient with an alcoholic wife once said that he was a man who liked to have his own way but his wife always won by getting drunk. His wife, who was present in the therapy session, became indignant and said she won nothing but unhappiness by her involuntary drinking. Yet obviously she did win something by it. In this case she won almost complete control of her relationship with her husband. He could not go where he wanted because she might drink; he could not antagonize her or upset her because she might drink; he could not leave her alone (unless he could encourage her to pass out) because of what she might do when drunk; and he could not make any plans but had to let her initiate whatever happened. In other words, she could bring him to heel merely by picking up a glass. She might suffer distress and humiliation and even provoke her husband to beat her, but *she* provoked those situations and thereby controlled what was to happen. Similarly, her husband could provoke her to drink at any time, either by exhibiting some anxiety himself or forbidding her drinking. Each partner must make a contribution to perpetuating the symptom and each has needs satisfied by it. However, they both have other needs and although the symptom may work out as a compromise it tends to be an unstable one. Yet when the wife goes to a therapist, she is immediately threatened by the same situation she has with her husband—how much control is she going to let someone else have over the relationship with her.

Let us take a somewhat extreme example of the initial process in therapy to illustrate the struggle for control which must inevitably take place. A woman calls a therapist and asks for an appointment, and the therapist says he will see her on Monday. She asks if it can be Tuesday since she has not been feeling well and hopes to feel better by then. Let us suppose he agrees to Tuesday and says he will see her at 10 o'clock on that day. She asks if she can see him in the afternoon since mornings are difficult for her. Let us suppose he agrees to an afternoon appointment and gives her his office address. She replies, "I'm really so frightened about leaving the house, I wonder if you could come to my home."

Although this example is exaggerated, it illustrates a process that goes on in more subtle ways in the opening interchange between therapist and patient. Immediately the issue between therapist and patient is this: who is to control what kind of behavior is to take place between them. The patient who will maneuver to set the time and place will also maneuver to control what is said when they begin to interact. It is the importance to the woman of controlling her relationships which makes her a candidate for psychotherapy. One can assume she must have suffered many disappointments with people to so desperately try to circumscribe their behavior, yet it is her insistence on this type of control which inevitably makes her relationships unfortunate.

It is not pathological to attempt to gain control of a relationship, we all do this, but when one attempts to gain that control while denying it, then such a person is exhibiting symptomatic behavior. In any relationship that stabilizes, such as that between a husband and wife, the two people work out agreements about who is to control what area of the relationship. They may agree that the nature of the husband's work is within his control and he has a right to circumscribe his wife's behavior on this issue. Should he fail in his job or make insufficient income, this agreement may be called in question by the wife. They must either change the agreement then, or reinforce the old one. Difficult relationships are those where the two people cannot reach agreement on a mutual definition of areas of the relationship. When one bids for control of an area, the other bids for control and they are in a struggle. The struggle may be conducted by open battle, by sabotage, or by passive resistance, just as it may be crude and obvious or infinitely rich and subtle.

However, difficult relationships do not necessarily produce psychiatric symptoms. A relationship becomes psychopathological when one of the two people will maneuver to circumscribe the other's behavior while indicating he is not. The wife in such a relationship will force her husband to take care of the house in such a way that she denies she is doing so. She may, for example, have obscure dizzy spells, an allergy to soap, or various types of attacks which require her to lie down regularly. Such a wife is circumscribing her husband's behavior while denying that *she* is doing this; after all, she cannot help her dizzy spells.

When one person circumscribes the behavior of another while denying that he is doing so, the relationship begins to be rather peculiar. For example, when a wife requires her husband to be home every night because she has anxiety attacks when she is left alone, he cannot acknowledge that she is controlling his behavior because *she* is not requiring him to be home—the anxiety is and her behavior is involuntary. Neither can he refuse to let her control his behavior for the same reason. When a person is offered two directives which conflict with each other and which demand a response, he can respond by indicating he is not responding to a directive. The formal term for such a communication sequence as it is described here is a paradox.

The idea of paradoxical communication patterns derives from the Russellian paradoxes in classification systems. As it is used here, the term paradox is a term for describing a directive which qualifies another directive in a conflicting way either simultaneously or at a different moment in time. If one person directs another to do a particular act, a paradox is not necessarily evident, but when one person directs another not to follow his directives, the paradox is obvious. The receiver cannot obey the directive nor disobey it. If he obeys the directive not to follow directives, then he is not following directives. This paradox occurs because one directive is *qualified* by another in a conflictual way. If it is qualified by another, it is at a different *level* of classification from the other. In contrast, if two directives are at the same level of abstraction, such as "do it" and "don't do it," they contradict each other. No contradiction is involved when they are at different levels, just as a class and the item within it cannot contradict each other, they can only conflict in a paradoxical way. For example, if one says to another "Do a certain thing," and qualifies this directive with "Don't obey my orders," there is no contradiction, but only a conflict at different levels. Similarly, if one says, "I am directing you to respond spontaneously." a paradox is posed—one cannot obey a directive "spontaneously." This type of communication sequence is common in human relationships and is particularly evident in certain types of relationships.

The communication sequence which occurs when one person offers conflicting directives will be described here as the posing of a paradox. The response of the receiver may be of various types: he may terminate the relationship, he may comment upon the impossible situation in which he is placed, or he may respond by indicating that he is not responding to the other person. That is, he may respond with paradoxical communication. This latter response is typical of hypnotic trance, symptomatic behavior, and "spontaneous" change in psychotherapy. When a person responds by indicating he is not responding to the other person, a paradoxical relationship is established. One person is directing another, while indicating the other should not follow his directions, and the other person is responding by indicating he is not responding to the directives in this place at this time. When one notes that *any* message exchanged between people has directive aspects, then it is evident that the exchange of paradoxical communication will be common (and the description of human behavior will never be simple).

When two people are attempting to control the type of relationship by circumscribing each other's behavior, it is apparent that the person posing paradoxical directives will "win." The other person cannot define the relationship by obeying directives or refusing to obey them, because he is being asked to do both simultaneously.

The unfortunate thing about paradoxical relationships is that the person posing paradoxes wins control of a particular area of behavior, but in doing so he requires the other person to respond in a similar way and so perpetuates the conflictual relationship. The husband who must remain home every night with an anxious wife will qualify his staying home with an indication that *he* is not doing this in response to *her*, or out of choice, her anxiety is requiring this involuntary behavior from him. The wife cannot win an acknowledgment that he wants to be home with her or that he does not. She also cannot be sure that *she* has control over the relationship in this area. She wins only the response she offers; an action qualified by a denial that the person has voluntarily chosen to make that action. Consequently, as long as she behaves in a symptomatic way, she cannot receive reassurance that he wants to be with her and would choose voluntarily to stay at home. She therefore cannot be reassured and so take responsibility for asking him to stay home for her sake, but continues to ask him to stay home for the anxiety's sake, and the perpetuation of the symptom is assured. When this type of communication sequence is initiated, it becomes pathogenic.

The primary gain of symptomatic behavior in a relationship could be said to be the advantage of setting rules for that relationship. The defeat produced by symptomatic behavior is that one cannot take either the credit or the blame for being the one who sets those rules. If a person is unable to ask something for himself and must deny that *he* is asking, he also can never take the responsibility of receiving. It seems to be a law of life that one must take the responsibility for one's behavior in a relationship if one is ever to receive credit for the results.

Since whatever a person communicates to another person is setting the rules for how that person is to behave, the interchange between therapist and patient will inevitably center upon who is to set those rules. Although psychotherapy involves many factors, such as support, encouragement of self-expression, education, and so on, it is of crucial importance that the therapist deal successfully with the question whether he or the patient is to control what kind of relationship they will have. No form of therapy can avoid this problem, it is central, and in its resolution is the source of therapeutic change.

If the patient gains control in psychotherapy, he will perpetuate his difficulties since he will continue to govern by symptomatic methods. If one describes successful therapy as a process whereby a therapist maintains control of what kind of relationship he will have with a patient, then it becomes necessary to consider the tactics which a person can use to gain control of the relationship with another person and therefore influence his emotions and somatic sensations. Those tactics which have developed in various methods of psychotherapy are the subject of this book. A number of types of psychotherapy will be mentioned in passing, but particular emphasis will be placed upon directive psychotherapy, awareness therapy, the therapy of schizophrenics, marriage therapy, and family therapy. A purpose of this work is to suggest that therapeutic change results from the set of therepeutic paradoxes which these various methods of psychotherapy have in common. The nature of the therapeutic paradox will be explored in relation to various methods used by psychotherapists.

CHAPTER II

How Hypnotist and Subject Maneuver Each Other

ANY PSYCHOLOGICAL theory which presumes to explain man must include an explanation of that peculiar phenomenon the hypnotic trance. Psychiatry owes a great debt to the field of hypnosis; much of the descriptive theory of intrapsychic processes which is now common parlance was developed in the attempt to explain the behavior of subjects in trance. As far back as 1884, Bernheim[9] and others were postulating the existence of a conscious and an unconscious to explain amnesia and selective awareness in hypnotic subjects. The idea that thoughts follow associative pathways was postulated because of similar observations. When Freud developed this theory of an unconscious intrapsychic structure he came from an hypnotic orientation and his clinical contributions were obvously influenced by the investigations of hypnosis in the nineteenth century. In the literature of the last two decades of that century there are debates about whether there is an unconscious part of the conscious or a conscious part of the unconscious as well as questions about the function of a discriminating ego in this structure, all of which seems reminiscent of some current discussions. Today, much of the theory about individuals, whether in the field of hypnosis or in psychiatry, appears to be revisions of, or attempts to test and document ideas developed during that fruitful period when the hypnotized subject was a puzzle to those who were investigating the nature of man's mental processes.

Just as the focus has been only upon the individual in psychiatric descriptions of symptoms, so has the focus been only upon the individual in descriptions of hypnosis. While intrapsychic theories were being postulated, there was no concurrent attempt to focus upon the hypnotic relationship. Investigators today continue in this determined struggle to confine theoretical descriptions of hypnosis to the single individual, even though the hypnotic trance more than any other psychological phenomenon has required a relationship for its appearance. When Mesmer proffered his magnets and subjects responded with trance behavior, it seemed reasonable that theoretical questions should center upon the nature of magnetism and its influence on human beings, with little or no description of the subject's relationship to Mesmer. When Braid later induced trance behavior by eye fixation, the theories shifted from magnetic properties to ideas about the individual's nervous system because of the argument that trance was obviously the result of the physiological effects of tiredness of the eyes. Later when it was found that trance could be induced in other ways, such as by having the subject merely imagine that he was fixating his eyes upon a point, the focus shifted to an investigation of "suggestion." One would expect that at this point the subject of investigation would be the relationship between the suggester and the person suggested to. For example, it would be noted that in all trance inductions the hypnotist tells the subject what to do. Instead, the focus upon the individual continued and the theoretical problem became one of classifying *individuals* as more or less suggestible. A "suggestion" then came to be described as a magnet had previously been described—a thing in itself which influenced people independent of the relationship. This peculiar avoidance of the nature of the hypnotic relationship has paralleled the descriptive emphasis in psychotherapy where the focus is upon the patient rather than upon the therapeutic relationship.

Although the hypnotic trance as an individual phenomenon could be irrelevant to psychotherapy, as a model for describing the maneuvers of one person attempting to bring about changes in another it is most pertinent. If one assumes that in the hypnotic relationship an individual can change his perception, his emotions, and his somatic sensations there is no greater argument for the influence one person can have in relation to another. The similarities between the process of trance induction and the process of psychotherapy are apparent when one views the relationship. Each situation is usually conducted with a patient or subject who sought this experience, and each consists essentially of a conversation between two people with one attempting to induce change in the other. Those who assume that the hypnotic and the psychotherapeutic situation are different have never examined both. In the past the hypnotic relationship might have appeared unique if one thought of an authoritarian hypnotist giving his "sleep" commands to a passive subject, but that type of induction is only one of many. In the last 30 years induction techniques have become so various that it is difficult to differentiate the hypnotic relationship from other kinds by any obvious means. Today a trance can be induced with an apparently casual conversation, or in one member of an audience while the lecturer is talking to the group, or in one person while the hypnotist is dealing with another. A trance can even be induced when the hypnotist does nothing. For example, Milton H. Erickson once invited a subject up to the lecture platform for a demonstration. When the woman joined him on the platform, Erickson merely stood and did nothing. The woman went into a trance. When asked why this happened, Erickson explained, "She came up before all those people to be hypnotized, and I didn't do or say anything. Someone obviously had to do something, and so she went into a trance." This method is particularly effective with a resistant subject; there is nothing to resist. In some ways the procedure is similar to the extremely nondirective therapist. The patient comes for help and the therapist does and says nothing. Someone has to do something, and so the patient undergoes a change. Of course, this is a somewhat facetious way to draw a parallel between psychotherapy and hypnotic induction, but the variety of ways trance can be induced today and the variety of psychotherapy situations raise serious questions about similarities.

A rather strange alliance has always existed between psychoanalysis and the theory and clinical use of hypnosis. Investigators have considerably oversimplified the hypnotic trance by focussing upon the individual alone and attempting to explain trance as a regression or in terms of transference. Yet there has been a certain reluctance on the part of such theoreticians to explain regression and transference during psychoanalysis in terms of trance induction. An obvious question posed when it is argued that regression and transference occur in both hypnosis and psychoanalytic therapy is this: Is the relationship between hypnotist-subject and analyst-patient formally the same so that the product of the relationship is similar type of behavior in subject and patient? For example, is the patient who has a vivid recall of an emotional experience in one psychoanalytic session which is not recalled in the next session exhibiting resistance or hypnotic amnesia? Is there a difference? It will be argued in this work that both types of relationships are formally similar if one examines them in terms of the paradoxes posed in the interaction, and therefore one could expect similar responsive behavior in patient and subject.

The clinical use of hypnosis has inevitably paralled the current ideas about the nature of psychotherapeutic change. When therapists are more directive, hypnosis emphasizes direction. When the current vogue is awareness or insight therapy, hypnosis is adapted along those lines.[59] Hypnoanalysis had its day, and that day now appears to have passed. When it was assumed that bringing unconscious ideas into awareness and relating them to childhood experiences was a basic cause of change, the use of hypnosis was obviously in order. With a good subject there are a variety of devices for bringing ideas into awareness and the recall of the past is facilitated with trance. One can even have a subject visualize parallel incidents in the present and past so that the connections are obvious, if one wishes to do so. However, psychoanalysts were not satisfied with mere lifting of repression or childhood recall, they argued that the focus of the therapy should be upon the resistance to these processes. It was the working through of these resistances which caused the change. The analytic emphasis was not upon the subject resisting the analyst, since only the subject was the focus of description, but upon the resistance of the subject to his own internal processes. It would appear that hypnosis made yet another contribution to psychoanalysis since the emphasis upon working through resistance and transference interpretations was apparently caused by the lack of therapeutic result with the hypnotic lifting of repression and childhood recall. Although a hypnotist would say that resistance, too, could be suggested to the subject, this was analytically unsatisfactory. The process of working through resistance should occur in the "natural" process between analyst and patient with the resistance arising when it should and being dealt with when it arose. Hypnotic techniques of directly suggesting resistance are considered more "unnatural" and different from advising the analysand that in the process of treatment he is expected to become resistant.

The question of how best to use hypnosis as a clinical tool can only be answered if one first describes the phenomenon of hypnosis. Clinically the use of hypnosis has appeared and disappeared during the years, almost being discarded entirely when Freud abandoned the use of overt hypnosis. The current acceptance of hypnosis will probably be upon a different basis than in the past. With the shift in focus from the individual to both persons, it follows that a description of hypnosis in terms of the relationship must be provided before we can discover its potential for bringing about therapeutic change. An interpersonal description of hypnosis will be offered here as a way of establishing certain premises about human relationships and to provide a model and some terminology which can be applied to the psychotherapeutic relationship.

As in most other psychological problems, theories of hypnosis have concentrated upon the state of the individual rather than the transactions between hypnotist and subject. The resulting literature consists of conjectures about the perceptual or physiological nature of hypnotic trance with a surprising number of conflicting ideas and insoluble contradictions. The various theoreticians have proposed at least the following descriptions of hypnotic trance. The trance is sleep, but it is not sleep. It is a conditioned reflex, but it occurs without conditioning. It is a transference relationship involving libidinal and submissive instinctual strivings, but this is because of aggressive and sadistic instinctual strivings. It is a state in which the person is hypersuggestible to another's suggestions, but one where only autosuggestion is effective since compliance from the subject is required. It is a state of concentrated attention, but it is achieved by dissociation. It is a process of role playing, but the role is real. It is a neurological change based upon psychological suggestions, but the neurological changes have yet to be measured and the psychological suggestions have yet to be defined. Finally, there is a trance state which exists separately from trance phenomena, such as catalepsy, hallucinations, and so on, but these phenomena are essential to a true trance state.

One can wonder if a rigorous answer is possible to the question: Is there a state called "trance" which is different from the normal state of being "awake?" The "trance" state is by definition a subjective experience. It can be investigated only if the investigator examines his subjective experiences when supposedly in such a state. This is a most unreliable method of research, particularly when one is dealing with the slippery perceptive experiences of hypnotic trance. Whether or not another person is in a trance state cannot really be known any more than what another person is thinking can be known—or even if he is thinking. We can observe the communicative behavior of a person, but we can only conjecture about his subjective experiences. A rigorous investigation of hypnosis must center on the communicative behavior of hypnotist and trance subject with, at most, careful conjecture about the internal processes which provoke the behavior.

Debate about hypnosis has always centered around the question of whether a subject is *really* experiencing a phenomenon or only behaving as if he is. Such a debate is essentially unresolvable. The few crude instruments available, such as the GSR and the EEG, indicate slight physiological changes, but no instrument can tell us whether a subject is really hallucinating or really experiencing an anesthesia. At most, we can poke him with a sharp instrument in the supposedly anesthetized area or amputate a limb, as Esdaile did, and observe his communicative behavior. Our only data are the communications of the subject, the rest is inevitably conjecture.

It would seem practical to begin an investigation of hypnosis with an analysis of what can be seen and recorded on film in the hypnotic situation and thereby limit what needs to be inferred from the subject's behavior. If an investigation centers on the process of communication between a hypnotist and subject, then answerable questions about hypnosis can be posed: Is the communicative behavior of a supposedly hypnotized subject significantly different from the communicative behavior of that person when not hypnotized? What sequences of communication between hypnotist and trance subject produce the communicative behavior characteristic of a person in trance? Answers to these questions will explain what is unique to the hypnotic relationship and differentiates it from all others. To answer such questions a system for describing communicative behavior is needed. An approach to such a system will be offered here with the argument that human interaction can be dissected and labeled and that a particular kind of communication sequence is characteristic of the hypnotic relationship.

In the literature on hypnosis there is sufficient repetition of ideas so that a few generalizations can be made about the hypnotic situation which would be agreed upon by most hypnotists. It is now generally accepted that hypnotic trance has something to do with a relationship between the hypnotist and subject. In the past it was assumed that trance was the result of the influence of the planets or merely something happening inside the subject independently of the hypnotist. Currently, it is assumed that hypnotic phenomena result from an interpersonal relationship as hypnotist and trance subject communicate with one another by verbal and nonverbal behavior. It is also generally agreed that "trance" involves a focusing of attention. The subject does not, while in trance, report about activities outside the task defined by the hypnotist, and his reports about the hypnotic task are in agreement with the hypnotist's reports. In addition, it is assumed that the relationship between hypnotist and subject is such that the hypnotist initiates what happens in the situation. He initiates a sequence of messages, and the subject responds. The common assumption that the hypnotist must have "prestige" with the subject seems to be an agreement that the subject must accept the hypnotist as the person who will initiate ideas and suggestions. Although the subject may respond to the hypnotist's messages in his own unique way, still by definition he is responding and thereby acknowledging the hypnotist to be the one who has the initiative in the situation. In those instances where the subject decides the task, it is implicitly agreed that the hypnotist is *letting* this happen. It is also accepted that in every induction the hypnotist at some point "challenges" the subject either explicitly or implicitly to try to do something he has been told he cannot do.

These few generalizations are acceptable to an investigator of hypnosis. There is one further generalization which makes explicit what is implicit in most techniques and theories of trance induction, and some consideration should make it acceptable to most hypnotists. Hypnotic interaction progresses from "voluntary" responses by the subject to "involuntary" responses. "Voluntary" responses are those which hypnotist and subject agree can be deliberately accomplished, such as placing the hands on the lap or looking at a light. "Involuntary" responses are those which hypnotist and subject agree are not volitional, such as a feeling of tiredness, levitating a hand without deliberately lifting it, or manifesting a hallucination. Involuntary responses, in general, consist of changes at the autonomic level, perceptual changes, and certain motor behavior. The motor aspects of trance are particularly obvious during a challenge

when a subject tries to bend an arm and cannot because of the opposition of muscles.

Every trance induction method known to this writer progresses either
rapidly or slowly from requests for voluntary responses to requests for
involuntary ones. This alternating sequence continues even into the
deepest stages of trance. When the sequence occurs rapidly, as in a
theatrical induction, the hypnotist quickly asks the subject to sit down,
place his hands on his knees, lean his head forward, and so on. Following these requests for voluntary behavior, he states that the subject
cannot open his eyes, or move a hand, or bend an arm, or he requests
similar involuntary behavior. In a relaxation induction the sequence occurs
more slowly as the hypnotist endlessly repeats phrases about deliberately relaxing the various muscles of the body and follows these suggestions with others suggesting a feeling of tiredness in his body or
some other involuntary response. The most typical hypnotic induction,
the eye fixation, involves a request that the subject voluntarily assume
a certain position and look at a spot or at a light. This is followed by a
request for an involuntarily heaviness of the eyelids. A "conversational"
trance induction proceeds from requests that the subject think about
something, or notice a feeling, or look here and there, to suggestions that
require a shift in the subject's perceptions or sensations. The trance
state is usually defined as that moment of shift when the subject begins
to follow suggestions involuntarily. Either the subject struggles to move a
hand and cannot because of an involuntary opposition of muscles, or
he reports a perception or feeling which he presumably could not voluntarily produce.

Before discussing hypnosis in more interactional terms the hypnotic
situation can be summarized according to these general statements of
agreement. In the hypnotic situation the hypnotist initiates ideas or suggestions which are responded to by the trance subject. The hypnotist
persuades the subject to follow voluntarily his suggestions and concentrate upon what he assigns. When this is done, the hypnotist requests
involuntary responses from the subject. The progress of the hypnotic interaction progressively defines the relationship as one in which the hypnotist is in control of, or initiating, what happens and the subject is responding more and initiating less.

The particluar kind of relationship of hypnotist and subject can be examined against the background of types of relationships discussed in
Chapter I. In summary, it was suggested thåt relationships could be
simply divided into *complementary* and *symmetrical* with the type of relationship an ongoing subject of definition between any two people.
The type of relationship becomes a particular issue when one of the two

people makes a maneuver, defined as a request, command, or suggestion that the other person do, say, think, feel, or notice something, or a comment on the other person's behavior. A maneuver provokes a series of maneuvers by both participants until a mutually agreed-upon definition of the relationship is worked out between them. These maneuvers involve not only what is said, but the metacommunication of the two people or the way they qualify what they say to each other. A third type of relationship was proposed, a metacomplementary relationship, to describe that interaction where one person permits or forces the other to use maneuvers which define the relationship in a certain way. The person who acts helpless in order to force someone to take charge of him is actually in charge at a metacomplementary level.

THE HYPNOTIC PROCESS

With these types of relationships as background, hypnotic interaction can be described as apparently taking place in a complementary relationship. The hypnotist suggests, and the subject follows his suggestions so that each person's communicative behavior is complementary. The act of making a suggestion is a maneuver to define the relationship as complementary, and the act of following the suggestion is an acceptance of that definition of the relationship.

In hypnotic literature a suggestion is defined as "the presentation of an idea" as if a suggestion is an isolated unit unrelated to the relationship between the two people. Actually the act of making a suggestion and the act of responding to one is a process which has been going on between the two people and will continue. It is a class of messages rather than a single message and is more usefully defined in that way. A "suggestion" is defined here as a maneuver: that class of messages which make an issue of what type of relationship exists between the person who offers and the person who responds to the suggestion. A suggestible person is one who is willing to accept the interpersonal implications of doing what he is told. This idea is stated implicitly in such comments as "He willingly follows suggestions." It is possible to follow suggestions unwillingly, as well as not to follow them at all, but when a person willingly follows suggestions he is accepting a complementary relationship with the person who is telling him what to do. There are several crucial points about the hypnotic interaction which differentiate it from other relationships.

1. It has been said that certain kinds of messages exchanged between two people make an issue of what kind of relationship they have. The hypnotic relationship consists *entirely* of the interchange of this class of messages. The hypnotist tells the subject what to do with his suggestions

and comments on the subject's behavior. There are no other kinds of messages involved; talk about the weather is not interchanged.

2. When the hypnotist tells the subject what to do, he is defining the relationship as complementary. The subject must either accept this definition by responding and doing what he is told, or he must respond in such a way that he defines the relationship as symmetrical. Some subjects are resistant. Every subject is resistant to some degree. The central problem in hypnotic induction is overcoming the resistance of the subject. In communications terms "resistance" consists of countermaneuvers by the subject to define the relationship as symmetrical. No person will immediately and completely accept the secondary position in a complementary relationship. The hypnotist must encourage or enforce a complementary relationship by countering the subject's countermaneuvers. Whereas in ordinary relationships between people, both persons may initiate or respond with either symmetrical or complementary maneuvers. In the hypnotic situation the hypnotist concentrates entirely on initiating complementary maneuvers and influencing the subject to respond in agreement with that definition of the relationship. When the subject is "awake," or when the two people are maneuvering differently, the hypnotist may behave symmetrically with a subject, but during the hypnotic relationship his efforts are devoted entirely to defining the relationship as complementary. A complication will be added to this description later, but for the moment let us describe the hypnotist-subject relationship as complementary.

When he meets with particular kinds of resistance, a hypnotist may explicitly place himself in a secondary position with a subject while implicitly taking control at the metacomplementary level. That is, if the subject insists on defining the relationship as symmetrical, the hypnotist may appear to hand control of the relationship over to the subject by saying that he is only guiding the subject into trance and must follow the subject's lead with whatever he wishes to do. Having placed himself in the secondary position of a complementary relationship, the hypnotist then proceeds to give the subject suggestions and expects him to follow them, thus defining the relationship as complementary with himself in the superior position. Whenever the hypnotist behaves in a symmetrical or secondary way, it is to take control at the metacomplementary level.

3. When a subject accepts a complementary relationship, whether he likes it or not, it becomes possible for him to misinterpret messages from the environment, from another person, or from inside himself. This statement is conjecture, since it describes the internal processes of an individual, yet such an inference seems supportable on the basis of the subject's communicative behavior. When the hypnotist suggests a hallucination, the subject will misinterpret the messages from the environment which

contradict the hallucinatory image. The same is true of bodily sensations, emotions, and memories. The more the subject is unable to counter the metacomplementary maneuvers of the hypnotist, the more trance manifestations he is capable of experiencing. To describe his behavior from an interactional point of view, it is necessary to discuss what the evidence is for "involuntary" behavior.

THE INVOLUNTARY IN TERMS OF BEHAVIOR

An attempt to bring rigor into the investigation of hypnosis requires us to deal with observable behavior rather than to conjecture about the internal processes of a subject. When it is said above that the trance subject experiences involuntary phenomena, this statement is unverifiable. We cannot know whether or not a subject is experiencing an hallucination or various bodily sensations and emotions. For example, when a subject's arm begins to levitate we might say that this is an involuntary phenomenon and therefore a manifestation of trance. As a hypnotic subject, we might ourselves experience that hand levitation and feel that the hand was lifting up and we were not lifting it, thus we would subjectively know that this was involuntary. However, as investigators of hypnosis we cannot rely on our subjective experiences. Ideally, we should be able to describe the processes of trance induction and trance phenomena while observing a film of hypnotist and subject interacting. Confined to our observations of the film, we could not observe "involuntary" activities by the subject. We could only observe behavior which we *inferred* was involuntary. Our problem is to describe the communicative behavior of a subject at that moment when we draw the inference that he is experiencing an involuntary trance phenomenon.

To describe communicative behavior one must take into account the fact that people not only communicate a message but qualify or label that message to indicate how the message is to be received. A message may be qualified by another which affirms it, or it may be qualified by one which denies it. A person can step on another person's foot and qualify this message with a "vicious" expression which indicates "I'm doing this on purpose," or he may indicate he does not know it is happening. Thus a qualifying message may either deny or be incongruent with another message, or it may affirm or be congruent with the other message. When we observe a film of two people interacting and we conclude that something one of them does is "involuntary," we draw that conclusion from the *way* the person qualifies what he does. If we see a trance subject levitating an arm and hear him say in a surprised way, "Why, my arm is lifting up," we conclude that he is experiencing an involuntary phenomenon. Our conclusion is drawn from the fact that the subject is doing something and denying that *he* is doing it. He may make this denial with a verbal comment, with a surprised expression, by the way he lifts the arm, by commenting on it later after he was awake, and so on. He may also say, "Why, my arm is lifting up," and thereby deny that he is lifting it, but say this in an "insincere" tone of voice. That is, he qualifies the arm lifting with two statements: one says "I'm not doing it," the other says, "I'm doing it." When we observe this incongruence between his tone of voice and his statement we conclude that the subject is simulating an arm levitation and that it is not *really* involuntary. Our conclusion is based on the fact that two incongruences are apparent in the ways he qualifies his messages: (a) he lifts his hand and says he did not, (b) he says he did not in a tone of voice which indicates he did. If he should express astonishment at the lifting of his hand in words, in his tone of voice, and in his postural communication so that all of his messages are congruent with a denial that he is lifting his arm, then we say it is *really* an involuntary movement.

Besides the fact that we detect simulation of hypnotic behavior by noting two incongruences in the ways the subject qualifies some activity, it seems clear that the goal of hypnotic induction from the behavioral point of view is to persuade the subject to deny fully and completely that *he* is carrying out the activity. That is, the hypnotist pushes the subject towards qualifying his behavior with messages congruent with each other and which as a totality deny that the subject is doing what he is doing. When the subject behaves in this way, an observer reports that the subject is experiencing an involuntary phenomenon.

As an illustration, let us suppose that a hypnotist wishes to induce a hallucination in a subject. After a series of interactional procedures from hand levitation through challenges, the hypnotist suggests that the subject look up at a bare wall and see that painting of an elephant there. He may do this abruptly, or he may suggest that the subject watch the painting develop there and later press for an acknowledgment that the painting *is* there. The subject can respond in one of several ways. He can look at the wall and say, "There is no painting there." He can say, "Yes, I see the painting," but qualify this statement in such a way, perhaps by his tone of voice, that he negates his statement. In this way he indicates he is saying this to please the hypnotist. Or the subject can say there is a painting on the wall and qualify this statement congruently with his tone of voice, posture, and a contextual statement such as, "Naturally there's a painting there, so what," or "Our hostess has always liked elephants." This latter kind of behavior would be considered evidence of trance.

Characteristic of a person in trance is (a) a statement which is (b) incongruent with, or denies, some other statement, but which is (c) qualified by all other statements congruently. The subject in trance (a) reports a picture (b) on a bare wall, thus making a statement incongruent with the context, and (c) he affirms his statement that there is a picture on the wall with other verbal messages, his tone of voice, and body movement. As another example, the subject lifts his hand during a hand levitation and indicates *he* is not lifting it. This statement, which is incongruent with the lifting hand, is supported or affirmed by the ways he says it. If a subject is experiencing an anesthesia, he responds passively to a poke with a pin, thereby responding incongruently, and he affirms his response with congruent words and tone of voice.

The behavior of a subject in trance is differentiable from the behavior of the subject awake by this single incongruence. A person in normal discourse may manifest incongruences when he communicates his multiple messages, or all of his messages may be congruent or affirm each other. The single incongruence is characteristic of trance behavior. Even though several hypnotic tasks may be assigned a subject simultaneously, each is characterized by a single incongruence.

The single incongruence of trance has another characteristic which differentiates it from incongruences in normal communication. This incongruence consists of a denial that he is responding to the hypnotist. The subject is doing what the hypnotist suggests while denying that he is doing what the hypnotist suggests. If a subject levitates a hand, he qualifies this with a denial that *he* is lifting it. When he does this he is indicating that he is merely reporting an occurrence, he does not qualify the lifting hand with an indication that it is a response to the hypnotist even though at that moment the hypnotist is suggesting that the hand lift. Should the subject act like a person awake and lift the hand while indicating that he is lifting it, he would be acknowledging the hand lifting as a message to the hypnotist. By qualifying the hand lifting with a denial that *he* is doing it, he manifests an incongruence which indicates that he is merely making a report. In the same way the subject merely reports the existence of a painting on the wall instead of indicating that his seeing the painting there is a statement to the hypnotist.

To formalize the behavior of the trance subject, it can be said that any communicative behavior offered by one person to another can be described in terms of four elements: a sender, a message, a receiver, and a context in which the communication takes place. In other words, any message can be translated into this statement:

> "I am communicating something
> (a) (b)
> to you in this situation."
> (c) (d)

Since communicative behavior is always qualified, any element in this message will be qualified by an affirmation or a denial. In a hypnotic trance, the subject denies these elements and does not affirm them. Trance behavior denying each element can be briefly listed.

(a) Whenever he requests an "involuntary" response, the hypnotist is urging the subject to deny that *he* is responding or communicating something. The first element of the statement mentioned, "I am communicating," is qualified with a denial and therefore changed to "It is just happening."

(b) The hypnotist not only urges the subject to deny that *he* is originating a message, such as an arm levitation, he may also urge the subject to deny that anything is happening, i.e., being communicated. The subject may appear to be unaware that his hand is lifting, thus qualifying the lifting hand with a statement that it is not lifting. Or he may show a similar denial by manifesting amnesia. If he qualifies his behavior with a denial that it happened, then nothing was communicated. He cannot only say "*I* didn't lift my hand," but he can say, "My hand didn't lift," and thereby manifest an incongruence between his statement and his lifting hand. When a subject's tone of voice and body movement is congruent with the statement that he does not recall something, or congruent with the absence of a report of some activity during trance, then observers report that he is experiencing amnesia.

(c, d) It is also possible for the subject to deny the final elements in the diagrammed essential message. He may indicate that what he is doing is not a communication to the hypnotist in this situation by qualifying, or labeling, the hypnotist as someone else and/or the situation as some other. Hypnotic regression is manifested behaviorally by the subject qualifying his statements as not to the hypnotist but another person (after all if he is regressed he has not met the hypnotist yet), perhaps a teacher, and the context as not the present one but perhaps a past schoolroom. When all of his communicative behavior is congruent with one of these incongruent qualifications, then an observer will report that the subject is experiencing regression.

In summary, a subject in trance as well as a person awake exhibits behavior toward another person which is describable as the statement "I am communicating something to you in this situation." The trance subject qualifies one or all the elements of this statement incongruently so that the statement is changed to "It is just happening," or "Nothing happened," or "I am communicating to someone else in some other place and time."

The problem posed by hypnotic induction is this: How does one person influence another to manifest a single incongruence in his communicative behavior so that he denies that *he* is communicating something, that something is being communicated, or that it is being communicated to the hypnotist in this situation? More simply, how is a person influenced to do what he is told and simultaneously deny that *he* is doing anything?

TRANCE INDUCTION IN TERMS OF BEHAVIOR

When hypnotic trance is seen as an interaction consisting of one person persuading another to do something and deny he is doing it, then it would seem to follow that trance induction must consist of requests for just that behavior from a subject. The hypnotist must ask the subject to do something and at the same time tell him not to do it. The nature of human communication makes it possible for the subject to satisfy these conflicting demands. He can do what the hypnotist asks, and at the same time qualify this activity with statements denying that he is doing it or that it is being done. Thus he does it, but he does not do it.

To simplify the rich and complex interchange which takes place between a hypnotist and subject, let us describe a hand levitation induction. The hypnotist sits down with the subject and tells him to place his hand on the arm of the chair. He then says something like, "I don't want you to move that hand, I just want you to notice the feelings in it." After a while the hypnotist says, "In a moment the hand is going to begin to lift. Lifting, lifting, lifting." If we could divest ourselves of theories and naively observe this interaction between hypnotist and subject, it would be obvious to us that the hypnotist is saying to the subject, "Don't lift your hand," and then he is saying, "Lift your hand." Since our observation is biased by theories of human behavior, we see this behavior in terms of the unconscious and conscious or in terms of autonomic processes, and so the obvious incongruence between the requests of the hypnotist is not so obvious. Yet we are faced with the inevitable fact that if the subject's hand lifts, he lifted it. He may deny it, but no one else lifted that hand.

There are only three possible responses by a subject to a request that he lift his hand and not lift it. He can refuse to do anything and thereby antagonize the hypnotist and end the trance session. He can lift his hand and simultaneously deny that *he* is lifting it, or conceivably that it is lifting. (The use of the term "denial" here does not imply that the subject is calculatedly denying that he is lifting his hand. He may subjectively be certain that the hand is lifting itself. The emphasis here is on his behavior.) A third possibility would be for him to lift it and say he did, and then the hypnotist would say, "But I told you not to lift it," and the procedure would begin again.

Every trance induction method involves this kind of incongruent request. Indeed whenever one requests "involuntary" behavior from another person he is inevitably requesting that the subject do something and simultaneously requesting that he not do it. This is what "involuntary" means. To say that something is "involuntary" is to say that it happens of itself and if one *demands* that something happen of itself he is posing a paradox.

Not only is the double-level request apparent in trance induction, but during the process of deepening the trance it becomes even more obvious. At some time or other in hypnotic interaction the hypnotist tests or challenges the subject. These challenges are all formally the same: the hypnotist asks the subject to do something and simultaneously directs him not to do it. The most common is the eye closure challenge. The hypnotist asks the subject to squeeze his eyes tightly closed during a count of 3, and at the count of 3 the subject is to try to open his eyes and fail. He is told that the harder he tries to open them the more tightly they will remain closed. When the directive "Open your eyes" is qualified by the directive "keep your eyes closed" or "don't obey my directive," the subject is being told to obey the suggestion while being told not to obey it. When the test is successful and the subject keeps his eyes closed, he is said to be "involuntarily" unable to open them. Observing his behavior we would say he is keeping his eyes closed and qualifying this behavior with the statement that *he* is not keeping them closed, it is just happening. When one sees this set of directives in terms of a learning context, it is apparent that it occurs outside of the hypnotic situation as well. Many mothers of disturbed children, for example, appear to set up a learning situation where the child is not rewarded for succeeding but is rewarded for trying and failing. When this happens, both mother and child agree the child is not failing deliberately, it is just happening.

THE IMPOSITION OF PARADOX

Whenever a hypnotist poses directives which are incongruent, he is imposing a paradox upon the subject. The subject must respond to both directives, he cannot leave the field, and he cannot comment on the fact that his situation is impossible. It is difficult for the subject to leave the field because he has usually requested a trance to begin with. Most hypnosis is done with voluntary subjects. It is also difficult for him to comment on the incompatability of the hypnotist's directives because of the hypnotist's general approach. If a subject is asked to concentrate on his hand and he comments on this suggestion by asking why he should, he is usually informed that he does not need to inquire into the matter but merely should follow suggestions. The behavior of the hypnotist rather effectively prevents conversation about the hypnotist's behavior.

Although the imposition of paradoxical directives is implicit in every hypnotic induction, in some situations it is more obvious than others. For example, during a lecture on hypnosis a young man said to Milton H. Erickson, "You may be able to hypnotize other people, but you can't hypnotize me!" Dr. Erickson invited the subject to the demonstration platform, asked him to sit down, and then said to him, "I want you to stay awake, wider and wider awake, wider and wider awake." The subject promptly went into a deep trance. The subject was faced with a double-level message: "Come up here and go into a trance," and "Stay awake." He knew that if he followed Erickson's suggestions, he would go into a trance. Therefore he was determined not to follow his suggestions. Yet if he refused to follow the suggestion to stay awake, he would go into a trance. Thus he was caught in a paradox. Note that these were not merely two contradictory messages, they were two *levels* of message. The statement "Stay awake" was *qualified* by, or framed by, the message "Come up here and go into a trance." Since one message was qualified by another they were of different *levels* of message. Such conflicting levels of message may occur when verbal statement, tone of voice, body movement, or the contextual situation, qualify each other incongruently. A double-level message may occur in a single statement. For example, if one persons says to another, "Disobey me," the other person is faced with an incongruent set of directives and can neither obey nor disobey. If he obeys, he is disobeying, and if he disobeys, he is obeying. The statement "Disobey me" contains a qualification of itself and can be translated into "Don't obey my commands," and the simultaneous qualifying statement, "Don't obey my command to not obey my commands." A hypnotic challenge consists of this type of request.

When the hypnotist presents incongruent messages to the subject, the subject can only respond satisfactorily with incongruent messages. The peculiar kinds of behaviors exhibited by a hypnotic subject are reciprocals to the hypnotist's requests.

The letter A can represent the hypnotist's statement, "Keep your eyes open and stare at this point." This statement is qualified by B, "Your eyelids will close." The subject cannot respond satisfactorily if he responds to A and keeps his eyes open. Nor can he respond satisfactorily by responding to B and closing them. He can only respond with incongruent messages when asked to close his eyes and not close them. He must close them, C, and qualify this closing with a denial that *he* did it.

Should the subject respond to only A or B, and thereby respond congruently, the hypnotist is likely to point out to him that he is not cooperating and begin again. Or a hypnotist might handle a congruent response in other ways. For example, if a subject should stubbornly keep his eyes open, thus responding only to A, the hypnotist might suggest that he keep them open as long as he can, no matter how much of an effort this is. In this way he ultimately produces the eye closure and accepts the weariness as an "involuntary" response.

Essentially the hypnotist is saying to the subject, "Do as I say, but don't do as I say," and the subject is responding with, "I'm doing what you say, but I'm not doing what you say." Since human beings can communicate on multiple levels, this type of interaction becomes possible.

THE HYPNOTIC RELATIONSHIP

The relationship between hypnotist and subject was previously described as the enforcement of a complementary relationship by the hypnotist. When the subject responds to the hypnotist's messages rather than initiating his own, he is joining the hypnotist in a mutual definition of the relationship as complementary. When the subject "resists," he is opposing the hypnotist's complementary maneuvers with countermaneuvers. Characteristically these define the relationship with the hypnotist as symmetrical—one between equals—rather than complementary. The hypnotist counters these maneuvers with maneuvers of his own which define the relationship as complementary. He may, for example, ask the subject to resist him. In this way a symmetrical maneuver is redefined as complementary. It becomes behavior requested, and therefore to respond symmetrically is to do as the hypnotist says and so behave as one does in a complementary relationship. This "topping" or countering the maneuvers of the subject was described as essentially an attempt by the hypnotist to win control of what type of relationship he and the subject are in.

The particular paradox posed by the hypnotist makes it impossible for the subject to counter with a maneuver which defines the relationship as symmetrical. If one is asked to do something and simultaneously asked not to do it, one cannot refuse to follow suggestions. If the subject responds or if he does not respond he is doing what the hypnotist requests and when one does what another requests, he is in a complementary relationship. The subject can only behave symmetrically by commenting on the situation or leaving the field and ending the relationship. If he leaves the field, the relationship is ended. If he comments on the hypnotist's statements and thereby behaves in a symmetrical way, he is likely to meet a countermaneuver which enforces a complementary relationship. The hypnotist might, for example, suggest that he comment on his behavior, thereby stepping to the metacomplementary level and defining the comments as responses to his suggestions. Then, if the subject comments, he is doing what he is told and therefore defining the relationship as complementary.

A complication must be added to this description of hypnosis. To say that the hypnotist imposes a complementary relationship and the subject in trance is agreeing to this definition is to leave hypnosis undifferentiated from other types of relationship. Conceivably, there are many other situations in which one person tells another what to do and the other willingly does what he is told so that they mutually define the relationship as complementary. Yet in these other situations trance behavior is not apparent. The person doing what he is told does not manifest denials that he is doing so. It seems apparent that trance behavior is not explained by saying that the subject and hypnotist behave in those ways which define their relationship as complementary. The complication is this: the hypnotist not only prevents the subject from behaving in symmetrical ways, thus forcing him to behave in complementary ways, but he prevents the subject from behaving in complementary ways as well.

If the subject resists the hypnotist, thus behaving in a symmetrical way, the hypnotist may ask him to resist, thus forcing him to behave in a complementary way by defining his resistance as the following suggestions. However, if the subject behaves in a complementary way and follows suggestions willingly, the hypnotist then asks him to behave symmetrically. He asks the subject to refuse to follow his suggestions. Essentially a challenge is a request that the subject resist the hypnotist, since the subject is asked to do something the hypnotist has told him not to do. Actually the paradox posed prevents both complementary and symmetrical behavior. Just as one cannot refuse to respond to paradoxical directives and is thereby prevented from behaving symmetrically, one cannot behave in a complementary way by responding because he is also being told not to respond. The subject is also prevented from achieving the third type of relationship, the metacomplementary. Conceivably, he could *let* the hypnotist tell him what to do and in this sense be labeling what the hypnotist does as done with his permission. However, when he behaves in this way, the hypnotist requests that he try to prevent himself from doing what the hypnotist asks and acknowledge that he cannot. The challenge forces him to abandon metacomplementary behavior. Whichever way the subject tries to define his relationship with the hypnotist, he finds the hypnotist refusing to accept that type of relationship.

The hypothesis offered here seems to have reached an impasse at this point. It was said earlier that all behavior of a person defines his type of relationship with another and it was then said that all relationships can be classified as either symmetrical, complementary, or metacomplementary. Now it is said that the trance subject's behavior does not define the relationship in any of these ways. A way out of this impasse is possible when it is seen that *the subject* is not behaving. All of his behavior is labeled as *not his behavior,* and so he cannot be indicating what kind of relationship he is in. The goal of the hypnotist is precisely this: to prevent the subject from defining the relationship as symmetrical, complementary, or metacomplementary by inducing him to qualify his messages in such a way that he is indicating he is not defining the relationship. If Mr. A is responding to Mr. B, the very existence of that response defines the relationship. However, if Mr. A responds to Mr. B and denies that *he* is responding, then his response is not defining his relationship. The behavior of the subject in trance does not define a particular kind of relationship but indicates that the subject is not defining the relationship at all. The control of what type of relationship it is rests with the hypnotist.

What differentiates the hypnotic relationship from others is the mutual agreement which is worked out that the hypnotist is to control what type of behavior is to take place. All behavior from the subject is either initiated by the hypnotist, or if the subject does initiate some behavior it is labeled as not being initiated by him. To avoid controlling what kind of behavior is to take place, the subject must qualify what he does with denials that he is doing it, that it is being done, or that it is being done in this place and time. Thus at the qualifying level he is behaving in those ways which avoid defining the relationship by avoiding the implication that his behavior is done in relationship to the hypnotist. The hypnotist takes control not only of the behavior which takes place but of the qualifications of that behavior. This is, of course, a statement about a hypothetically ideal hypnotic relationship. In practice no subject will let a hypnotist take complete control of the relationship.

When the hypnotic subject avoids defining his relationship with the hypnotist, he appears to experience a variety of subjective experiences at the perceptual and somatic level. His perception of himself, the world, time, and space, and the behavior of other people undergoes distortions which seem to occur outside of his control and often outside of his awareness. This chapter has not dealt with the nature or extent of these presumed distortions but rather an attempt has been made to describe the interpersonal context in which they occur. Such an attempt has relevance not only in the field of hypnosis but in the etiology of psychiatric symptoms and the processes of change in psychotherapy.

In the field of hypnosis the emphasis has always been upon the individual with a special concern with the problem of classifying individuals into good and bad hypnotic subjects. Attempts to find a correlation between personality types and susceptibility to hypnosis have largely failed, despite the use of great numbers of attitude and projective tests. This failure is expectable if one assumes that hypnotic behavior is responsive behavior in a relationship rather than an aspect of a person's "character." The only test which would differentiate good and bad hypnotic subjects would be a test which measured responsive behavior in a relationship. The tests of "waking" suggestion, or suggestibility tests, approximate this type of measurement. Yet often these tests are applied without any awareness that they are synonymous with a hypnotic induction. When one simplifies trance induction down to the formal pattern of a request for voluntary behavior qualified by a request for involuntary behavior, one can see the parallel with a suggestibility test. For example, in the sway test, the subject is asked to stand still and then he is told that he will begin to sway backwards involuntarily. It does not seem surprising that subjects who respond appropriately to this test also respond appropriately to an hypnotic induction when it is seen that this test is a form of hypnotic induction. It would appear that certain people respond with hypnotic behavior when faced with paradoxical directives. One might hypothesize that people who respond in this way have "learned" to do so from past experience. An appropriate investigation of the "cause" of hypnotic suggestibility would focus upon the family patterns in the relationships of good subjects. Presumably paradoxical directives would be evident there. However, such an investigation would require examination and testing of the subject with his family members since the subject could hardly be expected to be aware of or recall the patterns in his family organization.

The relevance of hypnotic behavior to psychiatric maladies has appeared sufficiently clear so that hypnotic trance is often used to illustrate symptomatic behavior for teaching purposes. One might expect that the interpersonal context which induces symptoms will be formally similar to the relationship which induces hypnotic behavior. As will be discussed later, neurotic and psychotic symptoms occur in relationships where paradoxical directives are common. The directive that someone do something "spontaneously" appears often in human life, and the appropriate response to such a paradoxical request is to qualify one's response as "just happening." Such a response is a formal definition of a symptom.

When one examines methods of psychotherapy in terms of the relationship, paradoxical directives appear throughout the procedures and so are relevant to the processes of change in psychotherapy. Psychoanalysis is described from this point of view in a later chapter, but the question can be raised here whether or not the psychoanalytic procedure is not obviously similar to indirect methods of trance induction. If one directs a good subject to lie down on a couch in a quiet atmosphere and then to "spontaneously" say whatever comes to mind, he has provided an hypnotic context. The subject is being directed to respond involuntarily and the paradox is posed. The fact that the analyst may be relatively inactive does not indicate the procedure is not hypnotic; with resistant subjects the most effective induction is one where the hypnotist is relatively inactive, after setting up the context, so that the burden of response is upon the subject.

However, the most effective clinical use of hypnosis would not appear to be in relation to psychoanalysis or those methods which emphasize bringing about greater awareness in a patient. The best clinical use of hypnosis appears when (a) hypnosis is described in terms of tactics for defining a relationship and dealing with the resistance of subjects who counter with definitions of their own, and (b) psychiatric patients are described as people who use symptomatic behavior to gain an advantage in a relationship and to resist the definitions of others. It would follow that an effective use of hypnosis would center in dealing with symptomatic behavior as one would with resistant behavior, and the following chapter discusses such techniques as they are used in brief psychotherapy.

CHAPTER III

Techniques of Directive Therapy

IT HAS BECOME PART of psychiatric tradition to try to avoid giving a patient direct advice and to avoid telling the patient what to do. However, there are many psychotherapists who are willing to direct a patient. When directives are used, they are usually rather subtle and complex and not merely suggestions for ways of improving the patient's life.

The directive style of therapy will be described here using as illustrative data some of the methods of brief psychotherapy. Brief therapy, defined as from one to 20 sessions of treatment, does not consist of doing less of what is done in long-term therapy. The approach is different in theory and method from psychotherapy based upon theories of intrapsychic process. Usually brief therapy is brought to clearly defined symptoms. Whem more vague "character" problems are involved, then specific and limited goals are defined.

A variety of therapeutic methods are designed to deal with a patient in a minimum of time and several of these methods will be discussed here with emphasis upon what they have in common. The first method presented might be called new style directive therapy. One of the leaders in this method is Dr. Milton H. Erickson and illustrations of some of his techniques will be offered. Dr. Erickson, who is in private psychiatric practice in Phoenix, is primarily known as a leading medical hypnotist. He has developed a style of psychotherapy which has its roots in hypnosis, although actual trance induction may not take place. This description of some of his methods might or might not agree with his own description. When reference is made to a case he has published, this will be noted in the bibliography; otherwise, the descriptions are based upon tape recorded personal communications.

THE INITIAL INTERVIEW

The brief therapist attempts to induce change from the moment of his first contact with a patient. In the initial interview, information gathering is combined with maneuvers to point the direction of change. The type of information wanted by the brief therapist is rather different from that wanted by a long-term therapist. There is less concern about the past and more concern with the present circumstance of the patient and the current functions of his symptoms. Since this method does not involve bringing into a patient's awareness any connections between his past and the present, there is no exploration of childhood.

41

The brief therapist must gain the information he needs quickly. It would be convenient if patients were willing to offer all the necessary information at once, but they are not. In fact, they characteristically withhold information which is important to the therapist and they will do so even if they are asked not to withhold information. In brief therapy there is no time to wait out a patient, nor is there time or interest in discussing with the patient his resistances to revealing information. An Erickson technique to gain the information he needs is typical of his methods. He points out that the therapist wants the patient to talk under therapeutic direction, but since the patient is going to withhold information, the therapist should take direction of that withholding, too, by either directly or indirectly suggesting that the patient withhold information. For example, Erickson may directly advise the patient that this is only the first interview and, of course, there are things the patient will be willing to say to him and things he will want to withhold, and he should withhold them. Usually the patient withholds them until the second interview.

Many people would feel that advising a patient to withhold information would encourage him to do so. This is not necessarily so with the typical psychiatric patient. Although patients may have a variety of reasons for retaining information about their problems, one major factor of such retention is the advantage it gives them in dealing with the therapist. Psychiatric patients characteristically attempt to control what is to happen with the therapist and withholding information gives them some degree of control. The maneuver cannot be used successfully if the therapist directs the patient to behave in that way. Should the patient talk or withhold under those circumstances, he is conceding that he is following the therapist's directions.

The psychoanalytic therapist ostensibly uses quite the opposite approach when he tells the patient to say everything that comes to mind and withhold nothing. Apparently he is not encouraging the patient to withhold. However, when the patient inevitably does withhold information, he finds out that the analyst considers his withholding a necessary part of analytic treatment. The analyst indicates to the patient that his resistance to revealing information is necessary to the analytic process, and so the attempt by the patient to control what is to happen becomes labeled as occurring under the analyst's aegis.

An indirect suggestion that the patient withhold information is implicit whenever a therapist deals delicately with a patient who is inhibited in his offerings. By behaving delicately himself, the therapist is encouraging the hesitant patient to continue behaving in that way. Erickson describes such an approach as taking direction of the patient's inhibitions. For example, a woman came to Erickson with symptoms of choking and gagging which occurred shortly before bedtime and when people were telling off-color jokes. As stated by Erickson, the woman was demonstrating her inhibitions in the way she discussed this matter, so he also demonstrated inhibitions by assuring her he did not want to hear those jokes. At times he will even caution an inhibited patient that he is about to reveal something and perhaps he should not. Once the patient can rely on Erickson to protect the inhibitions, Erickson can then shift to a more open attitude and lessen the inhibitions. As this case of the woman suffering from hysterical gagging developed, Erickson used her inhibitions to produce a change. He accepted the woman's idea that she must not only undress in the dark but in another room than her bedroom. He then arranged that the woman "spontaneously" think of dancing into the bedroom in the dark when her husband could not see her. After all, she could do this in an inhibited way since the room was totally black. When she did this, she went to bed giggling. She could not be giggling and gagging and choking simultaneously, and so as she revised her attitude about inhibitions she also began to deal with her husband in other than symptomatic ways.

The difference between Erickson's way of maneuvering a patient and maneuvering a patient by waiting him out in long-term therapy can be illustrated with an example of a schoolteacher who came to Erickson and was unable to speak in the initial interview. Rather than interpret this as resistance, or wait until the patient provided the information he needed, Erickson complimented the woman on being able to communicate by nodding and shaking her head. He then suggested the possibility that she could write, and she nodded her head at this. Having noticed that the woman was right-handed, Erickson placed a pencil in her left hand. He then said to the woman, "How do you feel about that," and she began to talk, telling him that she feared she was going crazy and had been afraid to ask if this were so. Erickson points out that he arranged the situation so that the woman had to speak. She was communicating wrongly by only nodding her head when she was able to verbalize, and so he placed the pencil in her left hand to arrange that she communicate wrongly. Since the woman was a teacher with years of experience with a pencil in her hand, this maneuver was particularly effective.

While gaining the information he needs, the brief therapist also begins immediately to establish a context of therapeutic change. Rather than first getting the information and then proceeding, the therapy begins with the way the information is gathered. For example, a history may be taken in such a way that the idea is established of progressive improvement occurring in the patient, if this is at all possible. The therapist then works within a context of continuing improvement. Quite the reverse situation may also be utilized. If a patient is indicating a consistent worsening of his situation, the brief therapist may accept this idea fully and completely and then follow it with the suggestion that since things have become worse and worse it is certainly time for a change. The therapist then works within a context of highly motivated desire for a change.

The encouragement of a patient's commitment to a change is established as quickly as possible. Erickson was once asked what information he would want from a woman who entered therapy because she had lost her voice 4 years previously and was unable to speak above a whisper. "For brief therapy," said Erickson, "I would immediately pose her several questions. 'Do you want to talk aloud? When? What do you want to say?' These questions are important because in answering them she is committing herself. The burden of responsibility is being placed upon her shoulders. Does she really want to talk? Today, tomorrow, next year? What does she want to say—something agreeable or something unpleasant? Does she want to say 'yes' or does she want to say 'no.' Does she want to speak aloud expectedly or unexpectedly?"

When the patient discusses the circumstances under which she wishes to speak aloud, the groundwork is being laid for ways the change might occur. By dealing with *when* she wishes to talk, and whether she wishes to find herself talking unexpectedly, she is participating in establishing a premise of change. Once the patient can accept the premise that a change might occur, the therapist can work within a framework where each change experienced by the patient occurs as a part of a continuing progressive change.

Among the many ways to demonstrate in action the possibility of change to a patient is the use of direct hypnosis. Hypnosis was once discredited as a method of treatment with the argument that a patient might lose his symptom in trance, but it would return later and therefore only temporary relief could be achieved. Erickson considers this argument a misunderstanding of the best use of hypnosis. One does not use hypnosis to suggest away a symptom, but to establish a certain kind of relationship and to convince a patient that his symptomatic behavior can be influenced. If a patient with a compulsion is hypnotized and his symptom alleviated while he is in trance, the therapist is not curing the patient but establishing the possibility of change under his direction. When the skillful hypnotist relieves a symptom in trance, he does not banish it but rather insists that it occur again later only under special circumstances. The change which was produced in trance is then extended outside of the hypnotic situation.

Erickson's work is replete with examples of relieving a symptom in trance and then suggesting that it recur later under controlled circumstances. For example, in patients with functional pain, he will accept the pain as real and necessary but shorten the time of it, change the moment of occurrence, shift the area in which it occurs, or transform it into a different sensation. He cites the case of a woman with incapacitating headaches which lasted for hours who now has one every Monday morning, when this is convenient. She suffers the headache for as long as a minute, sometimes for as long as 90 seconds, yet with time distortion she can subjectively feel that it lasted for hours if she wishes to.

Although pain is considered by the subject to be an involuntary affliction and, therefore, unchangeable, the possibility of change can be established with it as one would with other involuntary symptoms. Erickson may, for example, ask a patient when he would prefer to have his pain. Would he prefer it in the daytime or the nighttime, on a weekday or on week ends? Would he rather have it severely for a short time and then be without it, or have it mildly all the time? As the patient grapples with the problem of when he would really prefer to have the pain, he is accepting the premise that his current pain program can undergo change.

DIRECTING THE PATIENT

Brief therapy is inevitably directive therapy. The patient must be persuaded to participate in bringing a change about. In long-term therapy the patient may participate by attending regular sessions and expressing whatever comes to mind. In brief therapy he is asked to follow specific directions which involve him in a cooperative endeavor to change his symptomatic behavior. As stated by Erickson, the patient must be told to do something and that something should be related to his problem in some way.

When asked what he thought crucial to inducing therapeutic change, Erickson replied that he thought it was like teaching a child in school. It is not enough to explain to the child that one plus one equals two. It is necessary to hand the child some chalk and have him write "one" and then write "one" again and make a plus sign and write "two." Similarly, it is not enough to explain a problem to a patient or even to have the patient explain a problem himself. What is important is to get the patient to *do* something. Erickson points out that it is insufficient to have a patient with an oedipal conflict discuss his father. Yet, one can give the patient the simple task of writing the word "father" on a piece of paper and then have him crumple it up and throw it in the wastebasket and this action can produce pronounced effects.

One of the difficulties involved in telling patients to do something is the fact that psychiatric patients are noted for their hesitation about doing what they are told. Yet, Erickson deals with patients in such a way that they feel they must follow his suggestions. There would seem to be several factors involved in Erickson's success in getting suggestions followed. One factor is Erickson's sureness. He is willing to take full responsibility for a patient and his problems and also is willing to indicate that he knows precisely what must be done. (However, he is also willing to be unsure if he wishes the patient to initiate something.) Often the patient will be encouraged to follow Erickson's suggestion in order to prove him wrong. Erickson also encourages patients to follow his directions by emphasizing the positive aspects of the patient's life so that they are pleased to cooperate with him. As is typical of most hypnotists, he places tremendous emphasis on the positive. If a patient points out he always tries and fails, Erickson will emphasize his determination and his ability to try. If a patient behaves passively, Erickson will point out his ability to endure situations. If a patient is small, he finds himself thinking about how fortunate it is to be small and agile instead of large and lumbering as he talks to Erickson. If a patient is large, his solidity and strength are emphasized. This emphasis on the positive is not mere reassurance, but statements supported by evidence which the patient cannot deny. By being sure of what the patient needs to do, and emphasizing the positive aspects of the patient's behavior, Erickson makes suggestions in a context where they are most likely to be followed. Besides this context, he makes suggestions which the patient can easily follow and, in fact, emphasizes how the patient is doing this anyway.

Typical of Erickson's directives to patients is his accepting the patient's behavior, but in such a way that a change is produced. At the most abstract level, his directives can be seen as encouraging symptomatic behavior by the patient, but under therapeutic direction. He never, of course, tells the patient to cease his symptomatic behavior. Rather, he directs the patient to behave in a symptomatic way, at times adding something else to this instruction. Since the behavior occurs under therapeutic direction, it becomes a different kind than when it is initiated by the patient.

Typical of Erickson's directives to a patient is that given to a patient who came to him reporting that he was lonely and had no contact with other people. All he did was sit alone in his room and waste his time. Erickson suggested he should go to the public library where the environment would force him to be silent and not have contact with others. At the library he should waste his time. The patient went to the library and, since he was an intellectually curious fellow, he began to idle away his time reading magazines. He became interested in articles on speleology, and one day someone at the library asked him if he was interested in exploring caves too, and the patient became a member of a speleological club which led him into a social life.

What is typical about this example is the acceptance, in fact encouragement, of the patient's symptomatic behavior, but the rearrangement of that behavior in a situation where a change is possible. The patient could hardly refuse to follow the directive since he was only being asked to follow his usual routine of wasting time and avoiding contact with others.

Besides arranging that the environment produce a change, Erickson may also use the mere fact of *his* directing the patient to behave in a symptomatic way to produce a change in the symptom. For example, with one patient who weighed 270 pounds and was an expert on diets, Erickson instructed her to "overeat enough to maintain a weight of 260 pounds." The woman returned to the next session, having lost 10 pounds, and curious to see whether Erickson would have her overeat enough to lose 10 pounds again, or would it be 20 this time. He suggested she overeat enough to maintain a weight of 255 pounds, thus suggesting a loss of only 5 pounds. Such an approach offers satisfaction of the woman's need to overeat, her need to lose weight, and also her need to rebel.

The writer utilized this type of direction with a patient who was a free-lance photographer and whenever he received an assignment he made some silly blunder which ruined the picture. As a result, he was so busy concentrating on avoiding errors in setting up his camera that he could not take a satisfactory picture. He was instructed to go and take three pictures suitable for sale to an architectural type of magazine, and each of these pictures was to be taken with a deliberate error. He could forget to close the back on one, set the shutter speed wrong on the next, or any errors which he was likely to make. The patient found it difficult to do this assignment, but he brought in three badly taken photographs and from then on had little difficulty with the technical side of his assignments. Symptomatic behavior under duress often produces marked change.

Besides directing a patient to do some activity, Erickson may also direct a patient to think of something related to his symptom, or to experience some sensation related to his symptom. Inevitably the patient must go through the symptomatic behavior, under direction, in order to think about it. Such a process is characteristic of any occurrence in therapy where the patient is directed to think about his symptom, including free association.

A common Erickson technique is to have the patient not only go through his symptomatic behavior, but also to add something to it as he does so. An example is offered here of a patient treated by the writer with this Erickson method. The patient was relieved of lifelong enuresis in two sessions.

The patient, a 17 year old youth, was in psychotherapy for some months with a psychiatrist who was dissatisfied with his progress. The youth had entered therapy under duress from his parents and liked to be independent and not ask for help or discuss his problems. He had been wetting the bed all his life at least 50 per cent of the time. He was referred to the writer for relief of his enuresis with hypnosis while he continued his therapeutic sessions with the psychiatrist. The young man was elaborately casual about most things in his life, but intensely worried about his bed-wetting. He wished to go away to college and he could not live in a dormitory with this embarrassing symptom. He proved to be an almost impossible hypnotic subject, and so he was led to agree both that he very much wanted to get over the symptom and that it made him feel helpless and childish. He was advised that if he were hyp-notized and the symptom suggested away he would only be encouraged to feel more helpless, but he could easily get over the enuresis himself if he really wished to. When he said he did, he was asked what he considered a long walk. He sug-gested that 2 miles was indeed a long way to walk. He was then told that he should go to bed that night, and when he awakened during the night with a wet bed he should get up and take a 2-mile walk. Then he was to return, climb into the wet bed, and go to sleep. Further, if he slept through the night and found his bed wet in the morning, he should set the alarm for 2 o'clock the next morning and get out of bed and take his walk. He was assured that if he followed this procedure with determination, he would rapidly get over his symptom without help from anybody. The youth went home, dutifully clocked 2 miles of distance with his car, and the first night he awakened with a wet bed he got up and got dressed and took his walk. He continued this procedure, and some time later he called the writer and said he was now wetting the bed only once every 2 or 3 weeks and was this as much as he could expect. He was advised to continue the regime and he would get over his enuresis completely. A year later he was still not wetting the bed.

The relief of this symptom was accomplished by a method which is simple and apparently neglects those factors which long-term therapists consider most important. Obviously, the boy was involved in conflicts within himself and in an intense relationship with his parents over this bedwetting. He was also threatened with the possibility of leaving home and going away to school if he had no symptom, and so on. However, this method not only took into account his desire for independence and self-help, but it was the kind of arrangement which was difficult enough that he would not go through with it unless he was willing to give up his symptom and replace it with a feeling of pride in accomplishment.

Although this method is simple, it can be applied to a variety of kinds of problems. Erickson reports a case of a 65 year old man who was suf-fering from insomnia. The patient had been taking 45 grains of sodium amytal nightly and still could get only an hour or two of sleep. When he asked for an increase, his physician became frightened at the addiction and referred him to Erickson. Judging him to be both honest and de-termined, Erickson told him he could recover from his insomnia easily if he was willing to give up 8 hours sleep. The old gentleman was willing to make that sacrifice. Erickson had learned that the man lived alone with his son, and that he did not like to do housework. He particularly did not like to wax the floors because he objected to the smell of floor wax. Erickson instructed the patient to go home and prepare for bed by put-ting on his pajamas at his usual time of 8 o'clock. However, instead of go-ing to bed he was to get out a can of floor wax and polish the hardwood floors all night. At 7 in the morning he was to stop, have breakfast, and get ready for his usual day's work. The next night, after working all day, he was to repeat this procedure and polish the floors all night again. The third and fourth night he was to do the same, and at the end of that time he would only have given up 8 hours sleep since he was only sleeping 2 hours a night anyhow.

The patient went home and dutifully polished the floors the first night, the second night, and the third night. The fourth night he said to himself, "I'm so weary following that crazy psychiatrist's orders, but I suppose I might as well polish again tonight since I still owe him two hours sleep." Then he decided that he would lie down and rest his eyes for just half an hour. He awakened at 7 the following morning. That night he was in a dilemma: Should he go to sleep or spend the night polishing the floor as he had promised. He decided to go to bed at 8 o'clock, and if he could read the clock at 8:15 he would get up and polish the floors all night. A year later he was still sleeping soundly every night. He reports that he does not dare suffer from insomnia since if he does not fall immediately asleep he must spend the night polishing floors. As Erickson describes the case, "You know the old gentleman would do anything to get out of polishing the floors—even sleep."

Although this method must be designed for the individual patient, in general, it involves committing the patient to wanting to give up his symptom, drawing him out on some activity which he does not like (but preferably feels he should accomplish), and persuading him to go through with the activity as directed. In another case, Erickson had the patient spend the nights reading those books he had put off reading, and since he might fail asleep reading them he was to stand up at the mantle and read all night. The cure involves the patient accomplishing it himself and thereby gaining respect for himself.

In both of these cases, the emphasis is apparently upon the patient's activity other than his symptomatic behavior. However, the instruction to the enuretic youth was that he was to take his walk *when* he wet the bed, and in this sense his bedwetting came under direction of the therapist as well as his self-punishment for bedwetting. Similarly, when the old gentleman is told by Erickson to stay awake and polish the floors, he is being told to behave in a symptomatic way by staying awake at night instead of going to sleep.

At times, Erickson's directive to a patient may include not only going through his symptomatic behavior with an additional suggestion, but that additional suggestion may be placed in such a way that the patient does not know he is receiving it. For example, Erickson once suggested to a woman who had weekly recurrent headaches that she carefully study her headache that week in case a month from then she should want to alter it. He points out that this suggestion is actually a suggestion that she skip 3 weeks of headaches. Just as he is an expert at getting over suggestions indirectly to hypnotic subjects, Erickson also likes to direct patients in such a way that they cannot recognize they are being directed and so cannot resist the directive. At times he may do this by dropping a casual comment, at other times he may arouse the patient emotionally on one topic and then mention another, apparently unrelated topic at that moment. The patient will "unconsciously" connect the two topics.

Another way which Erickson will use to get over a suggestion indirectly is to tell anecdotes to patients. These anecdotes may be experiences of his own or experiences with previous patients. Often they will include an idea which the patient can recognize and defend himself against, but while defending himself against that idea he is accepting others which encourage change.

Similarly, Erickson may persuade a patient to accept a suggestion by making it seem quite minor in nature. He will induce a cumulative change but base it upon so small a change that the patient can accept it. He may ask a patient with insomnia to report to him next time that he believes he slept one second longer one night. No matter how extreme the patient's protests that he rarely sleeps, he is still willing to concede so small an improvement. The groundwork is then laid for further improvement. Should a therapist ask immediately for a larger change with certain patients, he is likely to find himself doing long-term therapy.

Erickson may also bring in the relatives of a patient to enlist their cooperation in producing a change. Since most symptoms are imbedded in a relationship, a change can often be worked more rapidly by working with an intimate relative of the ostensible patient.

THE HYPNOTIC RELATIONSHIP AS A
MODEL FOR PSYCHOTHERAPY

Sigmund Freud once suggested that if the general population was ever to be reached with psychotherapy it would be with hypnosis. Typically, discussion of brief methods of psychotherapy include some aspects of hypnosis as a major factor. The techniques of Erickson which have been discussed here have developed out of his orientation in hypnosis. It would seem appropriate to consider the formal similarities between hypnotist—subject and psychotherapist—patient, not with the idea of hypnosis as a method of cure, but with the idea that it can be a model for therapeutic types of relationships.

A particularly important similarity between the two situations rests in the fact that attempts by a hypnotist to influence a subject may be met by resistances which are essentially similar to the resistances offered by a patient to a psychotherapist. The intensity of the relationship between hypnotist and subject and psychotherapist and patient rests upon the fact that both relationships sharply focus upon one of the most important questions in human life: How much influence will one person permit another to have over him?

If one examines all methods of psychotherapy at the most general level, a similar pattern can be seen. The patient is first persuaded that a positive change in himself might occur. The patient then participates in bringing the change about. This participation may include following a directive therapist's instructions, taking a journey to Lourdes, free associating daily in an analyst's office, and so on. Finally, the patient begins to look for and notice changes when they do occur.

If this process is translated into more interpersonal terms, it can be said that a patient is first persuaded that a therapist might influence him, he then participates in helping the therapist influence him, and he finally acknowledges, if only to himself, that he is not functioning entirely on his own terms. These steps are also the stages in the induction of hypnotic trance.

When traditional techniques of hypnosis are used, the hypnotist is clearly directing the subject, and the subject is clearly following directions. However, Erickson has pioneered in a variety of indirect methods of trance induction with his naturalistic techniques,[14] and as a result the line between a hypnotic relationship and some other influencing relationship has become quite vague. Erickson may, for example, induce trance behavior in a subject by having what appears to be a general conversation with him. He may also begin a long monologue which the subject finds tedious and wonders when he will get to the point, but interspersed in the monologue are certain phrases given certain emphasis which produce trance behavior in the subject.

When hypnosis is broadened to include indirect as well as direct methods of trance induction, questions are raised about the hypnotic nature of other types of relationships where one person is attempting to influence another. The definition of hypnosis then shifts from a description of a supposed state to a description of responsive behavior. The responsive behavior of a subject is in some ways formally similar to behavior of other people in other situations. The similarity between the responsive behavior of a resistant subject and a person exhibiting symptomatic behavior is particularly striking.

A hypnotist always meets some degree of resistance in a subject, and dealing with resistances is central to trance induction. The resistant subject may, at one extreme, be too cooperative and at the other he may be uncooperative. If he is too cooperative, the hypnotist requires that he try to resist him by "challenging" him. If he is uncooperative, other methods are used. Typically, the resistant subject who is asked to place his hands on his knees will do so with some indication that he is doing it in his own way in his own time. Often he will not do something, or partially do it, and be surprised if this is pointed out to him. Or he may be asked to sit still and yet he will move nervously about while insisting he cannot help himself. The resistant subject does not directly refuse to follow suggestions or the hypnotic induction would be over. He does not follow suggestions, but he indicates that he cannot help himself.

Techniques of handling the resistant subject have been discussed by Erickson more fully than by any other hypnotist. Essentially the way he recommends handling a resistant subject is to accept the resistance and even encourage it. He calls this a Utilization Technique[16] in the sense that he is utilizing the behavior offered him by a subject. For example, a patient came to Erickson for hypnotherapy and immediately began pacing up and down as he entered the office. He reported that he could not sit down but had to pace up and down and, therefore, he had been discharged by various psychiatrists as uncooperative. While he paced the floor and repetitiously explained this, Erickson said, "Are you willing to cooperate with me by continuing to pace the floor as you are doing now?"

The patient replied, "Willing? Good God, man! I've got to do it if I stay in the office."

Erickson then asked the patient if he could participate in his pacing by partly directing it. The patient agreed, and Erickson suggested that the patient pace over here, and then pace back and forth over there, and so on. After a while, Erickson began to hesitate in his directions, and the patient began to pause in his pacing and wait for them. Then Erickson seated the patient in a chair where he continued to go into a trance.

There are two major steps involved in this method: Erickson first asks the subject to do what he is already doing to resist him, and so do it under his direction. Then he begins to shift the patient's behavior into more cooperative activity until the patient is fully following his directions.

Erickson may accept a patient's resistance in a variety of ways. He may, for example, accept the patient's resistance in that chair, and then suggest the patient move to another chair, thereby identifying the resistance geographically and separating it from the patient. He may also accept the resistance as occurring at this time, but not at some other time. With one woman he attempted a method of induction which he knew would fail, and he then apologized to the woman for using that technique with her. In the discussion of his inadequacy she went into a trance. As he pointed out, the woman needed to defeat him, but she also wanted a trance, and by letting her defeat him first, she could have both.

These various ways of handling resistance become relevant to Erickson's psychotherapy when it is seen that he utilizes similar techniques for handling symptomatic behavior by a patient. For example, a woman came to him for help in losing weight who had tried every form of diet and medical treatment. She could lose the weight, but she immediately gained it back again. In fact, the moment she dieted until she reached the chosen weight, she was compelled to rush for food and eat compulsively until she was overweight again. Erickson asked the woman if she was willing to lose weight in a way that met her personality needs, and she agreed. He then instructed her to go out and gain from 15 to 25 pounds. While she was gaining this weight she could organize her thinking to be prepared to lose weight. The woman gained a few pounds and then became most reluctant about gaining more. Yet, Erickson insisted she gain more. He finally compromised when she had gained 20 pounds and *permitted* her to stop gaining weight. She then went on a diet, lost the weight she wanted to lose, and has continued to maintain a low weight.

In this example, Erickson deals with the patient's compulsion to eat in ways similar to the ways he deals with resistant subjects. He accepts her need to gain weight and even encourages it, but under his direction. She must then wait for further direction from him, and at a certain point he provides a shift. He also utilizes a typical pattern of the woman: she usually loses weight and then gains it, and he has her gain weight and then lose it.

In Erickson's case histories a formal pattern appears in case after case despite his diverse methods. He gains control of a patient's symptomatic behavior by encouraging it, thereby posing a paradox, and then he shifts his direction. In brief form, this method illustrates the essential interpersonal context of any therapeutic change.

THEORY AND METHOD

It would appear to follow logically that Erickson would develop a school of psychotherapy which would draw upon his experience in dealing with resistant hypnotic subjects. The attempt to change the behavior, perception, or sensations of a normal person with hypnotic techniques inevitably suggests ways of changing the behavior, perception, or sensations of people suffering with neurotic problems. When the resistance and the cooperation of the hypnotic subject is seen as a factor in the relationship with the hypnotist, then symptoms in neurotic individuals can be seen as ways of dealing with the therapist and with other people. An obvious similarity exists between the patient who "involuntarily" circumscribes both his own and other people's behavior and the resistant hypnotic subject who "involuntarily" will not respond on the hypnotist's terms. Although neither hypnotist nor therapist would ever concede to a patient that a contest is involved, inevitably there is a contesting process over how much influence the subject or patient will let another person have over him. There is going to be a struggle, which may never be labeled as such, over who is going to determine what is to happen between the two people. However, neither hypnotist nor therapist is likely to be merely authoritarian and insist they are in charge or they will be defeated in their endeavor. The patient or subject has only to refuse to do what they say to provoke them and thereby control what happens. Both hypnotist and therapist must circumscribe the subject's behavior in a permissive way. This permissiveness may be active or it may be the silence of psychoanalysis. It is at the point where permitting symptomatic or resistant behavior shifts to encouraging such behavior that the control of the relationship comes into the hypnotist's and therapist's hands.

When a hypnotist encourages a subject to resist him, after asking the subject to cooperate with him, the subject is in a peculiar situation and cannot easily gain control of what is to happen. If the subject resists, he is doing what the hypnotist asks, and if he cooperates he is doing what the hypnotist asks. He must follow the hypnotist's direction no matter what he does and so he cannot gain control of the relationship. Similarly, if a therapist encourages a patient to deal with him by symptomatic means, within a framework of helping the patient give up his symptomatic means, the patient cannot help doing as the therapist directs. If the patient continues with his symptoms, he is conceding that he is following therapeutic directions; if he ceases his symptomatic behavior, he is conceding that he is following the therapist's direction since this is the larger goal of the therapist. If one describes symptoms as the ways the patient has learned to circumscribe the behavior of others, he is unable to use these means if the therapist is directing him to do so. Different types of therapy can be defined as different methods of direction by the therapist. The psychoanalytic therapist encourages the patient to behave in symptomatic ways by directing him to lie down on the couch and say whatever he wishes, while the analyst maintains a permissive silence. Since the patient deals with others by means of symptomatic behavior, he inevitably will offer such behavior when he is asked to say whatever he wishes. In this sense, his symptomatic behavior occurs at the direction of the analyst. For example, although this is a crude oversimplification, it is clear that if a patient's symptom is constant complaining about his lot and he is asked to lie down and say whatever comes to mind, he will be complaining at the behest of the psychoanalyst.

The brief therapy of Erickson can be seen as formally similar—he might help the complaining patient complain in a more effective manner, thus encouraging the behavior, but under his direction.

The stages of brief therapy which have been described here all involve taking direction of the patient's behavior. In the initial interview, encouraging the patient to talk and suggesting that he withhold information results in directing both what he says and what he does not say. Specific instructions to a patient typically involve asking the patient to do something he is doing anyway, but to do it under direction and, therefore, change the character of the activity. Usually these directions involve a shift to a higher level of abstraction: the patient who is punishing himself *with* some distressing symptom may be asked to punish himself *for* treating himself badly with the symptom. In this procedure, the therapist is accepting the patient's need to punish himself but changing the purpose and result of the punishment. In addition, to go through with the punishment on instruction, the patient must go through with the symptomatic behavior he is punishing, and so the symptom comes under the direction of the therapist. Similarly, the therapist takes control of the symptom when he requests that the patient exhibit it at a different time than usual or in a different context or for a different purpose. If the therapist thinks the patient is likely to relapse, he may also suggest such a relapse and the conditions for it so that relapsing, if it then occurs, becomes part of a cooperative endeavor rather than resistance by the patient. The basic rule of brief psychotherapy would seem to be to encourage the symptom in such a way that the patient cannot continue to utilize it. One of the quickest methods is to persuade the patient to punish himself when he suffers from the symptom, thereby encouraging him to give up the symptom.

It is possible to describe any form of therapy as a self-punishment for the patient. After all, it is difficult to go and discuss one's weaknesses and inadequacies with a therapist (who ostensibly has none). To be successful, therapy must in some sense be an ordeal. If an expatient says of his psychoanalysis that it was a pleasure, he obviously did not have a typical experience. When one observes that psychotherapy is hard on the patient and that the patient seeks out this ordeal, one can wonder if the type of people who seek psychotherapy are not somewhat prone to self-punishment, whether one operates upon a theory of guilt as the "cause" of symptoms or not. If psychotherapy can be seen as a punishing situation which the patient seeks, then it seems reasonable to make this self-punishment more explicit and actually direct the patient to punish himself for his distress.

The range of possible self-punishment for a patient is quite wide. Ostensibly the best self-punishment would be that which is of benefit to the patient and/or meet his psychodynamic needs. If the man who feels he should exercise more is required to get up in the middle of the night and do a number of deep knee bends whenever he experiences his symptom, then he is benefiting whatever he does. If he gives up the symptom, that is beneficial; if he does not, then he is exercising, and that is beneficial. A part of the effect or this form of treatment seems to be the withdrawal of some of the "bad" aspects of the symptom by making the appearance of the symptom result in something good for the individual. If a man who feels he should do more writing is required to get up in the middle of the night and write for an hour on any day that he suffers symptomatic distress, then the symptomatic distress becomes defined as producing a beneficial effect. Thereby many of its functions are eliminated. Often the threat of a possible punishment can have effects upon a patient. For example, a writer constantly postponed writing so that he never accomplished anything, and he also avoided social life with women but felt he should experience more relationships with women. When he agreed that if he did not write a precise number of pages each week, the number he felt he should write, then he would ask a precise number of girls for dates the following week, he was quick to spring to his typewriter to avoid such a punishment. However, either way he would benefit: if he wrote, that was what he wanted, if he did not, then he would have to socialize with women, which was what he wanted. In either case, there would be a change in his life pattern.

When a symptom is seen as a way a patient gains an interpersonal advantage, it seems logical to resolve the symptom by arranging a situation where the symptom places the patient at a disadvantage. A prescription for self-punishment is one way of arranging such a situation, but the mere fact of making the therapeutic relationship a benevolent ordeal can also set up this situation. For example, a patient suffered from an involuntary squint which occurred whenever anyone behaved hostilely with him. He was a young executive in a selling situation where he needed to appear self-confident and sure of himself, and so the squint was a handicap. However, the squint also gained him some advantage; he was able to disarm anyone who was hostile to him because it is difficult to be hostile to a man who squints as if he has been struck by you. The patient wanted to get over this symptom quickly, and it was clear that an approach in terms of self-understanding of his fears would not be quickly productive because he had been through 3 years of psychoanalysis with that emphasis.

When the patient was referred for hypnotic treatment he came in somewhat reluctantly and condescendingly because he felt that hypnosis was really not quite respectable. In his past he had always sought the best and most respectable treatment, and with the recurrence of depression, as well as this squinting symptom, he had sought out a phychiatrist of high status in the community. The referral by the psychiatrist for hypnotic treatment was not welcomed by the patient, but he was agreeable about it.

The fact that the patient felt condescending about a relationship with a hypnotist made it possible to arrange his situation so the squinting was a disadvantage rather than an advantage to him. He did not prove to be a good hypnotic subject, and so another tactic was used. First, a question was raised whether or not he had ever dealt with his name in his psychoanalysis, since it was such an odd name. We will call him Mr. Elephant. He replied that he had not. He became somewhat defensive about this, pointing out that he had probably not dealt with many things in his analysis. His feelings were aroused by having his analysis questioned by someone who used a less respectable procedure. He was then told that for this particular treatment it was extremely important that he know he squinted each time it happened. When asked how often he had squinted during the interview up to that point, he was uncertain. He was advised that it was important that he know exactly when he squinted, in fact, so important that it was necessary to point the squint out to him each time in such a way that he would be increasingly aware of it. The suggestion was made that each time he squinted, the therapist would squint back at him, thereby calling the squint forcefully to his attention. It was pointed out that this procedure might be painful to him, but it was for a good cause. He readily agreed to this procedure, being an agreeable and tolerant man. However, the question was then raised: How could the therapist know if the patient had noticed him squinting back at him? It was decided, after some discussion, that the patient would acknowledge that he noticed the therapist squinting back at him by stating his name each time it happened.

In a few moments the patient squinted, the therapist squinted back, and the patient said "Elephant." He asked politely if that was what was wanted, and he was assured that was exactly it. Once again he squinted, the therapist squinted back, and the patient said "Elephant." Since the patient habitually squinted every few moments, this procedure was repeated every few moments as the conversation progressed. The patient began to get angry, but he continued to be determinedly polite and condescending. However, as the interview continued, the patient began to react to the squinting back as if it was an aggressive or hostile act. Since he typically squinted when faced with hostile acts, naturally his squinting increased. Yet the more it increased, the more he was forced to go through this unpleasant procedure. Toward the end of the interview the patient began to squint less and less. At the beginning of the next session, he was asked to go through the same procedure once again. He did not squint during an entire hour and a half session.

Although the treatment involved more than this procedure before the squint was eradicated, the rapid disappearance of the symtom during the interview would seem to have a great deal to do with this simple ordeal through which the patient was placed. In essence, it provides a paradigm for aspects of longer term methods of psychotherapy. Instead of giving him an advantage in a relationship, the symptom placed the patient at a severe disadvantage. He was faced with a therapeutic paradox: he was being helpfully ridiculed by a man he looked down upon. It might be added that as his symptom disappeared his depression was relieved as well, a typical response to these methods which is contrary to the popular belief that the relief of a symptom will result in a substitute symptom or precipitate a depression. (It should also be noted that the humiliation was not taken as exploitive; therapist and patient enjoyed each other socially after successful treatment.)

Another aspect of directive therapy illustrates an idea which is contrary to popular belief. Many directive therapists are willing to take charge and intervene in a patient's life, while nondirective therapists typically argue that telling the patient what to do will increase his dependency problems. From the point of view of directive therapy, the situation appears much like the mother-child relationship when a child is trying to get more direction from the mother and the mother is trying to avoid having the child so dependent upon her. The more the mother brushes off the child, the more dependent and demanding the child becomes. Often this is the case in psychotherapy. A willingness to let the patient be dependent upon the therapist temporarily will typically produce a lessening of the demands for dependency, while frustrating the patient's demands can increase them. Such frustration will induce transference behavior in a patient which can then be interpreted in terms of past frustration, but treatment is thereby extended and in the long run the experience can be too humiliating for a patient.

Directive therapy, in many modified forms, would seem to be becoming more typical in psychiatric practice. Those therapists who are dissatisfied with the length of treatment, failures, and the reaching of plateaus without progressive improvement, often try out some intervention in the life of the patient, or some directions for specific tasks, which force a more rapid change. Some of the methods of brief therapy are usable occasionally in the context of long-term therapy. Other techniques seem to require a style in themselves which is different from the style of the long-term therapist. One essential aspect of the brief therapy situation is the creation of an intense involvement between therapist and patient and then a rapid disengagement from that involvement. The separation of patient and therapist begins almost at the moment they have fully come together. By such a rapid disengagement, the patient is prevented from delaying or defeating his improvement because the premise is established that the therapist will not long be there to defeat.

OTHER METHODS

One of the more exasperating therapeutic problems is the phobic reaction. A way of discussing other brief methods of therapy is to deal with how they relieve the phobic patient. The usual emphasis placed upon relieving the unreasonable fear of a person with a phobia deals with the patient's ideas or emotions. The goal of the therapist is to help the patient understand what is behind it, distract the patient's attention, shift his perception, or change his affect in the situation. Such an emphasis is typical in the routine hypnotherapeutic approach and in deconditioning processes. However, it is argued here that these shifts in ideas and affect are a byproduct in the relief of phobias and that the essential goal is to induce the patient to enter the phobic situation while behaving on the therapist's terms. From Freud onward it has been acknowledged that "understanding" or "insight" of the cause of a phobia is not sufficient for a cure; the patient must enter the phobic area behaving differently than he has in the past. Many methods of relieving phobias appear to offer the patient some rationalization, or reasons, for entering the phobic area along with assurances that now the situation will be different. These rationalizations may include: the idea that the patient now has sufficient insight so he will not have the fear, the idea that he should enter the phobic area so that he will become anxious and better understanding can be achieved when his anxiety is intensified, the idea that his anxiety has now been deconditioned so it is safer for him to enter the phobic area, and so on. Usually if the patient will continue to enter the phobic area under direction his distress will be relieved. A major problem is how to motivate him to do so.

One way to arrange that a patient enter a phobic area can be illustrated with a patient who came to Erickson with a fear of riding in an elevator. Erickson induced a trance and directed the subject to go to a particular address with the suggestion that he be particularly fascinated by the sensations in the soles of his feet on the way there. The patient arrived at the address, thinking about the sensations, and then discovered that he had ridden an elevator to reach the address. He rode back down the elevator on his return home. The usual way to look at the resolution of this fear would be to say that the patient's attention was distracted by his concentration on his feet and he rode in the elevator without realizing it. Once having done so, he could do it again. An alternative explanation is possible, but before discussing it a similar case can be cited.

A woman once came for hypnotherapy for various problems, one of which was a fear of taking a shower with the bathroom door closed. She feared that if she closed the bathroom door and showered she would be unable to turn off the water or open the door and that she would drown. She was angry about this silly fear, yet if she attempted to overcome it she found herself tensing up and behaving in an agitated way and so was unable to turn on the shower if the door was closed. To help her solve this problem would set a precedent for solving more important ones, and so one day while she was in a good hypnotic trance it was suggested to her that one of these days she would realize she had taken a shower with the bathroom door closed.

The following session she came in rather angry. She said that one day that week while drying herself after a shower she noticed the bathroom door was closed and realized she had taken a shower under those circumstances. She thought the therapist had something to do with it, and she was angry because she had conquered this fear but gained no feeling of triumph in having done so. It had merely happened. To help her feel she had conquered the fear, the therapist suggested that during her next shower she would feel somewhat afraid and apprehensive with the door closed, but with courage she could overcome this fear. She followed directions and her apprehension vanished after several showers.

Once again, this resolution of a fear could be explained by saying the patient went through a fearful situation without "realizing" she did. Yet this explanation is doubtfully satisfactory. A person may have amnesia for an experience, but at the time of the experience he realizes what he is doing. The essential element here would not seem to be the distraction of attention.

We know that one of the peculiarities of hypnosis is the "post-hypnotic suggestion." When the subject in trance is directed to do something at a later time, he goes into a trance at that time to accomplish the task. Presumably, therefore, Erickson's patient was in a trance while riding the elevator. If he was in a trance, he was behaving differently. It seems possible that it was not merely the distraction which lessened his fear, but the fact that he rode in an elevator while behaving differently than he had in the past. He was not reinforcing his fear by his behavior, he was extinguishing it by behaving differently. Similarly, the woman patient had followed a posthypnotic suggestion and taken a shower in a trance and so was behaving differently. Both cases involve the patient (a) going through the fearful situation while (b) behaving differently. It can be argued that unreasonable fear can only persist if the feelings of fear are reinforced by the behavior of the fearful person. If the person is behaving differently he is feeling differently.

In both these examples the patients went through the fearful situation behaving at the therapist's directions and on his terms. Their behavior was "taken over" by the therapists. If this is typical of the resolution of this type of fear, one can wonder if it occurs in situations where it is argued that the relief occurs independent of the relationship with a therapist.

One of the current ways to resolve fear is by the method of deconditioning. An exponent of this idea is that of Wolpe who offers a full presentation of his method in *Psychotherapy by Reciprocal Inhibition*.[60] A partial description of it will be given here. According to Wolpe's theory, fear and anxiety are the result of previous conditioning to fearful situations. The therapeutic task is to decondition or desensitize the autonomic responses of the patient. His ideas developed from experimental work with animals, in which he made them anxious and cured their anxiety by progressively taking them step by step back through the anxiety situation.

After taking a patient's history, Wolpe instructs him to make a list of all the situations which make him anxious. Then he has the patient make a list of his fears from the least fearful to the most fearful. When this is done, Wolpe has the patient relax and imagine a series of scenes beginning with the least fearful situations. If the patient is afraid of blood, he is relaxed and told to imagine a small bandage with blood upon it, then a small wound with blood, and so on until finally he imagines a hospital full of bloody and wounded soldiers. Wolpe temporarily recesses the procedure the moment the patient indicates any anxiety. In addition, Wolpe sends the patient out to assert himself in interpersonal situations. He apparently has considerable success with his method.

Wolpe's argument is typical of those who follow conditioning theory. He believes he is desensitizing processes which occur inside the individual. If we examine this deconditioning method from an interpersonal point of view, it appears similar to the previous examples of the relief of fear by taking control of a patient's behavior in the fearful situation. Wolpe is a gentle rather than an overtly dominating person, but he takes rather full control of a patient's behavior. The patient must follow Wolpe's directions by making his list of anxiety situations, he must relax or be hypnotized on Wolpe's terms, and he must imagine what Wolpe tells him to imagine. It is Wolpe who describes and designates the fearful scenes, and the patient has only a veto power by manifesting some anxiety. The patient is taken through the anxiety situations in imagination while relaxed or behaving as Wolpe directs. Then he is directed to go out into the realistic fearful situation with strong reassurances, both direct and implicit, that he will now behave differently in those situations. He goes through them with the expectation of returning to Wolpe for congratulations for experiencing the situation without fear. Although the method is presented by Wolpe as a procedure focussed upon the internal processes of the patient, a fuller description would indicate that the patient's behavior is "taken over" by the therapist in the process of treatment. If one examines the interpersonal context of this subjective change in the patient, it would appear that the problem posed the patient is a most paradoxical one. He enters treatment to recover from, and therefore to avoid, feeling anxious. He is asked to think about those situations which provoke him to feel anxious (according to Wolpe the method is most effective with patients who can become anxious merely by imaging an anxious situation). Yet he is not allowed to feel anxious. If he exhibits the least anxiety, the treatment session is stopped. When this occurs, he must return again, paying an additional fee, and again be faced with a situation which makes him anxious. Yet if he becomes anxious, he is again dismissed and must return. Faced with a benevolent therapist who is placing him through an anxiety arousing ordeal, the patient is forbidden to feel anxious, and the procedure will only be terminated when the symptoms cease.

Wolpe, as well as Freud and many other therapists, provides a rationalization for the patient to proceed into the phobic area. Typically the therapist does not order the patient into the phobic situation, even after the rationale is provided. He "advises" him to voluntarily seek out the phobic situation. Yet such advice in a helping context is directive, and insofar as it is directive the patient is faced with a typical therapeutic paradox; he is being *directed* to *voluntarily* do something. If he was merely directed to enter the phobic area, he could do so and return, pointing out that the experience was fearful and the therapist had disappointed him. Yet when he "voluntarily" enters the phobic area, he is not only likely to be less fearful but if he should experience anxiety he can be advised that what he did was voluntary and perhaps he was not quite ready for it yet—sometime in the future he can voluntarily do it again.

The importance of the interpersonal aspects of deconditioning therapy is best illustrated by a point in the theory of the method. Such therapists, and Wolpe in particular, emphasize that anxiety "spreads." The cause of phobic anxiety is typically said to be the result of a trauma where the person became anxious and this anxiety spread to the phobic area. Therefore the patient should never be allowed to become anxious in the treatment or the spread continues. There is careful avoidance of requiring the subject to think of something anxiety provoking when he is not yet ready for it, because encouraging anxiety spreads it over the neural pathways and increases the patient's problem. Psychoanalysts are criticized for allowing a patient to become anxious on the couch because they are thereby increasing the severity of the patient's symptoms. Yet the writer has found, and so have others, that a patient's anxiety can decrease if it is *encouraged.* In fact, the more one asks a patient to become anxious, including helping him become so by asking him to think of anxious situations, the less anxious he becomes. This would follow if "anxiety" is responsive behavior, but not if it is the result of trauma and neural pathways.

The relief of irrational fear and anxiety occurs in an interpersonal context where the therapist is influencing and controlling the behavior of the patient. This influence and control occurs when the therapist accepts the patient's behavior and defines it as cooperation rather than opposition. If a person is behaving in an anxious way, he will not stop on command. Fearful behavior can be seen as a style of maneuvering other people, although the results subjectively may be distress. To control such a person's maneuvers, it is necessary to acknowledge and accept his behavior and thereby "take it over." Often one can, for example, suggest that a person's anxiety will increase—momentarily. If he then behaves in a more fearful way, the therapist has gained control of his behavior and so can direct him successfully to behave in a less fearful way. Traditionally it has been said that the therapist is dealing with an increase and decrease in the quantity of fear inside the person, yet it is more apparent that he is setting the terms as to how that person is to behave with him. Since the patient is not setting the terms, he cannot reinforce by his behavior his feelings of fear, and when the fear is irrational it will not be reinforced by the realistic situation.

Another method of relieving a patient's symptoms quickly was developed by Cowles who apparently had success with a considerable number of patients.[11] Once again, his method included providing the patient with an explanation of his problem which included a procedure for relieving it, and then the patient was sent out to behave in a symptomatic way and come back and report changes. Cowles' theory centered in a depletion of "nerve energy." When a patient arrived, Cowles would explain to him that his symptoms were the result of a loss of nerve energy and that when this occurred he would naturally have a history of having symptoms each rather worse than the previous one. His analogy was progress down an elevator. He thereupon gave the patient a nerve tonic and then a powerful suggestion. This suggestion was given in a particular kind of way. The patient was told to lie down, and then Cowles would press his thumb and forefinger between the eyes of the patient, pressing the occipital nerve. At the same time he would press with his other hand on the patient's stomach. Simultaneously, he would say loudly to the patient a suggestion which was essentially a suggestion that he would get better and better. The first few treatments it is doubtful if the patient could hear the suggestion; the pain of the pressure on the nerve is considerable. Then Cowles would send the patient out to "fight his fears" and return with a report. He was told that he would go back up the elevator of symptoms rapidly until ultimately he was symptom free.

The patient of Cowles came for treatments which lasted as little as 5 minutes, each one like the time before. He was required to wait in a waiting room full of improving patients. Regularly he went to a meeting of improving and recovered patients who gave testimonials to their successful treatment. The general atmosphere was one of improvement, and excuse for improvement, and a requirement that the patient show some effort to improve. In this procedure the patient is essentially instructed to go out and behave in a symptomatic way, and only improvement will release him from the rather punishing treatment process.

One of the more entertaining examples of taking control of a patient's behavior appeared in Lindner's article called "The Jet Propelled Couch."[41] A borderline psychotic patient presented delusionary material to Lindner about his contact with other planets. He presented this in such a way that Lindner was excluded and the patient was in charge of this subject. In more orthodox therapy a therapist would gain control of this material by interpreting it to the patient and relating it to the patient's past life. Lindner, however, encouraged the patient to bring in the material and then proceeded to correct him on it and suggest additions. The more Lindner took the initiative with the planetary discussion, thus gaining control of the behavior the patient offered, the more reluctant the patient was to make an issue of the matter, and eventually he abandoned this psychotic behavior.

Although delinquency is not technically a psychiatric problem, treatment for delinquent behavior meets similar difficulties to those encountered in more legitimate psychiatric complaints. It seems about as useless to tell a delinquent to stop behaving badly as it is to tell a compulsive patient to stop ritually washing his hands. A method of treatment for antisocial behavior makes overt many of the implicit processes in other forms of psychotherapy. The method described is to have the therapist accept and take over the delinquent behavior within an institutional setting.[45] The youth is not advised to give up his delinquent behavior, such as a plan to escape, rather he is encouraged to talk about his plan with the therapist. The therapist then points out how inadequate this plan is and suggests changes to help him escape more successfully. However, he draws the line at personal participation. He will not provide a key, pointing out that he is not fool enough to get actively involved in this endeavor and jeopardize his position. In this situation the therapist maintains his superior position in the relationship by not letting the patient place him at a disadvantage, while redefining the rebellious or resistant behavior as cooperating with him in a joint plan. The result is the abandonment of unsocial behavior and a rather intense involvement of the youth with his therapist so that more traditional therapeutic techniques can be used.

Recently the writer discovered another method of brief psychotherapy, one where the symptomatic behavior is directly prescribed. The procedure was developed by Frankl as a technique of logotherapy[20] and he calls it "Paradoxical Intention." A summary of the method is provided by Gerz,[27] with examples of 24 patients treated for phobic and obsessive-compulsive complaints. As mentioned by Gerz, anticipatory anxiety frequently will cause a symptom to actually materialize. "The more the patient fears the occurrence of the symptom and the more he tries to avoid it, the more liable it is to occur. For example, the patient who has a fear of blushing will actually do so as soon as he tries hard not to blush. How would it be, then, if instead of trying *not* to blush, the patient would *try to blush;* or if, instead of trying not to pass out, or not to get panicky, etc., he would try to do that which he is so afraid of? Since we have no voluntary control over our autonomic nervous system, naturally the patient will not be able to blush as soon as he tries to do so, and it is precisely this phenomenon which is used in the technique of Paradoxical Intention." In the procedure, the therapist takes a case history, explains to the patient the basic principles of Paradoxical Intention, and he discusses successful cases with him. Then the patient is asked to have his symptom right there. As Gerz reports, in a case of a patient afraid to pass out, "To evoke humor in the patient I always exaggerate by saying, for example, 'Come on; let's have it; let's pass out all over the place. Show me what a wonderful 'passer-out' you are.' And, when the patient tries to pass out and finds he cannot, he starts to laugh." The procedure is continued in the office and the patient is advised to try to have his symptoms elsewhere. Gerz says that it is necessary for the procedure to be repeated over and over until finally the neurotic symptoms cease.

This technique developed by Frankl is imbedded in the mystique of existentialism and so has a decidedly individual orientation; the patient is seen as struggling against his fears and desires with relief coming when he attempts to do what he fears. As Frankl describes the procedure, the method is doubtfully the posing of a paradox in any formal sense. To fear something and then to deliberately do what one fears is not paradoxical behavior in terms of a logical definition (in German "paradox" would appear to be synonymous with "absurd"). The obvious paradox in the procedure only appears if one shifts from the individual to the relationship point of view. When a therapist indicates he will help a patient over a problem and within that framework he encourages the patient to have the problem, he is posing a formal paradox. The messages at one level conflict with the messages they qualify, just as a class can conflict with the items within it, and when this occurs paradox is generated.

When one examines the various methods of psychotherapy, a difficulty in discovering what they have in common is the problem of getting an accurate description of what actually happens in a particular form of therapy. The therapist's reports are usually couched in the language of his particular method rather than being a description of the interchange which actually takes place. This is less true of brief methods than of long-term therapy, but the problem still remains. For example, one can observe a psychodrama session by Moreno and receive a different impression than one does when those sessions are written up in the framework of psychodramatic theory. The amount of control which a therapist takes of a patient's behavior in psychodrama is particularly impressive. Not only is the patient often required to act out his usual behavior under direction, but also the behavior of his family members and even his dreams. At times he may be provided with an alter ego which is articulating what he is "really" thinking, so that his thoughts are even defined for him. It can also be argued this experience can be punishing and will continue until the patient undergoes a change. In an intensive psychodramatic session, the patient is helped to recover from his symptomatic behavior while behaving symptomatically under direction, a procedure typical of therapy methods.

In summary, directive therapy places the patient in a paradoxical situation which he cannot resolve as long as he continues with his symptomatology. Rather than giving him an advantage in controlling the relationship with the therapist, his symptoms place him at a disadvantage as long as they continue. Defining the situation as benevolent, the therapist provides an ordeal. The patient is thereby caught in an "impossible" situation, a therapeutic paradox. If the therapist was benevolent only, the patient could deal with him. If the therapist was only treating the patient badly, the patient could deal with this. However, when the therapist is hard on the patient within a framework of benevolent help as long as the symptoms continue, the patient can only abandon his symptomatology.

Throughout these illustrative methods of directive therapy it is evident that "insight" or attempts to bring about self-awareness and understanding are not part of the procedure. There are no transference interpretations or connections made between the patient's past and present life from the usual intrapsychic point of view. Often the therapist may see a variety of kinds of intrapsychic or interpersonal data which he does not reveal to the patient. His goal is to bring about a change, not to focus the patient on his mental or emotional structure. The therapist in some methods of brief therapy may also terminate treatment while still aware of other problems the patient may have. His goal is to produce a rapid change in one aspect of a patient in such a way that progressive change will occur in other aspects of the patient's life after therapy has terminated. When the therapist is successful, the patient is "normal" in the sense that he has as little concern with insight as the general population and is dealing with other people in ways that bring him more satisfaction.

CHAPTER IV

Strategies of Psychoanalysis and Other Awareness Therapies

THE TECHNIQUE of psychotherapy one prefers will depend upon his theory of psychopathology and the function of symptoms. Different therapists exposed to a similar patient will have quite divergent assumptions about the nature of the problem as well as procedures for treatment. For example, faced with a woman patient whose symptom is extreme anxiety whenever she attempts to leave her house alone, the brief therapist would assume that the woman herself and other people in her environment were reinforcing this symptomatic behavior. He would direct the woman to stay at home in such a way that she could not continue to do so. The family therapist would assume the woman's symptom was part of an implicit contact with other family members and would argue that the woman's husband should be treated for this symptom as well as the woman herself. The awareness, or nondirective, therapist would have quite a different view of the problem. He would assume that the woman's symptom had a "cause" in her intrapsychic structure. He would accept the woman's desire to stay at home while exploring the reasons behind her symptom. In theory and practice he would exclude other family members. His emphasis would be upon bringing into the patient's awareness her repressed ideas and the relation between her current behavior and her fantasies and childhood experiences. This emphasis upon the individual and the refusal to overtly direct the patient are both characteristic of the nondirective school.

Those who prefer a nondirective strategy in psychotherapy, particularly the psychoanalysts, usually disapprove of brief methods of treatment or telling a patient what to do in his personal life. The psychoanalyst will argue that a directive therapist merely removes symptoms and does not *really* change the patient. Should a patient appear to change quickly in another form of psychotherapy, the psychoanalyst will argue that merely a "transference cure" and not a basic change has occurred. The idea that there is no point in relieving a patient of his symptoms, in fact that it is not wise, is deeply imbedded in psychiatric thinking. Two assumptions are present in this point of view: (a) relieving symptoms is not particularly difficult if one chose to do it, and (b) if a patient is relieved of a symptom he will merely have another, probably a worse one, since the underlying "causes" have not been resolved. The validity of both these assumptions is currently being questioned and the evidence for them is slight, if existent.

Nondirective therapy is usually distinguished from other methods by the refusal of the therapist to tell a patient what to do outside the consulting room and by his impassive passiveness within the room. The psychoanalyst typically feels that intervening in the life of a patient distorts the therapeutic process. Psychoanalysis in Freud's time was not only more brief, but it was more active. Freud would select the topic for a patient to free associate about, and when the patient gained some "insight" into a problem, Freud would suggest that he take action in his personal life now that he had this new knowledge. The long length of treatment and the extreme unwillingness of a psychoanalyst to require specific behavior from a patient would seem to be a later development.

A problem in describing psychoanalysis, as well as other schools of psychotherapy, is the fact that reports of therapists emphasize the theory of a school rather than what actually happens between therapist and patient. Although there is a voluminous literature on psychoanalytic theory, there is a decided absence of descriptions of what actually takes place in the psychoanalyst's office. There is even some question whether psychoanalysts are not typically more directive than they would admit for publication.

The emphasis upon thought processes and the development of fantasy life would seem to be related to Freud's fascination with the processes of human thinking. One cannot read Freud without admiring his tenacity and skill as he traces a patient's ideas through all their symbolic ramifications. There is no intent in this chapter to disagree with Freud's formulations about individual personality development or his analysis of symbolic material. Rather, it will be suggested that the exploration of the human psyche may be irrelevant to therapeutic change. Although Freud assumed that the patient's self-exploration produced change, it is argued here that change occurs as a product of the interpersonal context of that exploration rather than the self-awareness which is brought about in the patient. Freud appeared during a period when it was assumed that man could change through self-understanding, and it seems more apparent today that the ability of a person to change because of self-knowledge is definitely limited. A description of psychoanalytic therapy which includes both analyst and patient, rather than only the subjective processes within the patient, makes apparent other possibilities besides self-understanding as the source of therapeutic change.

Despite the absence of descriptions of what actually happens between therapist and patient in psychoanalysis, it is possible to describe this form of therapy on the basis of the general ideas of what is supposed to happen. It is also possible to find in this method similarities with other, apparently quite different, methods. Since various forms of therapy effect changes in the same type of patients, the question can be raised whether or not there are similarities between (a) the directive therapist's advice to a complaining patient that he complain more effectively, (b) the repeating back of the patient's statement of complaint in the nondirective therapy of Carl Rogers, and (c) the silent reception of complaints by the psychoanalyst.

According to the psychoanalysts, therapeutic change takes place when a patient free associates in the presence of the analyst. The conflict between the patient's instinctual drives and the necessities of social existence have produced in his unconscious repressed ideas, distorted perception, and misdirected libidinal energy. Working through his transference to the analyst, the patient discovers the various repressed ideas carried over from childhood and is freed from them. His difficulty in therapy is working through his resistance to the discovery of these distorted ideas. With the occasional interpretations of the analyst he learns to face them, trace them to their roots, and find relief. There are three rather important premises in the psychoanalytic point of view: (a) the patient's problem is largely one of distorted perception and affect, (b) the patient's struggle is largely with himself and with his resistances to discoveries about himself, and (c) it is assumed that any advantage a patient gains in his environment from his symptoms is mere secondary gain; the primary emphasis is upon his defenses against ideas within himself.

This emphasis upon only internal processes in a patient was not always so in the history of psychoanalysis. One of the more important moments in that history was Freud's courageous reversal of his position on hysteria. From asserting that hysterics had suffered an actual sexual assault in the past, as they reported, he shifted to the argument that their statements represented fantasies involving wish fulfillment. From this emphasis came the presentation of the Oedipal conflict. However, this shift also centered psychoanalysis upon the fantasy life of the patient rather than his behavior in relation to other people. If Freud had emphasized the possibility of the hysteric's parents behaving in a particular way with the patient, he would have entered the field of family study and classification. If he had emphasized the way the hysteric was manipulating him by falsely telling him about such an assault, he would have examined psychotherapy in terms of tactics between patient and therapist. Instead, he centered upon the patient's misinterpretations of his past and so entered the field of symbolic process. The emphasis upon the distorted perception of the patient, rather than upon the patient's behavior, shifted the concern of psychoanalysis to the fantasy life of the patient rather than the patient's responsive behavior to what the analyst was doing or not doing.

Inevitably, distorted perception must be considered in any study of human beings. No one can deny that patterns of perception persist in people after the patterns were learned. Otherwise we would meet each new person without any expectations of what that person is like. For reasons of economy alone we must codify our information about people so that we do not have to start fresh each time someone says something to us. It also seems apparent that our codification system will at times not be in actual agreement with the situations we are in. We misperceive people because our expectations are not complete enough to account for the new things which occur in our lives. Whenever we enter a new relationship we perceive it in terms of previous relationships, and we will both modify our previous perceptions and maneuver the new relationship to meet our previous perceptions. However, granting the persistence of patterns of perception, and granting their inappropriateness in some situations, we need not confine the study of therapy to the processes in the interior of an individual. A person perceives, but he also behaves, and the responses he gets to his behavior will affect his perception. The de-emphasis of behavior in psychoanalysis has almost produced the argument that psychoanalytic therapy is a one-person system of interaction. When it is assumed that the patient's struggle is largely with overcoming resistances to discoveries about himself, the behavior of the analyst is neglected. In fact, some analysts seem to be arguing that when an analyst says nothing at a particular moment he is not influencing the patient. Similarly, Rogers will argue that the therapist is merely a mirror held up to the patient so that the patient can see himself.

Actually nondirective therapy is a misnomer. To state that any communication between two people can be nondirective is to state an impossibility. Whatever a therapist does not say to a patient as well as what he says will circumscribe the patient's behavior. If a therapist says, "I'm not going to direct you what to do," when a patient asks for direction, the therapist is obviously directing the patient not to ask him what to do. If a patient complains to a therapist and the therapist is silent, this silence is inevitably a comment on the patient's behavior. The crucial aspect of nondirective therapy from the point of view offered here is the fact that the patient cannot gain control of the psychoanalyst's behavior. If a therapist both directs and denies he is directing, he will be in control of the relationship.

THE THERAPIST'S SUPERIOR POSITION

To control a relationship a person must be in a position to establish the rules for what is to happen between himself and another person. The fact that a therapist must be in a superior position and take charge in therapy is obvious when one considers how impossible the situation would be if he did not. A patient views the therapist as an authority who can help him, and should the therapist behave in an inadequate way the patient will go elsewhere. However, it does not necessarily follow that the therapist makes an issue of being in charge, because, after all, he is dealing with people who are peculiarly sensitive in this area. The therapist assumes a position of obvious advantage in the interchange and claims the right to set rules for the relationship, while at the same time treating his superior position lightly and perhaps even denying it.

The context of the relationship emphasizes the therapist's position in such a way that he can treat it lightly. Patients are usually referred to him by people who point out what a capable authority he is and how much the patient needs help. Some therapists have a waiting list, so that the patient is impressed by standing in line to be treated while others may imply that patients with similar symptoms were successfully treated. Furthermore, the patient must be willing to pay money even to talk to the therapist, and the therapist can either treat him or dismiss him, and so controls whether or not there is going to be a relationship. Not only the therapist's prestige is emphasized in the initial meeting, but also the patient's inadequacy is made clear. The patient is at a disadvantage, since he must emphasize his difficulties in life to a man who apparently has none.

The physical settings in which most therapists function also reinforce their superior position. In many instances the therapist sits at a desk, the symbol of authority, while the patient sits in a chair, the position of the suppliant. In psychoanalytic therapy the arrangement is more extreme. The patient lies down while the therapist sits up. His chair is also placed so that he can observe the patient's reactions, but the patient cannot observe him. Such an arrangement gives him an advantage, since both people must observe their effect on each other to control each other's behavior. Patients most concerned about controlling others may panic at talking to anyone they cannot see and may refuse the couch.

Finally, the initial interview in therapy usually makes quite explicit the fact that the therapist is in charge of the relationship by the rules for treatment he lays down. He suggests the frequency of interviews, implies he will be the one who decides when treatment will end, and he usually instructs the patient how to behave in the office. He may make a general statement about how the patient is to express himself there, or he may provide specific instructions as in the analytic situation where the patient is told he must lie down and say whatever comes to mind.

Although the therapist begins with an advantage in setting the rules for the interaction, any or all of his advantages may be tested or questioned by the patient before therapy is completed. The patient may neglect to pay his fee, not show up at the proper time, imply that other patients of this therapist were not cured, walk about instead of sitting where he is supposed to, refuse to talk, and indicate that he is probably more adequate than the therapist.

In every exchange with the patient the therapist will attempt to maintain his advantage and the patient will try to overcome his disadvantage, but this does not mean that an overt struggle for control of the relationship is the process of psychotherapy. The therapist who must make an issue of being in a superior position by insisting that the patient apply that label is going to provoke a sense of contest and be at a disadvantage in the relationship. Ideally, he should be able to *let* the patient appear to be in the superior position when the patient insists. Whenever a therapist demands that a patient behave in a certain way he is likely to be defeated, but whenever he *permits* the patient to behave in a certain way he is continuing to define his position as superior. For example, a patient may insist that his nondirective therapist talk to him. Should the therapist argue that he does not want to and the patient must talk, he will be at a disadvantage. However, he may say, "I wonder why you're so disturbed at my not talking," or "I'll be glad to talk, but it's how *you* see the problem that is important," and then he is accepting the patient's demand while still circumscribing the patient's behavior.

The permissive aspect of psychotherapy is perhaps most clearly represented in nondirective therapy. The therapist does not oppose anything the patient does short of physical assault. Whatever the patient may do, no matter how drastic, in his personal life, he does not provoke advice or opposition from the therapist. Whatever the patient says in the consulting room does not produce shock or protest from the therapist. Complaints of misery, or statements about how well life is going, produce an attentive silence. Obviously, if the patient cannot provoke an expected response from a therapist he cannot control, or circumscribe, the therapist's behavior. Typically the patient will try a wide range of behavior in the course of psychoanalysis, including many techniques of maneuvering which he has not used for years. (This is called regression in psychoanalysis.) By responding only in his own way and only on his own terms, the psychoanalyst maintains control of what is to happen between himself and the patient.

There is one type of behavior which will provoke a response from the psychoanalyst, but the response is of such a nature that the advantage still rests with the therapist rather than the patient. If the patient refuses to report his dreams or to free associate, the psychoanalyst will point out that this behavior is an expression of resistance to gaining an understanding of himself. Usually the psychoanalyst at the beginning of treatment lays down in his ground rules the statement that at times the patient will feel angry and antagonistic to the analyst and think of not cooperating or even breaking off treatment. When this happens it will be a sign of resistance to change, and therefore subject to examination and analysis because it is so important to the process of treatment.

When the patient does begin to refuse to cooperate, the analyst does not take it personally—which would give the patient the advantage since he would have provoked a response. Instead the analyst points out that resistance to change and resistance to the ideas coming to light in the patient are essential to the process of cure. Resistant behavior by the patient thereby becomes defined as a cooperative endeavor in the treatment process. Should the patient continue to be resistant, the analyst continues to deal with this as a problem the patient has with himself and thereby prevents the patient provoking an exasperated reaction from him. Since the patient has produced exasperated reactions in his relationships in the past, he has gained control of his relationships in the past. However, he cannot use those methods successfully with the psychoanalyst.

If a patient says something unpleasant to a directive therapist, such as "I don't like you," the reply may be, "All right, you don't need to like me to make use of my help." The therapist defines what kind of relationship they will have by accepting what the patient says and "topping" it in such a way that he maintains control of the relationship. When a patient says to a psychoanalyst, "I don't like you," he may receive silence in reply or an "M hm." Such a reply also accepts the patient's maneuver and "tops" it. Since the analyst will not let the patient provoke him, he continues to define what kind of relationship they will have. Similarly, the Rogerian therapist who replies to such a statement, "You feel you don't like me," is maintaining control of the relationship by this acceptance of the patient's maneuver. There is an old saying that you cannot win a fight with a helpless opponent: when your best blows are unreturned, you can only feel guilty and try to provoke a response in another way. A patient is disarmed by permissive silence; he cannot win control of the therapist's behavior. Those ways the patient has maneuvered effectively in the past become unusable, although he may attempt them again and again in the course of a long analysis. The patient can only ultimately become frustrated and rather desperately seek ways of maneuvering differently. Yet the therapist has never suggested that the patient try a different line of approach, (the patient might be able to deal with this type of direction) he has only been permissive. The patient must "voluntarily" behave differently in the hope that he can discover, almost by a random process, some ways of gaining control of the responses of the analyst. Silence is not the only maneuver of the psychoanalyst, of course. More loquacious therapists may not reply to "I don't like you," with silence. They may say, "I wonder why you don't like me today? Is it because the last time you were here you criticized your parents and you feel a little guilty about it?" Such a reply also accepts what the patient says but indicates that it is a temporary derangement, and once again the therapist is maintaining control of what type of behavior will take place between them. It is the inability of the patient to gain control of what is to happen which makes the procedure such an ordeal for him; however, if the skilled psychoanalyst responds when the patient is behaving differently from his usual ways, the patient is inevitably led in the direction of change.

The important factor in this method of directing a patient is the therapist's denial that he is directing the patient. The patient cannot refuse to follow directions and he cannot cooperate on his own terms. The analyst maintains his position of power in the relationship by being permissive and unresponsive. Inevitably when the analyst says little, what he does say becomes of enormous importance. Similarly, when the Rogerian therapist repeats back what the patient says, his selection of what to repeat becomes extremely significant, not because of what he says but because of the moment and statement he emphasizes. This moment of repetition is one of the few indications the patient has of the direction in which he is being pointed. Ultimately the patient learns to win a response from the therapist but only on the therapist's terms. The denial of direction is implicit in the method; after all, the patient is freely selecting the topics of discussion and the therapist is merely responding occasionally to certain topics. It would seem obvious that this method of directing people would be designed for people who do not easily follow directions—a characteristic of psychiatric patients.

To both direct and deny that one is directing requires a particular style of speaking. If someone asks another person for a cigarette, he is directing that person to give him one. However, if someone says, "I wish I had a cigarette," he is not asking for one, and yet the other person cannot refuse him. The cigarette must be "voluntarily" offered, or the statement must be ignored. Typically the nondirective therapist does not say, "Tell me more about that," so the patient can obey or refuse to do so. He says, "I wonder why you say that?" or "Oh?" or "You seem to feel strongly about that," or he repeats what the patient has just said with a questioning inflection. The patient faced with this type of message has been asked to clarify his statement further, and yet he has not been asked to do so in a way that he can refuse to do so. He can only "voluntarily" clarify what he has been saying. This way of nondirectively directing can be described as a directive qualified with a denial that it is a directive. The patient cannot refuse to follow direction when no explicit request has been made. A further result of this procedure is the intense concentration of the patient on the therapist; he must struggle to find in what the therapist says some indication of what he should think about and do. He may come into a session and say, "I received the impression last time that you felt I should re-consider my plans." The nondirective therapist's response may be "Oh? Perhaps you have some doubt about your plans." Once again the therapist is denying a directive, but in many such situations the patient is accurate in his interpretation of the way the therapist is pointing him, despite the therapist's denials. Patients who have been through psychoanalysis and go to a directive psychotherapist may continue this procedure when it is inappropriate. The directive therapist may say, "I don't think your plans are wise and I want you to change them." The patient will return the following week and say, "I may be wrong, but I have the impression that you think I should re-consider my plans." After sufficient training in responding to nondirective requests, the patient may find it difficult to assume that a straightforward request is straightforward.

THE FRAMEWORK OF PSYCHOANALYSIS

Perhaps the most outstanding factor in nondirective therapy is the insistence by the therapist that the patient initiate what happens in the sessions. The patient comes to the therapist expecting an authority who can help him and tell him what to do, and he is promptly informed that he must do the talking and select the topics to talk about. This situation would seem to be unique in human life. Ordinarily when one seeks assistance from an expert, particularly in the healing arts, he explains his problem and is given instructions, medication, or at least advice. The situation is typically defined as one between a person in authority and a suppliant, and therefore a complementary relationship. In psychoanalysis, the therapist takes charge in the situation by placing the patient in charge of what is to happen. He instructs the patient to talk about whatever comes to his mind. Should the patient ask what he should talk about or what would be most important to discuss, the analyst declines to state and suggests that the patient is fully in charge of what is to be talked about. A part of the success of this form of treatment could be the uniqueness of the situation: the patient cannot deal with the psychoanalyst in his usual way because he has never been in such a relationship before. It is particularly difficult for the typical psychiatric patient to deal with a situation where he is in charge of what happens and yet he is not in charge. Analytic group therapy has adopted this basic strategy of psychoanalysis; the leader of the group takes leadership by disinvolving himself from leadership and requiring the group members to initiate what happens, thereby facing the group with a paradox.

Essentially the psychoanalytic situation depends upon the patient offering and the analyst countering what is offered. Most patients, particularly "helpless" patients, are accustomed to the opposite situation. The occasional patient who can only deal with people by countering what is offered will fail in this type of therapy. When the nondirective therapist meets the nondirective patient, such as a mute patient, they both become incapacitated.

Once the patient is initiating subjects of conversation, the psychoanalyst will begin to influence what should and should not be said. The therapist's control is directed less at what will be initiated and more on what direction it will take; therefore on what will ultimately be initiated. This is accomplished in such a way that the patient cannot say he is being influenced in what to talk about. The therapist's comments, such as "M hmm," or "Oh," when the patient mentions something the therapist considers important, occur within a framework of a lack of response at other times. Therefore the patient is placed in a position where he must attempt to gain a response without knowing what will be the type of behavior that can produce a response. The result is searching behavior which may include the patient's full repertoire of maneuvers that have provoked responses from other people in the past.

When the psychoanalyst does direct the patient what to communicate, he requests that the patient communicate in a particular style. This style is essentially the way the psychiatric patient is accustomed to communicating since he is being asked to say something while indicating he is not responsible for what is said. It was pointed out earlier that the typical psychiatric patient habitually insists on controlling other people's behavior in an indirect way—by symptomatic behavior which permits him to do something and deny that *he* is doing it. It would follow that he would inevitably communicate in this way in therapy, particularly if he is required to initiate what is to happen in the sessions. Yet if he is only allowed to communicate in his usual way, he will either win control of what happens in therapy or at any rate continue with symptomatic behavior. Psychoanalytic therapy has produced a way to solve this problem. The patient is directed to communicate indirectly—to say something and indicate *he* is not saying it, when the therapist directs the patient to communicate with him by dreams, fantasies, and free associative statements. The patient is being encouraged to say something and deny that *he* is saying it since, after all, he cannot be responsible for the dreams and free associations which come into his mind. When symptomatology is seen as a way of influencing people while denying this, it becomes apparent that encouraging indirect communication from the patient is a way of encouraging him to communicate in a symptomatic way. (The geography of the psychoanalytic setting also encourages indirect communication. The patient lies on the couch and talks to the ceiling rather than directly to the analyst.) When the patient qualifies his statements as not made by him but by his unconscious, on the instruction of the psychoanalyst, then the patient's way of labeling his communicative behavior as not originating with him is not opposed but encouraged *on the therapist's terms*. In this symbolic style of communication the psychoanalyst is an authority and the patient is not. (Jungian psychotherapy is not dealt with specifically here because the tactics are similar to other methods. The Jungian therapist also accepts the patient's behavior and wins control by translating that behavior into a theoretical structure which the therapist can ostensibly deal with but the patient can only gamely struggle to understand.)

Although the psychoanalyst encourages indirect communication from a patient, he is occasionally faced with direct statements. Often he is faced with direct statements about *himself*. These are less welcome than indirect statements which *the therapist* can define as comments upon the relationship. When the analyst indicates references to the relationship which occur in the patient's dreams and free associations, he is controlling how the patient defines the relationship. Should the patient define the relationship by commenting upon him directly, the analyst also takes control of the patient's definition, but in a different way. He indicates that the patient is really responding to a subjective image of him and therefore is really defining some other relationship. For example, if the patient says, "You don't have any interest in me," the therapist is likely to reply, "I wonder why you say that? Perhaps someone in the past didn't have any interest in you." The subject then shifts to the relationship between the patient and his parents. Although it is part of the theory of psychoanalysis that change in the patient is related to discoveries about similarities between the childhood past and the present, the fact of talking about the past can also be seen as a therapeutic tactic. The patient can make indirect comments about his relationship with the therapist by talking about his parents in a particular way. The therapist can then point out the similarity if he chooses to. He may do so if he wishes to emphasize that he is the one defining what the patient is *really* talking about.

If a therapist can arrange the situation so that the patient will concede that he is the authority on what the patient is *really* saying, then the therapist is in control of what kind of relationship they have. An obvious tactic which produces this situation is the emphasis the psychoanalyst places upon the unconscious. Since by definition the patient cannot be aware of what he is unconsciously doing or saying, he must rely upon the analyst to help him discover what he really means and what he is really doing. Inevitably, he must hand over to the analyst the authority to define what is happening and so the control of the relationship. The uncertainty of a patient about his own behavior can become profound when he is encouraged to believe that he is driven by forces beyond his control which the psychoanalyst can understand and interpret but he cannot. Inevitably if the patient is uncertain, he cannot win control of the relationship. Most of the techniques of psychoanalysis are designed to insure that the patient settles down to the secondary end of a complementary relationship. If the patient attempts symmetrical maneuvers and directly disagrees about a point with the therapist, his maneuvers will be defined by the analyst as a product of an unconscious wish and/or the manifestation of resistance to getting well. Symmetry as a type of relationship is forbidden until the termination of treatment, if then.

There is one further way that the analyst circumscribes a patient's behavior, which should be mentioned here. The analyst directs the patient to avoid communicating by, or about, his symptomatic behavior. Attempts by the patient to impose a paradoxical relationship are lessened when the patient cannot use his symptom to circumscribe the analyst's behavior. The analyst usually points out that the symptom is only a symptom and that they must deal with what is behind it and get at the cause. This prevents the patient from manipulating the therapist with this type of behavior and forces him to communicate differently. Avoiding this type of maneuvering by a patient may be seen as a practical necessity, since the patient has usually acquired considerable skill over the years in using his symptomatic behavior to control his personal relationships. However, rather elaborate psychological theories about cause and effect may be designed to rationalize this tactic.

Should a patient insist on using his symptomatic behavior in the therapy room or confine his discourse to that subject, the therapist will soon find the patient controlling the interaction. Rather than permit this, the analyst accepts the patient's behavior and redefines it. Should the patient insist upon talking about his compulsive behavior, for example, when the analyst is directing him to deal with other matters, the analyst may say, "Have you noted that whenever you discuss your wife you begin to talk about your symptom again." Or he might say, "Your symptom seems to increase whenever I mention your mother." In this way the therapist accepts the patient's resistance to talking about certain subjects, but he redefines that resistance as a cooperative indication to the therapist where sensitive areas are in the discourse.

In summary, the patient comes to the nondirective therapist, an authority who can tell him what to do to solve his problems, and is instructed to initiate everything that happens with the therapist. He is directed to communicate in other than his usual way by not using his symptomatic behavior and by communicating free associations and dreams. He must "voluntarily" change his type of maneuvering on the basis of minimal indications from the therapist, he is prevented from using the therapist's type of maneuvers by the structure of the situation, and usually his attempts to win control are anticipated in such a way that the therapist can label them as resistance to treatment.

When someone goes to an authority for advice and help and is told to do the talking himself, he is faced with a paradoxical situation. He is told to take charge of what happens in the interview, and the fact that he is *told to do so* means that he is not in charge. Whatever he says is thereby defined as being said on the instructions of the therapist. Since he enters therapy behaving in a symptomatic way, he is faced with a situation where his maneuvers to control the therapist are requested by the therapist. It was pointed out earlier that directive thrapy operates in a similar way: the therapist encourages the patient to behave in his symptomatic way. In nondirective therapy if the patient behaves in his usual way he is doing what the therapist is telling him to do, and if he behaves differently he also is doing what the therapist is telling him to do, since the goal of the therapist is to change him. The patient cannot win control of the relationship in such a situation.

Since everything the therapist does will indicate how the patient is to behave, and since the nondirective therapist denies he is indicating how the patient is to behave, the patient is faced with a therapeutic paradox. He must respond to an incongruent set of messages, and his attempts to leave the field are blocked off by the therapist's earlier statements that leaving the field will be a sign of resistance to treatment. The patient cannot control the therapist by his usual methods of behavior. If he insists on directing what happens in the relationship, he finds his effort accepted, and he is doing so at the therapist's implicit request. Should he insist that the therapist direct what happens in the relationship, the therapist declines this patient-instituted arrangement by saying that it is not his function to direct the patient. Whichever way *the patient* tries to control the relationship, his attempt will fail. He can only try again and again, until later in therapy when the therapist may acknowledge his maneuvers as acceptable. Yet the therapist does not indicate that the patient can solve the problems by maneuvering acceptably, because he denies that he is directing the patient to behave differently. When the patient changes his behavior, this is labeled by the therapist as spontaneous change originating with him.

Psychotherapy was developed to deal with a particular type of person, and there seems to be a formal similarity between symptomatic behavior and the style of therapeutic maneuver which counteracts such behavior. The therapeutic situation is so structured that when a patient behaves in his symptomatic way, thus imposing a paradox, he provokes a countering therapeutic paradox. His only possible responses are to leave the field, to comment on the impossible situation the therapist poses for him, or to cease offering paradoxical maneuvers himself. If he leaves the field, he must continue with his distress. If he comments on the therapist's maneuvers, not only will the therapist have a proper rationalization for his directives but the patient can only successfully comment by acknowledging that he is trying to control the therapist and so he takes responsibility for his actions. If he abandons his own paradoxical maneuvers he is giving up his symptomatic behavior. When he behaves and affirms that *he* is behaving in that way, therapeutic paradoxes cannot be used in response to him and the therapist is disarmed. Usually therapy is terminated when the patient is behaving this way.

Perhaps it is logical that the cure for a type of behavior should involve the imposition of similar behavior. If a patient's problem centers in human relationships it must be cured in a human relationship; and if it centers in particular methods of control it could well follow that the cure would involve similar methods of control. The difference lies in the result; the patient wins control in his relationships but cannot acknowledge doing so and thereby provokes misery in himself and others, whereas the therapist's methods provoke the patient to behave in ways which bring him greater satisfactions. However, it is conceivable that a nondirective therapist could provide a context for creating or perpetuating psychopathology. The therapist might provide a situation which forces the patient to change, for example, recover from a symptom, and then not accept the change but disqualify it as a sign of resistance or flight into health. Conceivably the patient could then experience the distress of a psychotic patient whose parents force him to behave differently and condemn him when he does. (This pathological paradox is discussed later under schizophrenia.) Should such distress occur, the therapist might argue that it is the result of the fragility of the patient without realizing that the result occurs because of the effectiveness of the method.

If one defines the behavioral goal of psychotherapy, it would seem to be this: the therapist must induce a patient to voluntarily behave differently than he has in the past. It is unsatisfactory if a patient behaves differently because he is told to do so: he must initiate the new behavior. Yet an essential paradox lies in this goal of therapy: one cannot *induce* someone to *voluntarily* behave differently. Such a paradox can only be resolved if it is seen that in nondirective therapy the patient is directed in such a way that the direction is denied and therefore his changed behavior is defined as spontaneous.

When Sigmund Freud developed the procedures of psychoanalysis he arranged a therapeutic setting which is a unique situation in human life. A crucial aspect of this setting was Freud's emphasis upon not intruding, or influencing, the productions of a patient so that the expressions of the patient could develop "naturally." (It now appears generally recognized that a patient's productions are always being influenced by a therapist, which is why patients in Freudian analysis have dreams with more evident sexual content and Jungian patients dream in appropriate Jungian symbolism, thus substantiating the theories of the therapists.) Yet by making it clear that he was trying not to influence what the patient said and did, Freud posed an inevitable paradox because the context of the relationship was an attempt to influence what the patient said and did, because it was designed to change him. That is, within a framework constructed to influence a patient, Freud attempted to exert as little influence as possible and thereby caught the patient in the essential paradox of all nondirective methods of psychotherapy.

When Freud devised this extreme procedure he was dealing with patients who did not respond to other methods of treatment. At that time there were not many other methods of psychotherapy. Yet Freud pointed out that psychoanalysis should be tried only when other methods failed because of the time and expense involved. The indiscriminate use of this rather drastic procedure is, for many types of patients, a little like building an elaborate garage to repair a flat tire.

Although nondirective therapy as practiced by psychoanalysts once had the reputation of being the preferred form of psychotherapy for those who could afford it, this assumption is being questioned in recent years. However, the fact that it is successful in some cases would imply that it might have similarities in method with other types of psychotherapy which are also successful. Since other methods may not involve "insight," one must either argue that they do not really change a patient or one must assume that (a) "insight" can change a patient as well as other factors, or (b) it is not "insight" which produces a change in a patient but something that nondirective and directive methods of therapy have in common quite independent of "insight." It is argued here that there are important similarities between different types of psychotherapy if one examines them in terms of the interaction of patient and therapist. The difference between long-term nondirective therapy and the brief therapy described in the previous chapter is apparently great. Yet these two methods can be used to illustrate some rather important factors they have in common with each other and with other methods. Some of these similarities have been implicit in the previous discussion, but a few formal points that psychoanalysis and brief therapy have in common can be briefly listed.

Psychoanalysis provides (a) an explanation, or rationalization, for the patient to explain why he is the way he is and why he will improve in treatment. The explanation provided by psychoanalysis tends to be more complex than other forms of therapy and encourages excessive introspection which often continues with a patient long after treatment is discontinued. Whereas brief therapy may provide a patient with rather simplified rationalizations for establishing the possibility of change, psychoanalysis provides the patient with an education in dissecting himself (and other people). Some kind of explanation for undergoing change seems necessary for all methods of treatment. (b) In psychoanalysis the responsibility for change is placed upon the patient, as it is in brief therapy. Requests by a patient for assistance with a problem are met with such statements as "How do you feel about it," and so on, which are countering suggestions that the patient deal with the problem. From the opening framework where the psychoanalyst places the patient in charge, throughout treatment the burden is placed upon the patient to initiate what occurs. This, too, is the case in brief psychotherapy—often this is said explicitly when the therapist says "I cannot help you, but I can help you help yourself." However, the brief therapist may more actively point out the direction in which the patient should carry his burden of responsibility for inducing change in himself. (c) Psychoanalysis provides an ordeal for the patient which could be described as a form of self-punishment. The patient must talk about the most sensitive areas of his life to an unresponsive man, he must detail all his inadequacies, weaknesses, and unsavory thoughts to a man who apparently has none, and he must do this daily while paying a considerable amount of money for an indefinite period of time. (It is generally said by psychoanalysts that the fee must represent a sacrifice on the part of a patient, a part of the ordeal the patient must go through.) The ordeal of treatment can only be ended by the patient giving up his symptomatic behavior and undergoing change. In fact, the psychoanalytic ordeal may continue even after the patient shows marked improvement because of the argument that "basic" change does not occur quickly but slowly over long periods of time. Rapid change is called the "honeymoon" in psychoanalysis, or "transference cure," or "flight into health." Yet questions can be raised whether it might be the perpetuation of treatment which perpetuates the problem. Often a patient may appear to undergo more change after terminating analysis than when involved in it. In brief therapy the therapist intervenes in the patient's life, produces a change, and then rapidly disinvolves himself so that the change can continue independent of him.

If psychoanalysis is a pleasant experience to a patient, it is not effective. Insofar as it is a punishing experience, and since the patient seeks out that experience, the procedure can be seen as a form of self-punishment by the patient. It might even be argued that the patient undergoes improvement when he has punished himself sufficiently by going through the ordeal long enough—quite independent of how much self-awareness he has achieved in the process. When the procedure is seen as an ordeal, it is obviously related to the specific self-punishment provided a patient by a brief therapist. (d) The psychoanalyst is permissive and does not oppose a patient or forbid him behaving in a symptomatic way. Whereas the psychoanalyst permits symptomatic behavior, the brief therapist goes further and encourages it. The two methods can be seen as similar if it is argued that permitting a patient to deal with you in a certain way is encouraging him to behave in that way. Certainly when we observe parents permitting a child to have temper tantrums we argue that the parents are encouraging such behavior. Similarly, it could be argued that the psychoanalyst is encouraging symptomatic behavior by his extreme permissiveness and by ostensibly placing the patient in charge. When psychoanalysis is seen in this way, the paradox which appears in brief therapy also appears in psychoanalysis. The patient cannot gain control of the relationship by symptomatic means if he is being encouraged to do so. If he continues with his symptomatic behavior, he is conceding that the therapist is in charge, and if he does not he makes a similar concession because the goal of the therapist is to induce a change in him. Related to this area of interaction is the way both the brief therapist and the psychoanalyst deal with resistance to change: both encourage it when it appears and define it as cooperation in a joint endeavor. When resistance is relabeled as cooperation it is effectively extinguished.

Although this list of similarities is hardly comprehensive, there would seem to be sufficient indication that a more thorough study of all forms of psychotherapy in terms of their similar formal patterns would be rewarding. A more rigorous science of psychotherapy will arrive when the procedures in the various methods can be synthesized down to the most effective strategy possible to induce a person to spontaneously behave in a different manner. "Spontaneous" behavior would seem to occur when a person is caught in an impossible situation—that is, a situation which he cannot resolve by his usual manner of behaving. He is thereby provoked to respond in ways which he has never responded before. From this point of view, psychotherapy can be seen as similar to the ways of achieving "liberation" or "enlightenment" in Eastern religions. Discussing this problem, Alan Watts says, ". . . the whole technique of liberation requires that the individual shall find out the truth for himself. Simply to tell it is not convincing. Instead, he must be asked to experiment, to act consistently upon assumptions which he holds to be true until he finds out otherwise. The *guru* or teacher of liberation must therefore use all his skill to persuade the student to act upon his own delusions . . ." He later says, "There is, then, nothing occult or supernatural in this state of consciousness, and yet the traditional methods for attaining it are complex, divergent, obscure, and, for the most part, extremely arduous . . . we must look for a simplified and yet adequate way of describing what happens between the *guru* or Zen Master and his student within the social context of their transaction. What we find is something very like a contest in *judo:* the expert does not attack; he waits for the attack, he lets the student pose the problem. Then, when the attack comes, he does not oppose it; he rolls with it and carries it to its logical conclusion, which is the downfall of the false social premise of the student's question."[54]

If one should simplify the context of psychotherapy and ways to achieve enlightenment, it could be said a similar paradox occurs in both situations. Within a benevolent framework, whether of healing or teaching, the suppliant is encouraged to behave in his usual ways, while he undergoes an arduous ordeal which makes it difficult for him to continue in his usual ways. The response to this paradoxical situation is a type of response which the individual has never made before and he is thereby freed from the repetitive patterns he has followed in the past.

CHAPTER V

The Schizophrenic:
His Methods and His Therapy

IN THIS DISCUSSION of the psychotherapy of schizophrenics there will first be a description of what there is about the schizophrenic that needs to be changed. Then there will be a presentation and analysis of methods of changing him.

Most theories of schizophrenia were proposed at a time when it was thought the schizophrenic patient could not be treated with psychotherapy because, according to those theories, he was out of contact with reality. In recent years a variety of therapists have been developing therapeutic techniques which seem to produce some results with schizophrenics. It has been difficult to see a connection between the ways these therapists actually deal with a patient and former theories of the psychopathology. Such therapists may have a violent struggle with a patient, they may have a quiet, insightful conversation with him, or they may spoon feed him like an infant. An attempt will be made here to demonstrate that the various techniques of therapy involve a similar pattern which can be related to both a developing theory of schizophrenia and a theory of psychotherapy.

SCHIZOPHRENIC INTERACTION

Despite all that is said about difficulties in interpersonal relations, psychiatric literature does not offer a systematic way of describing the interpersonal behavior of the schizophrenic so as to differentiate that behavior from the normal person. The schizophrenic's internal processes are often described in terms of ego weakness, primitive logic, or dissociated thinking, but his interpersonal behavior is usually presented in the form of anecdotes. An example of what needs to be classified is the following conversation between two hospitalized schizophrenics. A brief excerpt is offered here from the verbatim conversation which will be reproduced at greater length later in this chapter.

Smith: Do you work at the air base? Hm?
Jones: You know what I think of work, I'm 33 in June, do you mind?
Smith: June?
Jones: Thirty-three years old in June. This stuff goes out the window after I live this, uh—leave this hospital. So I can't get my vocal chords back. So I lay off cigarettes. I'm a spatial condition, from outer space myself, no shit.

In this conversation no intrapsychic processes are immediately apparent. There is no dissociated thinking, autism, or withdrawal from reality. From what the men say one might conjecture the presence of such processes as dissociated thinking, but even without conjecture it should be possible to state what is present in this interpersonal behavior which differentiates these men from other men.

There are at least three possible psychiatric approaches to these data. The classical approach would determine whether or not the two young men are in contact with "reality." When one of them says he is from outer space and the other says the hospital is an air base, the classical theoretician would draw his conclusion of schizophrenia. He would analyze the data no further, because classical psychiatric theory assumes that these men are not responding to each other or to their environment but are behaving in an essentially random way because of some organic pathology.

Another approach, the intrapsychic, would center around the thought processes of the two patients. The analyst would conjecture about what the patients must have been thinking, or what kind of peculiar logic might have produced these odd associations. The intrapsychic point of view would presume that the conversation is meaningful, that it is based upon distorted thought processes, and that it contains so many associations unique to these men that it is necessary to know their life histories to understand why particular statements were made. From this point of view an analysis of the data is pointless, since insufficient information is provided by the conversation alone. The young men are "obviously" schizophrenic, and their statements are symbolic manifestations of deeply rooted fantasy ideas.

Finally, there is the interpersonal approach to these data, which emphasizes the ways in which the two men interact, or behave, with each other. This approach assumes that the two men are responding to each other rather than merely to their own thoughts, and that they respond in ways different from normal ways. What is potentially most scientific about the interpersonal approach is its emphasis upon observable data. The ways in which people interact with each other can be observed, whereas the identification of thought processes is inevitably based on conjecture. What is lacking in the interpersonal approach is a systematic descriptive system differentiating the deviant from the normal ways in which people interact with each other.

An ideal classification of interpersonal relations would indicate types of psychopathology, or differentiate relationships into classes, according to the presence or absence of certain readily observable sequences in the interaction. If such an ideal system could be developed, it would not only clarify diagnosis, currently based upon an antiquated system, but also clarify the etiology of psychopathology. If one says that a patient is withdrawn from reality, one says nothing about the processes which provoked this withdrawal. If one says that a patient interacts with people in certain deviant ways, then it is potentially possible to describe the learning situation which taught the person to behave in these ways and to describe ways of changing this type of behavior.

AVOIDING CONTROL IN A RELATIONSHIP

It was pointed out in Chapter I that it is difficult for anyone to avoid working out what type of relationship he has with another person. However, there is one way a person can avoid indicating what is to take place in a relationship, and thereby avoid defining it. He can negate what he says. Even though he will be defining the relationship by whatever he communicates, he can invalidate this definition by using qualifications that deny his communications.

The fact that people communicate on at least two levels makes it possible to indicate one relationship, and simultaneously deny it. For example, a man may say, "I think you should do that, but it's not my place to tell you so." In this way he defines the relationship as one in which he tells the other person what to do, but simultaneously denies that he is defining the relationship in this way. This is what is sometimes meant when a person is described as not being self-assertive. One man might respond to a request by his wife by saying, "No, I won't," and sitting down with his newspaper. He has asserted himself in the sense that he has defined his relationship with his wife as one in which he is not to be told what to do. Another man might respond to a similar demand by saying, "I would like to do it but I can't. I have a headache." He also refuses to do the task, but by qualifying his message in an incongruent way, he indicates that *he* is not defining the relationship by this refusal. After all, it was the headache which prevented his doing the task, not him. In the same way, if a man strikes his wife only when drunk, the act of striking her is qualified by the implication that *he* is not responsible; the effect of the liquor is. By qualifying his messages with implications that *he* is not responsible for his behavior, a person can avoid defining his relationship with another. These incongruent qualifying messages may be verbal, such as, "I didn't mean to do it," or they may be conveyed by a weak voice or a hesitant body movement. Even the context may negate a maneuver to define a relationship—for example, when one boy invites another to fight in church where a fight is not possible.

To clarify the ways in which a person might avoid defining his relationship with another, suppose that some hypothetical person decided to entirely follow through with such an avoidance. Since anything he said or did not say would define his relationship, he would need to qualify with a negation or a denial whatever he said or did not say. To illustrate the ways in which he could deny his messages, the formal characteristics of any message from one person to another can be broken down into these four elements:

(a) I
(b) am saying something
(c) to you
(d) in this situation

A person can avoid defining his relationship by negating any or all of these four elements. He can (a) deny that *he* communicated something, (b) deny that something was communicated, (c) deny that it was communicated *to* the other person, or (d) deny the context in which it was communicated.

The rich variety of ways in which a person can avoid defining a relationship can be summarized briefly.

(a) To deny that *he* is communicating a message, a person may label himself as someone else. For example, he may introduce himself with an alias. Or he may indicate that he personally is not speaking, but his status position is, so that what he says is labeled as coming from the boss or the professor, for example. He may indicate that he is only an instrument transmitting the message; he was told to say what he did, or God was speaking through him, and therefore he is not the one who is defining the relationship.

A person may also deny that *he* is communicating by labeling what he says as effected by some force outside himself. He may indicate that *he* is not really talking, because he is upset or deranged by liquor, or insanity, or drugs.

He may also label his messages as being the result of 'involuntary' processes within himself, so that *he* is not really the one communicating. He may say, "You aren't upsetting me; it's something I ate," and deny that his sick expression is a message from him about the relationship. He may even vomit or urinate and indicate that these things are organically caused and not messages from *him* which should be taken as comments on a relationship.

(b) The simplest way in which a person can deny that he *said* something is to manifest amensia. By saying, "I don't remember doing that," he is qualifying an activity with a statement negating it. He may also insist that what he says is being misunderstood, and that therefore the other person's interpretations do not coincide with what he really said.

Another way to deny that something is said is to immediately qualify a statement with one which contradicts it. This negates everything said as irrelevant nonsense that is therefore not a comment on the relationship. Or a person may make up a language, simultaneously communicating and negating that communication by the very fact that the language cannot be understood by the other person. In another variant, a person can indicate that his words are not means of communication but things in themselves. He may make a statement while discussing the spelling of the words in the statement, and so indicate that he has not communicated a message but has merely listed letters of words.

(c) To deny that what he says is addressed *to* the other person, a person may simply indicate that he is talking to himself. He may also label the other person as someone else. For example, he can avoid talking to the other person by talking to the person's status position rather than to him personally. One can be sarcastic with a salesman at the door without defining one's relationship with that person, if the comments are about salesmen in general.

Or, if a person wishes to go to an extreme, he can say that the friend he is talking to is not really a friend but is secretly a policeman. Everything he says is then labeled as a statement to a policeman and therefore cannot define his relationship with his friend.

(d) To deny that what he says is said in this situation, a person can label his statements as referring to some other time or place. He can say, "I used to be treated badly and I'll probably be treated badly in the future," and these temporal qualifications deny his implication that he is treated badly at the present moment. Similarly, he can say, "A person I used to know did such and such," and by making it a past relationship he denies that his statement is a comment on the present relationship.

To negate a situational statement about his relationship most effectively, he can qualify it with the statement that the place is some other place. He may label a psychiatrist's office as a prison and thereby deny that his statements are about his relationship with the psychiatrist.

In summary, these are ways of avoiding a definition of the relationship: When everything a person says to another person defines the relationship with that person, he can avoid indicating what kind of relationship he is in only by denying that he is speaking, denying that anything is said, denying that it is said to the other person, or denying that the interchange is occurring in this place at this time.

INTERPERSONAL RELATIONSHIPS WITH SCHIZOPHRENICS

It seems apparent that the list of ways to avoid defining a relationship is a list of schizophrenic symptoms. A psychiatrist makes a classical

diagnosis of schizophrenia when he observes the most obvious manifestation of schizophrenia, an incongruity between what the patient communicates and the messages which qualify that communication. His
movements negate or deny what he says, and his words negate or deny
the context in which he speaks. The incongruities may be crude and
obvious, like the remark, "My head was bashed in last night," made by a
patient whose head is in good shape; or they may be subtle, like a slight
smile or odd tone of voice. If the patient denies that *he* is speaking, either
by referring to himself in the third person or calling himself by another
name, the psychiatrist notes that he is suffering from a loss of identity.
If the person indicates that "voices" are saying these things, he is described as hallucinating. If the patient denies that his message is a message, perhaps by busily spelling out his words, the psychiatrist considers
him delusional or perhaps "concretistic." If the patient denies his presence
in the hospital by saying that he is in a castle or a prison, the psychiatrist
notes that he is delusional or withdrawn from reality. When the patient
makes a statement in an incongruent tone of voice, he is manifesting inappropriate affect. If he responds to the psychiatrist's behavior with
messages which qualify that behavior incongruently, he is autistic. (This
description deals with the behavior of the schizophrenic and not with
his subjective experiences, which, of course, may be terrifying.)

The classic psychiatric symptoms of schizophrenia can be described
interactionally as indicating a pathology centering around a disjunction
between the person's messages and the qualifications of those messages.
When a person manifests such a disjunction so that what he says is sys-
tematically negated by the ways he qualifies what he says, he is avoiding defining his relationship with other people. The various and seemingly unconnected and bizarre symptoms of schizophrenia can be seen
to have a central and rather simple nucleus. If one is determined to avoid
defining his relationship, or to avoid indicating what kind of behavior
is to take place in a relationship, he can do so only by behaving in those
ways which are describable as symptoms of schizophrenia.

It was suggested earlier that nonschizophrenics may at times also
avoid defining their relationships with others. Someone may deny he is
doing something by qualifying his activity with the statement that a
somatic influence or liquor is doing it and not him. These are patterns
of other psychopathologies, and partial ways of avoiding defining a particular relationship at a particular time. At best they tend to be temporary,
since headaches ease up and liquor wears off. If a person is more determined to avoid defining his relationship with anyone at any time, and
if anything he says or does defines his relationship, then he must behave
like a schizophrenic and fully and completely deny what he is saying or
doing in his interaction with others. Different types of schizophrenics

could be classified in terms of different patterns, and some of their patterns are observable in normal people. The differences from the normal subject lie in the consistency of the schizophrenic's behavior and the extremes to which he goes. He will not only deny that *he* is saying something, but he will also deny it in such a way that his denial is denied. He does not merely use a name other than his own, he uses one which is clearly not his, such as Stalin, or in some other way negates his denial. Whereas more normal people will congruently negate something they say, the schizophrenic manifests incongruence even at this level.

To illustrate schizophrenic behavior let me cite a common occurrence. When a normal person takes out a cigarette and does not have a match he usually says to another person present, "May I have a light?" When he does this, he is qualifying a message concerning his unlighted cigarette with a congruent message about the need for a match, and he is defining his relationship with the other person by asking for a light. He is indicating, "This is the sort of relationship where I may request something." Under the same circumstances, a schizophrenic might take out a cigarette, look in his pockets for a match, and then hold the cigarette up in the air and stare at it silently. The person with the schizophrenic is faced with a rather peculiar sequence of communication. He is being appealed to for a match, and yet he is not. By merely staring at the cigarette, the schizophrenic is qualifying his message about an unlighted cigarette with an incongruent message. He is indicating that it is something to be stared at, not something to be lit. If he held up the cigarette "as if" it should be lit, he would be implicitly asking for a light and thereby defining his relationship with the other person. He can avoid indicating what type of behavior is to take place, and therefore what kind of relationship he is in, only by looking at the cigarette in a detached way. A more obvious example is the behavior of a schizophrenic in a room with a stranger. He may not speak to the stranger, but since not speaking to him indicates what kind of relationship it is, the schizophrenic is likely to appear excessively preoccupied with something in the room, or with his thoughts. In this way he denies that he is defining his relationship with the other person by the way in which he qualifies his behavior.

By qualifying his messages to other people incongruently, the schizophrenic avoids indicating what behavior is to take place in his relationships and thereby avoids defining his relationships. The current trend in psychotherapy for schizophrenics takes into account this interpersonal behavior. The experienced therapist tends to take the schizophrenic's statements as statements about the relationship, and to ignore the denials of this. If the patient begins to talk in an odd language, such a therapist is less likely to interpret the symbolic content of that language and more likely to say something like, "I wonder why you're trying to confuse me," or, "Why do you speak to *me* in this way?"

ANALYSIS OF A SCHIZOPHRENIC CONVERSATION

To illustrate how the foregoing description of interpersonal relationships applies to schizophrenics, a recorded conversation between two young men will be presented here and subsequently analyzed. The numbers in brackets will be used in the analysis following the conversation to identify the passages analyzed. This conversation between two hospitalized schizophrenics took place when the men were left alone in adjoining offices where they could see each other through a connecting door. The men were presumably talking together for the first time, although they may have seen each other previously when entering the same building.

Jones (1): (Laughs loudly, then pauses.) I'm McDougal, myself. (This actually is not his name.)

Smith (2): What do you do for a living, little fellow? Work on a ranch or something?

Jones (3): No, I'm a civilian seaman. Supposed to be high mucka-muck society.

Smith (4): A singing recording machine, huh? I guess a recording machine sings sometimes. If they're adjusted right. Mm-hm. I thought that was it. My towel, mm-hm. We'll be going back to sea in about—eight or nine months though. Soon as we get our—destroyed parts repaired. (Pause.)

Jones (5): I've got lovesickness, secret love.

Smith (6): Secret love, huh? (Laughs.)

Jones: Yea.

Smith (7): I ain't got any secret love.

Jones (8): I fell in love, but I don't feed any woo—that sits over—looks something like me—walking around over there.

Smith (9): My, oh, my only one, my only love is the shark. Keep out of the way of him.

Jones (10): Don't they know I have a life to live? (Long pause.)

Smith (11): Do you work at the air base? Hm?

Jones (12): You know what I think of work, I'm 33 in June, do you mind?

Smith (13): June?

Jones (14): Thirty-three years old in June. This stuff goes out the window after I live this, uh—leave this hospital. So I lay off cigarettes. I'm a spatial condition, from outer space myself, no shit.

Smith (15): (Laughs.) I'm a real space ship from across.

Jones (16): A lot of people talk, uh—that way, like crazy, but Believe It or Not by Ripley, take it or leave it—alone—it's in the *Examiner*, it's in the

		comic section, Believe It or Not by Ripley, Robert E. Ripley, Believe It or Not, but we don't have to believe anything, unless I feel like it. (Pause.) Every little rosette—too much alone. (Pause.)
Smith	(17):	Yeah, it could be possible. (Phrase inaudible because of airplane noise.)
Jones:		I'm a civilian seaman.
Smith	(18):	Could be possible. (Sighs.) I take my bath in the ocean.
Jones	(19):	Bathing stinks. You know why? Cause you can't quit when you feel like it. You're in the service.
Smith:		I can quit whenever I feel like quitting. I can get out when I feel like getting out.
Jones:		(Talking at the same time.) Take me, I'm a civilian, I can quit.
Smith:		Civilian?
Jones:		Go my—my way.
Smith	(20):	I guess we have, in port, civilian. (Long pause.)
Jones	(21):	What do they want with us?
Smith		Hm?
Jones	(22):	What do they want with you and me?
Smith	(23):	What do they want with you and me? How do I know what they want with you? I know what they want with me. I broke the law, so I have to pay for it. (Silence.)

As Smith and Jones communicate and thereby inevitably maneuver to define their relationship, they obviously and consistently qualify their statements with negations. On the recording from which this transcript was taken, the qualifying inflections of voice make the incongruencies even more apparent.

The following brief examination of the verbal aspects of the conversation will indicate the ways that each of the two schizophrenics denies that he is defining a relationship: denial that *he* is communicating, denial that something is communicated, denial that it is communicated *to* the other person, or denial of the context in which it is communicated.

Jones (1). The conversation begins when Jones gives a peculiarly loud and abrupt laugh followed by a pause. He then introduces himself in a friendly manner, but uses an alias, negating his move toward intimacy by the qualifying statement that *he*, Jones, is not making such a move.

Smith (2). Smith replies with a friendly inquiry about the other person, but calls him a little fellow, qualifying his overture with an unfriendly comment on the other's size. (Jones is actually a little fellow who indicates that he is not too happy about this by speaking in an artificially deep bass voice.) Smith also poses the friendly question of whether Jones works "on a ranch or something," when it is obvious that Jones is a patient in a mental hospital and incapable of making a living; thus he denies that he is replying to Jones, a hospital patient.

Jones (3). Jones denies that he is a patient by calling himself a civilian seaman, and then denies this by qualifying it with a statement that he is supposed to be high mucka-muck society. He has set up a situation in which no matter what he, Jones, says, it cannot be about his relationship with Smith because *he* is not speaking.

Smith (4). Smith mentions the recording machine (which is in the room but out of Jones' sight) and says that a recording machine can "sing," or inform. But this friendly warning, which would define their relationship as a sharing one, is qualified by a negation of it: he muses about the recording machine as if he were talking to himself and not the other person. He also denies that he is giving a warning by qualifying his statement with a quite incongruent one mentioning a towel. He next makes a possible statement about their relationship by saying, "We'll be going back to sea," but since they are not seamen the statement negates itself.

Jones (5). After a pause, Jones says he has love-sickness, a secret love. This is perhaps a comment on Smith's sharing statement about being seamen, yet he denies, or leaves ambiguous, the possibility that he is talking about Smith.

Smith (6 and 7). Smith apparently accepts this as a possible statement about their relationship since he laughs uncomfortably and says he doesn't have a secret love.

Jones (8). Jones then points that he isn't talking about himself or Smith but about someone who looks like himself walking around over there. Since no one is walking around over there he qualifies his previous statement about love with a denial that *he* or Smith was the one talked about.

Smith (9). Smith points out that his love is the shark and it's best to keep out of the way of him. He denies that he is defining his relationship with Jones by making it himself and a shark that is talked about.

Jones (10). Jones subsides with a statement about being picked on or rejected, but he denies that he is referring to Smith by saying, "Don't *they* know I have a life to live?"

Smith (11). After another pause, Smith makes a friendly overture but negates it as a statement about their relationship with an incongruence about the place. He calls the hospital an air base.

Jones (12). Jones replies rather aggressively with a statement about his age, thereby denying his patient status by making his age the reason for his inability to work—as if he were saying, "It's not me, it's my age." However, he counters this denial by a statement contradicting it when he states his age as 33. If he had said, "I am eighty-six," he would have been congruently stating age as a reason for not working. Thus he denies his denial. The incongruence of this third level of schizophrenic communication is one of the basic differences between the schizophrenic and the normal subject. Almost every statement in this recording consists not only of denials but of negations of those denials. When Jones introduces himself as "McDougal," he does so in a tone of voice which seems to indicate his name is not really McDougal. An examination of this third level probably requires kinesic and linguistic analysis and is merely mentioned here.

Smith (13). Smith chooses from his statement the least relevant part, the fact that in June the man will be 33. How different such a reply is from a possible one qualifying Jones' statement, "Do you mind?" Rather than acknowledge "Do you mind?" as a statement about what kind of behavior is to take place in the relationship, and perhaps apologize for bringing up work, Smith comments on the month of June. In this way he denies that Jones' "Do you mind?" is a statement defining the relationship.

Jones (14). Jones makes a congruent statement about the context, saying it is a hospital, but qualifies this with the statement that all he needs to do is give up cigarettes. He promptly negates this statement that implies there is nothing really wrong with him by saying he is a spatial condition from outer space.

Smith (15). Smith joins him in this with a laugh and says he is also a space ship. Although they are mutually defining their relationship, they are negating this definition by the statement that they are not two persons sharing something but two creatures from outer space. This turns their statements about the relationship into statements about a fictional relationship.

Jones (16). Jones again qualifies the context congruently by mentioning talking "like crazy," but he immediately qualifies this with a series of statements incongruent with it and with each other as he talks about Ripley, and the comic section, and ends up saying "too much alone."

Smith (17 and 18). Smith responds to these statements by talking to himself and not the other person.

Jones (19). When Smith mentions bathing, Jones joins his monologue and once again makes a comment that has implications about sharing their situation. This is negated by his qualifying it with a statement that they are in the service.

Smith (20). Smith joins him in a denial that this is a hospital by calling the place a port.

Jones (21 and 22). After a pause, Jones makes a direct, congruent statement defining their relationship, "What do they want with us?," and he even repeats this when it is queried by Smith. This statement and the way it is qualified are congruent and in this sense it is a sane statement. He maneuvers to define the relationship without denying that he is doing so.

Smith (23). Smith rejects this maneuver. He first says, "How do I know what they want with you? I know what they want with me." This statement is congruent with what Jones has said and defines his relationship with Jones even though he is rejecting Jones. In this sense it is a sane reply. However, Smith then qualifies his congruent statement with a thorough negation of it. By saying, "I broke the law, so I have to pay for it," he denies the place is a hospital, denies that he is talking about himself, since he has not broken the law, and denies that he and Jones are patients by making the place a prison. With one message he avoids defining his relationship with Jones and discards the attempt of Jones to work toward a mutual definition of their relationship. This denial ends the conversation and the relationship.

This brief analysis deals with only half the interaction between Smith and Jones. The ways in which they respond to the other person's statements have not been completely discussed. However, it seems apparent that they qualify each other's statements with messages which deny they are from that person, deny they are messages, deny they are addressed to the receiver, and deny the context in which they take place. The schizophrenic not only avoids defining his relationship with another person, he also can be exasperatingly skillful at preventing another person from defining his relationship with him. It is such responses which give one the feeling of not being able to "reach" a schizophrenic.

What makes it "obvious" that these two men behave differently from other men is the extreme incongruence between what they say and the ways they qualify what they say. Two normal men meeting for the first time would presumably introduce themselves and make some inquiry into each other's background as a way of seeking out some common interest. If the context was at all appropriate, they would work toward defining their relationship more clearly with each other. Should one say something that seemed out of place, the other would probably query it. They would not only be able to qualify what they said congruently, but they would be able to talk about their communications to clarify the relationship. Disagreements would tend to reach a resolution. However, when one of the participants in a conversation is determined to deny that what he says has anything to do with the relationship being worked out, then inevitably the conversation will have the disjunctive quality of schizophrenic communication.

If one should ascribe any goal or purpose to human relations, it would appear to be a highly abstract one. The wife who maneuvers to get her husband to do a certain act does not merely have as her end point his acquiescence in this act. Her larger goals seem to be related to an attempt to work out a definition of what kind of relationship they have with each other. Whereas more normal people work toward a mutual definition of a relationship and maneuver each other toward that end, the schizophrenic seems rather to desperately avoid that goal and work toward the avoidance of any definition of his relationship with another person. It would logically follow that psychotherapy with such a person must be of such a nature that the schizophrenic is required to concede that what he does is in relation to another person.

THE CONTEXT OF PSYCHOTHERAPY

Although ambulatory schizophrenics may occasionally be treated in private offices, the traditional context for treatment is an institution where the patient's entire life is circumscribed by the people in authority over him.[28a] What the patient eats, what clothes he is to wear, when and where he is to sleep, and what he is to do are in the hands of a supervisory staff. Within this context of total authority, a therapist attempts to change the patient by individual conversation with him. It is important to emphasize the context because it frames whatever is said between the two people. A quite different situation occurs with neurotic patients where the therapist has little or no actual control of the patient's life. Of course, therapists in many total institutions do not have total power because of administrative needs or conflicts among the staff, but from the patient's point of view the therapist is part of the staff hierarchy and so controls what is to be done with him. How different it is for a therapist to be permissive when he has power over the activities of a patient and when he has no more power than the patient is willing to grant him. Similarly, if the therapist insists the patient do something when he can back up his request by physical force, the message is a rather different type than when he cannot, even though that force might actually never be used.

Besides an authoritarian setting, the therapist of the schizophrenic works within a context where the control over the patient is said to be for his own good because he is within the institutional setting for help and treatment. This benevolent frame also effects whatever the therapist might do individually with the patient. If a therapist is harsh with a patient within a framework of benevolent help, his harshness is of a different kind than if it took place in a setting which was designed to mistreat people.

An equally important part of the context is the "involuntary" nature of the relationship. When a patient volunteers to be treated, as in other forms of psychotherapy, he accepts a certain kind of relationship by that act. The therapist of the schizophrenic must typically force himself upon the patient and impose a relationship on someone who has not sought his company.

AN AUTHORITARIAN APPROACH

The first example of a therapeutic interchange offered here is typical of one type of treatment of schizophrenics. It takes place in a benevolent context where the therapist maintains the patient in a private home with a staff in total charge of the patient's living conditions. This particular paranoid schizophrenic had previously escaped, was placed in a state hospital, and had just been brought back against his will prior to this interview. The session takes place in the living room of the home in the presence of several assistants and visitors. The patient's mother is present in the kitchen, within hearing distance, although it is unusual for a relative to be present during this therapist's treatment. This is an excerpt from a tape recording of the interview:[49]

Therapist: Do you think you're going to get well this time, or is it going to be another business of going off to the insane asylum?

Patient: Well, I started off from there, and uh—when I figure out how I—where's my mother?

Assistant: She's in the kitchen.

Therapist: She's here. I—I will send her out—and she has to do what I say.

Patient: No, no, you got to do what *she* says, I . . .

Therapist: Don't you know who God is around here?

Patient: I am God. (Laughter in background)

Therapist: You!

Patient: Yes.

Therapist: You crazy dope (laughs). Kneel in front of me!

Patient: No, you kneel in front of me.

Therapist: Boys, show him who's God.
(The assistants struggle with the patient, forcing him to his knees in front of the therapist)

Patient: Now listen . . .

Therapist: Kneel in front of me!

Patient: You're not supposed to use force against me.

Therapist: Don't be silly. I'm the boss.

Assistant: Now he's on his knees.

Therapist: Now ——— what are you doing?

Patient: Hey, mother!

Therapist: What are you doing to God?

Patient: Hey mother!

Therapist: Let him up, boys.
Patient: (As he rises) There are conditions under . . .
Therapist: Who's boss here ————?
Patient: You do what I say and we can make conditions for dealing . . .
Therapist: That's right, there's no conditions.
Patient: I am the creator and if you don't do what I say then uh—what can
            we . . .
Therapist: Who kneeled in front of whom?
Patient: Uh—I will destroy you.
Therapist: You can't destroy me because I'm God.
Patient: No, I am God.
Therapist: No, I am God.
Patient: Well, I happen to be a better thinker and more—more of a leader than
            you of human beings and I think what I am and I realize I'm God,
            and I see what you are and uh—
Therapist: Show him again, boys, there's no use arguing with a crazy man.
Assistant: Kneel to God.
Patient: Look uh—(calling) mother!
            (Confusion of struggle as they force him to his knees)
Therapist: Make it easy, make it easy.
Assistant: Why does God have to cry for mother? (more noise and confusion)
            Why does God have to cry for mother?
Therapist: That's true, I didn't think of that even. That's true what he says.
Patient: Look, you're not supposed to use force against me.
Therapist: I'm boss here.
Patient: You're not supposed to use force—you're not boss here.
Therapist: Who's God?
Patient: I am God.
Therapist: Well, why don't you get up then?
Patient: Well, I'll push them away—tell them to get away.
Therapist: All right boys, get away.
Patient: That was a mistake, I should have pushed them then. (the patient
            laughs and everyone laughs) I should have obliterated them.
Assistant: (Laughing) Obliterate, yeah.
Therapist: Obliterate, that's it. (pause) You're absolutely helpless. (The inter-
            view continues)

The subtle aspects of this type of interchange will be largely ignored
in this report and only gross formal themes will be emphasized. The most
obvious theme between the two men centers on who is in charge. Whether
the question is phrased in terms of who is God or who is the boss, the
apparent issue is which man is to govern the behavior of the other
and so set the conditions for what kind of relationship they will have
together. The therapist chooses to force this issue, apparently assuming it is a crucial one. The patient responds as if he too considers it of
vital importance. When the therapist says, "Kneel in front of me!" the
patient replies, "No, you kneel in front of me." When the patient says
he is God, the therapist says *he* is God. This kind of one-up-manship
struggle takes place between them with the patient attempting to win

despite his obvious disadvantage. The patient has only his wits, while the therapist has on his side not only medical authority but the patient's mother, a number of strong assistants, and about 40 pounds.

The simple way for the patient to win in such an interchange would be to say, "All right, if you want to be the boss, I will let you." By giving permission to the therapist to take charge, he himself would be in charge. Such a maneuver would incapacitate the therapist in this type of struggle. However, such a maneuver is not part of a schizophrenic's repertoire. To either take charge himself, or to acknowledge that the therapist is in charge, would require the patient conceding a relationship with the therapist. Instead, the patient rigidly insists that he is God (and therefore *he* is not relating to the therapist) and that the therapist must do what God says.

DEFINING A TYPE OF RELATIONSHIP

A basic characteristic of the schizophrenic, either chronic or in an acute episode, is his unwillingness to follow directions and do what he is told. However, he does not refuse to follow directions. The schizophrenic does not say, "No, I won't," to a request any more often than he says, "Yes, I will." When he is told to do something, the schizophrenic typically does not do it but does not take responsibility for refusing. He may indicate that he did not hear what he was told, or that he is too preoccupied with his thoughts or "voices" to do it, or that he is helpless and unable to move, or that he misunderstands because of delusory thoughts about the situation, or that he is too suspicious or too excited to do it, or he may offer an argument in the form of some fantastically implausible reason for not doing it.

When a schizophrenic actually does what he is told, it is usually when sufficient force is threatened so that he must, and then he will do it in his own time and in his own way. The doing of it even then may be labeled as accidental, e.g., when a schizophrenic is required to go somewhere with an aide and walks a desultory route, just "happening" to continue in the company of the aid. However, there are some schizophrenics who achieve a similar end by doing exactly what they are told. Waxy catalepsy is an example of this type of behavior; in milder form it was followed by rebellious soldiers in the army who followed orders so precisely that they caused confusion to their superiors. A pertinent example was a mute patient who was told to leave the ward and take a walk on the hospital grounds. It was necessary to push him out the door, and he walked straight ahead into a tree and stood there with his face against it, thus exasperating his helpful doctor.

It is not the existence of delusions or hallucinations which cause a patient to be hospitalized; a person can have those and still make his living in society. The schizophrenic is placed in a hospital in those periods when he cannot maintain the most ordinary types of relationships. One ordinary relationship he will not form is that type where one person tells another what to do and he does it.

Even though a person would not do what he was told, he might still survive as a social being if he could tell others what to do. However, if the schizophrenic is placed in charge, he rapidly arranges that he not be in charge. He does not take necessary action when he should, or he does not tell anyone to do what must be done, or he tells people to do things so fantastic that others are forced to take charge of *him*. The patient in this interview insisted that he be treated as God, which would seem to imply he would accept being in charge of his life and that of others. Yet when he was previously placed in charge or himself he went to the police and told them he had been kidnapped and was God, thus forcing them to lock him up under supervision.

A third necessary type of relationship is that which exists when two people behave as equals with each other. If one tries to behave as an equal with a schizophrenic, he soon makes it impossible. Typically when faced with a competitive relationship, the schizophrenic will fail, thus forcing a relationship between unequals. If asked as a peer to cooperate in some joint endeavor, he will not hold up his end. (If schizophrenics could cooperate as equals, they would probably form gangs and attack hospital staffs as delinquents and criminals do.)

It is the various ways of qualifying what he does which identifies the schizophrenic and also make it so difficult to "reach" him. From this point of view, the goal of psychotherapy for the schizophrenic could be phrased in this way: *it is necessary to persuade or force the patient to respond in such a way that he is consistently indicating what kind of relationship he has with the therapist instead of indicating that what he does is not in response to the therapist.*

With a neurotic, the therapist may attempt to bring about a change in the type of relationship consistently formed by the patient. With the schizophrenic, the therapist must require him to form *any* type of relationship.

GAINING CONTROL OF A RELATIONSHIP

The psychotherapy of schizophrenics requires unique techniques because of the peculiar unwillingness of the patient to indicate that what he does is in response to another person. To persuade the patient to indicate a type of relationship, it would seem obvious that the therapist must gain control, or direction, of the patient's responsive behavior.

Those methods of gaining control of another person's behavior which prove effective with normal people and neurotics are frustrated by the schizophrenic. For example, one can ask a person to do something, and if he does it then one has gained some control of his responsive behavior. Such an approach is not practical with a schizophrenic because he will not do what he is asked. It is also possible to gain control if the other person will refuse to do what is asked. By provoking rebellious responses, one can control what the other person does. However, the schizophrenic does not refuse to do what is asked, he just does not do it, and so one cannot easily influence him to rebel.

It is also possible to gain control if a person says he "cannot" do something. Typically neurotics, and resistant hypnotic subjects, do not do what is asked of them but indicate they are unable to. The hysteric "cannot" move a paralyzed limb, the phobic "cannot" enter a phobic area, the resistant hypnotic subject "cannot" levitate a hand or have a hallucination. A typical method of gaining control of such a person is to ask him to be unable to do what he is told. If he then indicates he is unable to, he is responding to direction. The resistant hypnotic subject, for example, is encouraged to resist the hypnotist's directions. If he does so, he is following the directions of the hypnotist who is thereby controlling his behavior. The schizophrenic, however, will not say he "cannot" do something. One discovers immediately how different is the schizophrenic response if one attempts to hypnotize such a patient. The usual techniques for dealing with resistant subjects simply do not work since the patient is likely to preoccupy himself by responding to his "voices" instead of the hypnotist. If the patient cannot say "Yes" and cannot say "No" and cannot say "I cannot," he must respond by labeling whatever he does as not related to the other person.

THE FORCED RELATIONSHIP

One way to gain control of a schizophrenic's behavior is to force him into a situation where he cannot deny he is responding to the therapist. Essentially the patient must be trapped so that he is following directions whatever he does and so is participating in a relationship. The physical assault by the therapist cited earlier requires the patient to respond to him. The patient may label himself as God and so indicate that *he* is not responding, but this contention is difficult to uphold when he is on his knees. This is a possible position for a helpless patient, but not for God. Not only is he forced to his knees, but his denials are brusquely dismissed by the therapist. When the patient says he is God, the therapist says, "Show him again, boys, there's no use arguing with a crazy man." The patient is in a rather hopeless dilemma; if he denies that *he* is relating to the therapist by labeling himself God, he must acknowledge that God is subservient to the therapist, an untenable position. If he does not deny that he is relating to the therapist, he is conceding that he is responding in a complementary relationship with the therapist and so no longer is behaving in a schizophrenic way. Much of the violence that takes place in this style of psychotherapy centers on forcing the patient to concede he is responding directly to the therapist.

THE BENEVOLENT APPROACH

Although one can force a direct response from a patient by physical assault, subtle procedures may achieve the same end. A quiet conversation can also make a patient's denials ineffective. Fromm-Reichmann[24] was once treating a patient who had a religious system which included an all powerful God. The patient labeled her responses as occurring in relation to this God rather than other people. Instructing the patient to go to her God, Fromm-Reichmann said, "Tell him that I am a doctor and you have lived with him in his kingdom now from seven to sixteen—that's nine years—and he has not helped you. So now he must permit me to try and see whether you and I can do that job." This patient is also in a position where she must acknowledge a response to the therapist whatever she does. If she does not go to the God and tell him what she is supposed to, she is rebelling against Fromm-Reichmann, as well as rendering questionable the existence of God. If she goes to God and says what she was told, she is not only conceding a complementary relationship, but she is conceding that the therapist is more powerful than God. If she acknowledges her God, she must deny him. If she denies Fromm-Reichmann, she must acknowledge her.

Quiet directives may contain a pattern formally similar to violently forcing a patient to his knees and so may the opposite extreme of violence. A presumably polar extreme would be a therapist soothingly nurturing a catatonic patient. Many therapists typically treat extremely withdrawn schizophrenics by a benevolent nurturing. This technique is succinctly described by Ferreira who considers the term "mothering" most appropriate for the interaction.[19] A few quotations from his article give the flavor of the technique. He describes the treatment of two mute, chronic schizophrenics and says of the first patient:

Disheveled, in a waxy immobility, she sat in a chair, aloof, staring fixedly into space while a tray of food was rapidly getting cold on her lap. I sat by her side and gently inquired as to why she would not eat. She gave me a slow-motioned glance but remained immobile. I began talking about her food, that it would get cold while she, probably hungry and thirsty, was afraid to touch it. I continued; that I would not let her be thirsty or die, that I would feed her myself. I raised a glass of milk to her half open lips, and continued talking in a soft and low tone of voice, tender and warm as if talking to a baby. "Come on . . . it's milk . . . so good, so white, so fresh . . . gee! it's good milk . . . it's *my* milk . . . I'll give it to you."

Although this "mothering" approach seems rather different from forcing a patient to his knees, the therapist is insisting upon a complementary relationship by indicating that he will take charge and the patient should follow his directions. He continues:

She looked at me with a somewhat curious expression, a quasi smile on her immobile lips, a spark of light in her eyes. Slowly she reached for the glass. I commented: "I know you can drink it by yourself," and relinquished the glass to her. She took a few sips, while I kept remarking about the "freshness" of the milk and the pleasant sensation of drinking it. I spoon-fed her some food. She took over slowly—more milk, then more food. It took her about half an hour to eat half of her food and drink a glass of milk. At that point, her negativisitic attitude became more pronounced again, and, without the least insistence, I left her with a smile and the promise of returning the next day to see her.

When the therapist holds the glass to the patient's lips, she is in a situation where it is difficult for her not to respond to him. If she drinks, she is accepting the complementary relationship. If she turns away her head or clenches her teeth, she is rebelling against him and so defining a relationship. Instead, the patient responds by taking the glass herself, and the therapist immediately accepts this symmetrical maneuver. In a similar way, when the patient dealt with the previous therapist directly by asking him to tell the assistants to get away, the therapist immediately complied. In both cases if the patient indicates he is not responding to the therapist, the therapist insists on a complementary response. If the patient then responds in a symmetrical way, the therapist accepts this definition of the relationship.

The nurturing technique includes "taking over" the patient's behavior in other ways:

I would talk directly to her almost constantly. Facing her, smilingly warm, I would intrude on her silence and mutism with many statements and questions for which I would then verbalize the follow up answers. "You always sit in the same chair? I guess you like this chair better . . . makes you feel it is *your* chair . . . do you? Oh, I know you won't tell me that . . . You don't have to . . . but I wonder how lonely it must make you feel to have only one chair to sit on . . . only one chair that *you* want, that is . . ."

The patient cannot easily refuse to behave in relation to the therapist when he is labeling all her behavior as responsive by taking personally not only her slightest response but even her lack of response. When he carries on both sides of the conversation with her, he defines her as a person in a complementary relationship with him and she cannot deny this without responding to him. She cannot even "happen" to be sitting in that chair after he has defined it as her chair. From that point on, whether she sits in that chair or not, she is threatened with this action being in response to him.

The patient's denial that she is responding to the therapist by indications that she is responding to "voices" is handled in this way:

> She nodded her head affirmatively when I stated (interpreting her silence): "Voices forbid you from talking?" Then I embarked upon a line of dramatization. In a soft, quasi-intimate voice I stated to her: "You and I will fight those voices." Whereupon I addressed myself to the empty corner of the room and, with shouts of rage, I blasted the air and those invisible voices; "Go away, don't bother Cathy!" The patient paid unusual and dramatic attention to my attitude, and later on began responding to such antics with loud outbursts of laughter. This was the first time the ward personnel and I had heard her laughing.

When a patient continues to respond to "voices," the therapist is relating to the patient but the patient is labeling what is happening as unrelated to the therapist. To frustrate such a maneuver, it is necessary for the therapist to gain control of this symptom. The therapist does so here by siding with the patient against the "voices." If the patient then responds to voices, she is also responding to the therapist who has labeled those voices as occurring under his aegis.

When the patient begins to accept a complementary relationship, he typically carries it to an extreme and so requires the therapist to continue to be disciplining or nurturing. In the second case reported by Ferreira, the patient not only began to accept things from him but even arranged to be placed in bed and tucked in by the patient therapist. He would also rather frantically masturbate in his presence which, instead of antagonizing the therapist, resulted in his verbalizing the pleasures of it for the patient. Besides accepting a complementary relationship, no matter how extreme, the therapist also accepts and encourages any move toward symmetry. For example, he first was willing to hand feed the patient milk, and then:

> I added a carton for myself, an action which increased the conventional tones in our relationship. Later, I replaced the milk with orange juice or coke, and as the patient improved, I began to omit the bringing of a beverage.

PSYCHOTHERAPY AND ETIOLOGY

Although it is an almost absurd simplification to synthesize months or years of psychotherapy down to a few formal patterns, it seems reasonable if these patterns can be shown to be relevant to the nature and etiology of the problem. The various theories of schizophrenia extant were proposed in a period when schizophrenics were considered unreachable by therapy. The first and still persistent theory of the problem, the idea that schizophrenia is based upon an organic defect, does not help explain why particular techniques of therapy now seem to produce improvement in a patient. The intrapsychic idea that schizophrenia is an immersion in archaic and primitive thinking also does not relate easily to techniques of therapy. If Ego should be where Id is, one can wonder how the two entities are reversed by feeding a patient or forcing him to his knees. Similarly, to argue that a patient was irrevocably scarred in the first months of life by maternal deprivation does not help in understanding the responses a therapist obtains from an adult patient. The argument that schizophrenia is a maturational defect would seem relevant if we had more understanding of the process of maturation. If one thinks of maturation as steps up the ladder of psychosexual development with the schizophrenic on the oral rung at the bottom, the process of bringing him up is not clarified. However, there is a theory of schizophrenia developing which is relevant to a maturational point of view and to the techniques of therapy described here.

If we define "maturation" as a sequence of learning experiences in a family, then a maturational defect could be seen as a defective family situation. Although we know little about the subtle processes of interaction in a family which permit a child to develop normally, we do know that it is necessary for a child to proceed from a complementary relationship with his parents when he is young to a more symmetrical relationship as he matures and goes his own way. It would seem that the psychotherapy of schizophrenics described here institutes that formal process.

A human child, by the nature of the organism, must be taken care of or he will die. He must be offered food and accept it, he must be supervised and respond to that supervision, he must be directed and follow that direction if he is to live with others. At the same time that he is learning to define his relationship with his parents as complementary, he must also begin to learn to behave symmetrically in preparation for that day when he leaves his parents and establishes a family himself. He must "assert" himself, walk without support, attempt to compete with others, try to be superior to others, and ultimately behave as an equal with his peers. The usual family somehow manages to provide a learning context where the child can learn to form both complementary and symmetrical relationships. Current research on the families of schizophrenics indicates that the schizophrenic child does not have that opportunity. Although a description of the family of the schizophrenic with a review of the literature on research in progress is not practical here, a few points about these families which are generally agreed upon and relevant to psychotherapy can be described briefly.

THE FAMILY OF THE SCHIZOPHRENIC

Perhaps most relevant to any therapy of schizophrenics is the fact that the patient's family is a part of the context of treatment. He came from a family when he entered an institution, and he typically must return home when treatment ends. Not only is he likely to have continuing contact with family members during therapy, but whether he improves or not may depend less upon therapeutic technique and more about his concern over the family waiting at the gate for him should he be released.

The influence of the family on this type of patient is particularly important because he usually has had little or no experience with people outside his family. In cooperation with his parents, the child who becomes schizophrenic does not have independent relationships outside his family. For many years he experiences only the responsive behavior peculiar to his family and suffers an almost total lack of experience with people who respond differently. When he is ultimately of the appropriate age and circumstance to leave home and go out into the world, he is incapacitated for normal social intercourse. Not only does he lack experience with people, but if he forms an intimate involvement outside the family he is breaking a deeply ingrained family rule against such relationships. It does not seem surprising that a psychotherapist must force his company upon a schizophrenic and so relieve the patient of the responsibility of forming a relationship which is forbidden and which he is ill equipped to form.

Therapeutic change in the patient also has repercussions beyond his own life. It is the contention of many investigators that schizophrenia in the child serves a supportive, or homeostatic,[34] function in this type of family. If the patient behaves more "normally," the parents become disturbed or a sibling may begin to develop symptoms. The continual conflict between the parents may also come out more openly and separation may be threatened. When the patient is ill, the family is drawn together by this burden they share in common. Family members can avoid facing their difficulties with each other by focusing upon their problem child. Although it is possible to conceive of schizophrenic symptoms as a defense against unacceptable ideas by the patient, it is also possible to see them as a way of perpetuating a particular kind of family system. Therefore therapeutic change may threaten a patient not only with a different way of life for himself, but the responsibility for a shattered family and the collapse of someone else.

For most people, family life is where they learn to form, and have freedom to practice, different kinds of relationships. The maturational defect in the family of the schizophrenic centers in the inability of the parents to let the schizophrenic child learn to experience complementary and symmetrical relationships, despite the millions of messages they exchange together over the years. Typically if the child behaves in a way which indicates he is initiating a complementary, or "taking care of," relationship, his parents will indicate he should be less demanding and so behave more symmetrically with them. If he behaves in a symmetrical way, they indicate that he does not seem to appreciate their desires to take care of him. This constant disqualification of his bids for relationship is a theme of their life together. If the child seeks closeness he is encouraged to be at a distance. If he attempts to place some distance between himself and his parents, they respond as if they have been criticized and indicate he should seek closeness. If he asks for something, he is too demanding. If he does not ask, he is too independent. The child is caught in a set of paradoxical relationships with all of his responses labeled as wrong ones. What other parents would consider normal behavior, such as the child making demands upon them, criticizing them, objecting to what they do, asserting his independence, and so on, these parents consider it impossible behavior. Even positive, or affectionate behavior by the child, is responded to by these parents in a negative way as if they feel that too much more will be expected of them. This constant disqualification may occur immediately in response to a patient, particularly those who later give up trying to reach their parents, or the disqualification may be delayed. Paranoid patients would seem to have experienced an apparent acceptance of their behavior and a later disqualification when what was previously done is labeled as something else, and so they live in a world of booby traps.

The child also does not easily accept the behavior of his parents; typically he disqualifies whatever they offer just as they do. Because of the family inability to maintain a type of relationship with the child, there is thorough confusion in this type of family over authority and benevolence. Attempts to discipline the child usually end in confusion, indecision, and conflict. When parents attempt to be authoritarian, the attempt usually dissolves into helplessness and benevolent overconcern for the child. When they attempt to be benevolent, the benevolence dissolves into exasperated and futile attempts at discipline. Rarely can the parents insist the child do something because they prefer it that way; they must insist it is for his own good no matter how obviously their request is to satisfy their own needs.

Self-sacrifice by the parents is considered a virtue in these families; mothers will even say that they have done nothing for themselves in their lives and everything for the child. Such mothers have been called "overprotective" because of their persistence in doing for this special child what other mothers would let him do for himself. Not only will they help adult children eat, but they will converse with a quiet child by carrying both sides of the conversation.

What discipline there is in the family is usually sporadic and occasionally violent. Some fathers give the appearance of being stern authoritarians, but their directives are usually unsuccessful. Mother either interferes and incapacitates father, or he backs down when his orders begin to be followed. The continual conflict between the parents over whether one or the other is too mild or too severe with the child is easily spurred on by the child who may prevent discipline by behaving in a helpless or disturbed way. Even parents quite determined to exert authority jointly will end in a row if the child becomes upset. Not only does conflict between parents disturb the patient, but by behaving in a disturbed way the schizophrenic can instigate conflict between parents.

The problem of who is to control whose behavior is a central issue in this type of family. The parents appear to receive any attempt by the child to initiate a type of relationship as a maneuver to control them. However, if the child responds appropriately to a relationship initiated by them, the parents also respond as if this is a maneuver to control them. For example, if the child asks mother to do something for him, she indicates by her reluctance that he is too demanding. Yet if she initiates doing something for the child, and he accepts her behavior, she responds as if he is demanding too much of her. Similarly, if he indicates he wishes to do something himself, she will respond by showing him that she should do it for him. Conflict over even minor matters becomes a major problem when every response is taken as an attempt to be in control of the relationship. The schizophrenic solution is to label all his responsive behavior as not occurring in relation to his parents and therefore not indicating a type of relationship. Yet this psychotic behavior is also not a satisfactory solution; his parents are then unhappy because he does not respond to them. Should he attempt to respond to them directly, they become disturbed and encourage him toward denials that what he does is a response to them.

PSYCHOTHERAPY AND THE FAMILY

There are several major differences between the treatment methods described here and the family system of the patient. From a learning point of view, it would seem logical that in these differences resides the source of therapeutic change. The psychotherapy situation is by no means totally different from the parent-child relationship in the family. The authoritarian technique of the first therapist described here is reminiscent of the kind of assault some patients might suffer at home. The "mothering" of the second therapist is reminiscent of the ways the patient's mother does for him what he is capable of doing himself. Not only has the institution for treatment a peculiar mixture of overprotection and authoritarianism, but often what is done for the needs of the staff is benevolently defined as done for the needs of the patient. It would seem paradoxical that there are similarities between the processes of relieving pathology and the process which nurtures it. However, besides the pressure which the schizophrenic places upon the world to build it in his expected image, one might assume that it is necessary to behave in a way familiar to a patient if there is to be understanding. The change would presumably come when the familiar is redefined and so becomes different.

THE THERAPEUTIC PARADOX

When a child is forced to respond to two different types of directives from his parents which are incompatible with each other, he is caught in a paradox. For example, he can be asked to respond in a more self-assertive way to them, but he is not to criticize them. Or he is asked to respond to them in a way appropriate to a certain kind of relationship, but he is not to indicate what kind of relationship he has with them. When faced with these incongruent demands for a response, the child solves the problem by indicating that his responses are not in relation to them and so appears withdrawn from reality.

The psychotherapist too could be said to be imposing paradoxes on the patient. However, the patient is not forced by these paradoxes to respond in a schizophrenic way, he is forced to concede that he is responding to the therapist. In the example cited, the therapist prevents the patient from indicating she is responding to "voices" and not to him. He "takes them over" by commanding them and siding with the patient against them. From that point on the patient cannot use "voices" to deny a response to the therapist; if she responds to the "voices," she is acknowledging a coalition with the therapist against them. If she does not respond to "voices," she is indicating a coalition with the therapist because his goal is to cure her of such symptoms.

A more clear example of the therapeutic paradox imposed by the acceptance of voices was once described by the first therapist cited here. He reports that with some patients who once heard "voices" and have improved, he will insist that the patient hear them again. If the patient hears the "voices" on command, he is following the directions of the therapist and so responding in relationship with him instead of using the "voices" as a denial of that relationship. If he does not hear the "voices" on command, he is also following the directions of the therapist who as a larger directive is encouraging the patient to stop hearing "voices." Whenever a therapist encourages symptomatic behavior, within a framework of helping the patient cease the symptomatic behavior, the patient is caught in this paradox. A similar example is the therapist who encourages the paranoid patient to be suspicious. The patient cannot keep him at a distance by suspicious behavior if he is being encouraged to behave in that way. Whether he is suspicious or not in this situation, he is following the therapist's direction and so is in a relationship with him.

Although the parents of the patient may feel more comfortable with him if he is denying a response to them, the therapist attempts to prevent that denial. Typically he either encourages the denial, and so takes it over, or he takes denials personally so they lose their effectiveness. For example, the therapist may say to the patient who is off in a psychotic flight, "Why do you deal with *me* in that crazy way." The patient cannot then define the flight as not a response to the therapist.

When the therapist forces the patient to concede that he is responding to him, no matter what the patient does, the patient can no longer continue with schizophrenic symptoms. The further process of therapy is the clarification of what kind of relationship they are having and the encouragement of the patient in searching behavior to learn to define different types of relationships with the therapist.

THE ACCEPTANCE OF A RELATIONSHIP

The therapist's willingness to accept the patient dealing with him directly may be severely tested. If the patient gives up his denials and indicates he wishes a taking care of relationship, the therapist will be nurturing. The patient may then persist in this demand to the limits of toleration of the therapist, if not beyond. Similarly, the patient will deal with discipline by provoking the therapist to continue it at length.

When the patient deals with him directly, it is often in such an intense way that the therapist will be tempted to encourage the patient back into schizophrenic behavior again. The reputed "insight" into the unconscious by schizophrenics can also be seen as a willingness to put the needle into a therapist's weaknesses to the point of provoking retaliation. Similarly, improvement in a patient may not only involve provocation of the therapist but also of conflict between the therapist and the patient's administrator. Quite a good relationship must exist between a therapist and ward doctor to weather the storms provoked by an improving patient.

Besides being willing to continue in a particular type of relationship, no matter how difficult the patient may make it, the therapist must also be willing to accept a shift in the type of relationship if the patient initiates it. Although the therapist may impose "mothering" on a patient, he does not insist upon this type of relationship if the patient indicates he would prefer another type. In the example cited, when the patient reaches for the glass of milk, the therapist immediately lets her hold it and drink it herself. The actual mother of the patient would be more likely to take the patient's indication that she wanted to do something herself as a criticism of mother and so prevent it.

Although the therapist is willing to let the patient initiate a type of relationship, this does not mean the patient is in control in the situation. The therapist indicates that he is *letting* the patient define the relationship in whichever way he chooses. The total authority which the therapist has over the patient's life provides a continuing context which indicates that whatever the patient does is done with the therapist's permission. Therefore no matter what type of relationship the patient initiates, it is within a complementary frame at a higher level. (A rather different interchange is involved when the therapist sees an ambulatory schizophrenic in private practice.)

THE FRAME OF PSYCHOTHERAPY

Perhaps the major difference between treatment method and family situation centers on the peculiar nature of psychotherapy as an interchange set apart from ordinary life. Neither patient nor therapist can actually be defining a "real" relationship with each other; they are not friends, not relatives, not acquaintances, not even doctor and patient in the ordinary sense. Typically the therapist behaves as if there is an intimate involvement with the patient, but actually there is not. Both patient and therapist will go about their own lives separately when they leave each other's company. The supposed intimacy which is defined between them terminates with the end of the interview, in contrast to a relationship between friends which extends into mutual social life or a relationship between relatives which includes sharing living conditions.

From the point of view of the patient, it is extraordinarily difficult to gain control of the relationship with a therapist when the nature of that relationship is so slippery. The patient cannot assume the therapist is merely harsh, because he is benevolently helping him. Nor can he assume that the therapist is only benevolently nurturing him, because their relationship is usually consummated in a rather grim authoritarian setting. Often the patient will attempt to relate to the therapist as a parent, and many therapists of schizophrenics will encourage this by literally saying, "I am your mother and I will take care of you," or they imply such a relationship by their behavior. Yet obviously the therapist is not a parent; there is no family life between them but only a series of interviews. Similarly, the patient and therapist may establish a relationship more like friends than other forms of psychotherapeutic relationships, and yet they do not move in the same circles socially. It is perhaps the multiple paradoxes in the relationship which make it so difficult for the patient to find a handle to manipulate the therapist.

Not only is their relationship not an ordinary one, but one of the premises they establish together is "this is not real life," or "this is a kind of game." Within that framework the two people may become quite emotionally involved with each other, but this is also true of many games. Like a game, the interaction is confined to specific periods of time; unlike a game, the only rules are those the participants work out together as they go along. Not only must they define the rules as they interact with each other, but also they must resolve the conflict over who is going to make the rules. They have no outside authority to consult on what rules their relationship should be built upon, nor can they apply the rules of other types of relationships because this one is like no other. In the process of learning this, the patient tries to, and finds he cannot, use the rules typical in his family relationships.

The play-like quality of the interchange between schizophrenic and therapist is more apparent in this type of psychotherapy than any other. In all psychotherapy the therapist is both "involved" with a patient and at the same time sufficiently detached so that he can observe the type of interchange taking place. In this type of psychotherapy the same behavior exists but in a more active way; the patient is faced with a man who is "acting out" different kinds of serious involvement while labeling the situation in a play-like way. In the first example, the therapist forces the patient to his knees and insists that he is God, yet he does so in such an exaggerated way, before an audience of people, that it is like a game. Despite the grim seriousness of schizophrenia, the interview is even playful with considerable laughter from everyone involved. At one point the patient himself laughs, indicating he made a mistake and should have obliterated the assistants.

With the second therapist, there is again this play-like quality to the interaction. By exaggerating the "mothering," the therapist indicates that it is not "real," as it cannot be. This framework is further emphasized when the therapist sides with the patient against the "voices" and dramatically tells them off, provoking laughter from the patient.

From a communication point of view, the incongruity in levels of message manifested by the schizophrenic is met by a similar incongruity on the part of the therapist. For example, the message of the patient who calls himself God might be verbalized in this way: I am speaking, qualified by the statement it is God speaking, qualified by the helplessness which indicates it is not God speaking. The therapist's answer is: I am

being harsh with you, qualified by the setting of benevolent help, qualified by an indication that it is a kind of game they are playing. Just as
the therapist has trouble dealing with any one level of the schizophrenic's
multiple message, so does the patient have difficulty selecting and responding to a single level in the therapist's message.

The play-like nature of the therapeutic interchange is particularly striking if one observes the grim, realistic struggle between the patient and
his actual parents. The therapist may insist the patient behave in a certain
way, or he may take personally whatever the patient does, but he can
shift his responses easily and treat the situation lightly. The parents of
the patient rigidly follow a pattern of objecting to whatever he offers
while encouraging him to offer more. The parents also become disturbed
if the patient makes any comment on their behavior. The therapist encourages such comments and can accept them or decline them as he
chooses so they do not interfere with the therapeutic framework. Of
course the therapist has an advantage in a prolonged struggle with the
patient that parents do not have. The parents may have to continually
live with the patient and feel continually responsible for him. The therapist can maintain the play-like quality by absenting himself when he
chooses and going about his own life, leaving the disciplinary problems
to a paid staff.

COUNTERTRANSFERENCE AND PARENTAL BEHAVIOR

When a therapist becomes "too involved" with a schizophrenic, the
therapy is in difficulty. The play-like quality is gone and the patient can
easily place the therapist at a disadvantage or provoke him to behave in
ways he would rather not. At this point, supervision of the therapist becomes important to help him detach himself from too personal an involvement and reinstitute a psychotherapeutic frame to the interchange. The
control of what kind of behavior is to be exchanged between therapist
and patient then shifts back to the therapist.

Psychotherapy with a schizophrenic is generally agreed to be going
badly if the therapist does any of the following things: (a) if the therapist lets the patient provoke him to retaliate in a way which encourages the patient to withdraw into schizophrenic symptoms, (b) if the
overdedicated therapist insists on continuing to take care of a patient
when the patient is indicating a desire for more equality, (c) if the
therapist pushes the patient toward equality or independence at a time
when the patient is indicating he wishes more nurturing, (d) if the
therapist institutes disciplinary measures and then retreats if the patient
becomes disturbed, and (e) if the therapist denies the patient's perceptions about him when they are accurate because he cannot tolerate cer-

tain types of comments on his own behavior. One of the more convincing arguments that schizophrenia is of family origin is posed by the fact that this list of ways a therapist should not behave with a schizophrenic and the list of ways the parents behave with the patient are synonymous.

Countertransference can be seen as misperceptions of the patient by the therapist, but the interpersonal context of such a phenomenon is important. Those moments when an observer would say countertransference is occurring can be seen as those moments when the therapist has lost control of the relationship and is being forced by the patient into certain types of behaviors. Subjectively the therapist may project various images upon the patient; in terms of formal behavior, he is behaving like the actual parent of the patient.

In summary, schizophrenic behavior can be described as a pattern of behavior in which the patient is consistently labeling what he does as unrelated to the relationship he is involved in. Such behavior on his part could be provoked by a family situation where he is required by the nature of the family system to avoid indicating what types of relationships he has in the family. The therapeutic tactics center in providing a paradoxical situation which the patient cannot resolve as long as he behaves in a schizophrenic way. The benevolent therapeutic paradox posed the patient by the therapist is reminiscent of the pathogenic paradoxes which occur in his family. In both situations there are benevolent frameworks within which the patient is placed through an ordeal. In both situations the patient is encouraged to behave in his usual ways within a framework of helping him change. However, when the patient responds to this "impossible" situation by responding normally and defining his relationship, the therapist rewards him and accepts his response.

Psychotherapists who have developed specialized techniques for working with schizophrenic patients have usually never observed the patient interacting with his family. Yet the accepted procedures for therapy they have developed include behaving in ways similar to the actual parents of the patient, while also behaving differently at crucial moments. It would appear that a more careful examination of the family system of the schizophrenic would lead to more effective treatment techniques.

CHAPTER VI

Marriage Therapy

ATHOUGH IT IS becoming more common for psychotherapists to interview married partners together, there are no orthodox procedures for the treatment of a marriage. In fact, there is no formal description of pathological marriages and so no theory of what changes must be brought about. The psychodynamic approach, or role theory emphasis, leads to discussions of the individual problems of husband and wife and not to descriptions of the marital relationship.

The emphasis here will be upon types of relationships in marriage, but no attempt will be made to present a full exposition of the complexities of marriage; the focus will be upon marital distress and symptom formation. After a description of certain types of relationships, there will be a discussion of the kinds of conflicts which arise, and finally a description of ways a marriage therapist intervenes to produce shifts in a relationship.

WHEN MARRIAGE THERAPY IS INDICATED

Marriage Therapy differs from individual therapy because the focus is upon the marital relationship rather than the intrapsychic forces within the individual. It also differs from Family Therapy where the emphasis is upon the total family unit with a child typically chosen to be the problem. Technically the term should be confined to that type of treatment where the therapist interviews the couple together. However, the variations are many: some therapists will see both marital partners separately, others will see one partner while occasionally seeing the spouse for an interview, and others will see one partner while referring the other elsewhere with collaboration between the two therapists. Actually the psychotherapist who only does individual psychotherapy and refuses to see the spouse of a married patient is involved in indirect marriage therapy. Not only is much of the time of individual treatment devoted to discussions of marital affairs, but if the individual changes the marital relationship will change—or terminate.

There are certain situations where Marriage Therapy is specifically indicated:

(a) When methods of individual psychotherapy have failed, Marriage Therapy is appropriate. Often in such cases the patient is involved in a marital relationship which is inhibiting his improvement and perpetuating his distress to the point where individual psychotherapy is too small a lever to make a large change. For example, a woman with constantly recurring anxiety attacks and insomnia failed to improve in individual psychotherapy despite considerable exploration of her childhood. When her husband was brought into the treatment it was discovered that he was continually behaving in an irresponsible and unpredictable way. He was not only failing in business without taking any steps to prevent this failure, but he was surreptitiously writing bad checks time after time despite his protests to his wife that he would never do so again. The onset of her anxiety attacks occurred with his first failure in business and his cavalier dismissal of this event. The continual conflict between husband and wife over his refusal to take responsibility in his business or in his family was handled by the wife with recurrent attacks of helpless anxiety, and her problem was more marital than individual.

(b) Marriage Therapy is indicated when methods of individual psychotherapy cannot be used. Since most individual psychotherapy consists of countering what a patient offers, the therapist is incapacitated if the patient offers nothing. Marriage Therapy then becomes one of the few possible procedures. For example, a woman had a fear of heart failure as part of a series of anxiety attacks which forced her to quit her job and remain at home unable to go out anywhere alone. She sought psychotherapy and the therapist asked her to say whatever came to her mind. She said nothing. She would answer specific questions as briefly as possible, but she would not volunteer statements about her feelings or her life in general. After two sessions in which the woman said nothing, and the therapist said nothing, the woman discontinued treatment and sought another therapist. Clearly the woman would not permit the therapist to wait her out in the hope that the cost of treatment would ultimately force her to say what was on her mind. When she began marriage therapy with her husband present in the interviews, the wife became more loquacious. As the husband was questioned about his wife's problems, the wife found it necessary to correct him. She could not let her husband's portrait of her difficulties stand. To revise his version she had to provide her own and demonstrate her feelings about him, providing the leverage to start a change.

(c) Marriage Therapy would seem indicated when a patient has a sudden onset of symptoms which coincides with a marital conflict. Although most patients with symptoms tend to minimize their marital difficulties—in fact the symptom is apparently used to deny marital problems—there are times when symptoms erupt in obvious relation to a spouse. For example, a husband experienced an anxiety state which confined him to bed and cost him his job. His collapse occurred when his wife went to work over his objections. In another case a woman had a variety of hysterical symptoms while on vacation with her husband.

They quarreled, and her husband gambled away the vacation money, knowing that because her father had continually gambled away all the family money her greatest fear in life was of gambling. Although the onset of a symptom can always be seen as a product of a change in a family relationship, in some cases the connection is so obvious that treatment of the marriage is indicated.

(d) Of course, this type of therapy is indicated when it is requested by a couple who are in conflict and distress and unable to resolve it. (However, it is not unusual even in this circumstance for some therapists to advise them to seek individual treatment separately.) Typically one spouse, usually the wife, seeks Marriage Therapy while the other comes in reluctantly. Usually both partners will ultimately come in, even though one may need a special request, because if one partner in a marriage is miserable the other is too.

Finally, Marriage Therapy is indicated when it appears that improvement in a patient will result in a divorce or in the eruption of symptoms in the spouse. If a patient with severe symptoms says his marriage is perfect, and if his spouse also indicates this idea, then it is likely that improvement in the patient will lead to divorce or a distressed spouse. Although it is difficult to estimate the repercussions of therapeutic change, one indication of ultimate pathology developing in a relative is the stout insistence by a patient that his family life is ideal. Therapists have a responsibility to the relatives of a patient if they bring about a change.

THE FORMAL THEMES OF MARRIAGE

A marriage is an extraordinarily complex and continually changing affair. To select a few aspects of the marital relationship and emphasize them is to do some violence to the incredible entanglement of two people who have lived together many years. A few formal themes, those most relevant to marital strife and symptom formation, will be mentioned here.

When a man and woman decide their association should be solemnized and legalized with a marriage ceremony, they pose themselves a problem which will continue through the marriage: Now that they are married are they staying together because they wish to or because they must? The inevitable conflicts which arise in a marriage occur within a framework of a more or less voluntary relationship. It is not so much whether a marriage *is* a compulsory or a voluntary relationship, but how the couple choose to define it. A woman may, for example, wish to stay with her husband but be unwilling to concede that her choice is voluntary and so say that they cannot separate for religious reasons. Another wife might insist that she could leave her husband at any time, defining the relationship as voluntary, although her history would indicate that she had a rather desperate need of him and could not leave him.

A marriage seems to function best when there is some balance between the voluntary and compulsory aspects of the relationship. In a successful marriage, the couple define their association as one of choice, and yet they have sufficient compulsion in law and custom to stay together through the conflicts which arise. If divorce is too easy, there is too little compulsion in the marriage to survive problems. When divorce is too difficult, the couple can begin to suspect that they are together because they must be and not out of choice. At either extreme, a marriage can be in difficulty.

An example of a marriage which was so voluntary that the wife did not feel committed to her husband can be used for illustration. A woman in business for herself prior to her marriage agreed to sell the business at her husband's request because he wished to be the provider for the family. However, she took the money obtained in the sale and placed it in the bank in her own name "just in case the marriage did not work out." The marriage foundered on this act. The husband felt the wife was unwilling to commit herself to him; the wife behaved as if the marriage was a voluntary association which she could leave at any time so she would make no concessions in her relationship with her husband.

At the other extreme is the type of relationship where the couple behave as if they are compelled to stay together. This type of relationship occurs when there are strict religious rules about marriage, when one of the spouses experiences incapacitating symptoms, or when one of them puts up with "impossible" behavior from the other.

A compulsory marriage is like that relationship between cell mates in a prison. The two people get along because they must, but they are uncertain whether they would choose to be together if they had a free choice. A wife who suffers incapacitating depressions will be indicating to her husband that she is unable to survive alone. A husband who turns to drink whenever his wife must go away for a day, or when she threatens to leave him, will persuade her that he cannot live without her. It is not necessarily taken as a compliment if a spouse indicates he cannot do without his mate; implicit in such an arrangement is the idea that they are only together because they must be and perhaps any other body in the house might do but no one else would have them. When spouses begin to think of their relationship as compulsory, bad feeling is generated.

A marriage may begin as a compulsory relationship. For example, a man attempted to discuss breaking off his engagement with his fiancee and the girl jumped out of his parked automobile into oncoming traffic and ran wildly down the street. Later she told him she would kill herself if he did not marry her. He married her. From that point on, he was in doubt whether she really wished to marry him or was only desperately trying to escape a dreadful home situation. The girl was in doubt whether he married her because he wanted to or because of fear she would kill herself.

When one spouse continues the marriage even though treated badly by the other, a compulsory type of relationship occurs. If a husband puts up with more than is reasonable from his wife, the wife may begin to assume that he must be staying with her because he has to, not because he wants to, and the marriage is in difficulty. Sometimes a spouse will appear to test whether he or she is really wanted by driving the other to the point of separation. It is as if they say, "If my mate will put up with anything from me, I am really wanted." However, if the spouse passes the test and puts up with impossible behavior, the tester is not reassured about being wanted but becomes convinced the spouse is doing so because of an inability to leave. Once this pattern has begun, it tends to be self-perpetuating. A wife who believes that her husband stays with her because of his own inner desperation rather than because he wants her will dismiss his affectionate approaches as mere bribes to stay with her rather than indications of real affection. When she dismisses her husband's affection, he tries even harder to please her and so increases her belief that he stays with her out of desperation rather than choice. When the husband can no longer tolerate the situation, he may make a move to leave her. The moment he indicates he can do without her, the wife begins to feel she may be a voluntary choice and be attracted to him again. However, such a wife will then test her husband again by extreme behavior. When he responds permissively she again feels he is unable to leave her and the cycle continues.

The extreme oscillation which can occur in a marriage is typical of those cases where a couple comes to a therapist for help in getting separated from each other. Some spouses will separate and go back together and separate again over the years, unable to get together and unable to get apart. The major problem in helping the separating couple is discovering which direction they seem most to want to go. Sometimes a couple merely wants an excuse from an outsider to go back together so that neither will have to risk being the first to suggest living together again. In more complex repetitive separations there is usually a pattern of one spouse wanting to end the marriage until the other also wants it; then there is temporary reconciliation. For example, a young couple began to have trouble after a few years of marriage and the wife had an extramarital affair. The husband forgave her. She had another affair; they separated. After a while they tried living together again but the affairs still rankled. The husband continued to blame her for her actions; the wife blamed him for depriving her in such a way that she turned to someone else. They separated but continued to associate. When they entered therapy the husband wanted to go back together again, but was uncertain about it. The wife, having taken up with another man, did not want to live with her husband, yet she wanted to associate with him and consider possible future reconciliation. At one moment the husband insisted on immediate divorce, at the next he asked for a reconciliation. Each time he spoke more firmly about his plans for a divorce, the wife began to discuss the great potential of their marriage and how fond she was of him. When the husband talked about going back together, the wife discussed how miserable their marriage had been. After several sessions attempting to clarify the situation, the issue was forced by a suggestion that if the couple continue treatment they do so in a trial period of living together. Faced with returning to her husband, the wife refused. The husband managed to arrange a divorce, although when he was no longer compulsively involved with her, the wife was finding him attractive again.

THE PROGRESS OF A MARRIAGE

Although their information about one another may be minimal, two people have already established ways of relating to each other at the time they marry. The act of marriage, typically an act of conceding they really want each other, requires a different type of relationship and can provoke rather sudden shifts in behavior. A woman, for example, might be forgiving of all her fiancee's defects until the marriage ceremony and then she might set about reforming him. A man might be quite tolerant of his fiancee's inability to show affection, but when they are married he might insist she undergo a major change. The man who was pleased to find such a submissive girl may discover after marriage that she is quite insistent upon taking charge of him. Usually, however, the patterns which appear in a marriage existed in some form prior to the ceremony. People have a remarkable skill in choosing mates who will fit their needs, although they may insist later they married the unexpected. The girl who needs to be treated badly usually finds someone who will cooperate, and if someone feels he deserves very little from life he tends to find a wife who feels she deserves very little; both get what they seek.

The process of working out a satisfactory marital relationship can be seen as a process of working out shared agreements, largely undiscussed, between the two people. There are a multitude of areas in living together which a couple must agree about. For example, is a husband to decide what kind of work he will do, or will his wife's concern about prestige dictate his employment? Will the husband be allowed to freely criticize his wife's housekeeping, or is that her domain? Who is to handle the budget? Is the wife to comfort her husband when he is unhappy or become exasperated with him? How much are outsiders to intrude into the marriage, and are in-laws outsiders? Will the wife or the husband be the irresponsible one in the marriage?

Each situation that a newly married couple meets must be dealt with by establishing explicit or implicit rules to follow. When the situation is met again, the rule established is either reinforced or changed. These rules are the following: (a) those rules the couple would announce, such as a rule that the husband can have a night out with his friends each week, (b) those rules the couple would not mention but would agree to if they were pointed out, such as the rule that the husband turns to his wife when faced with major decisions, and (c) those rules an observer would note but the couple would probably deny, such as the rule that the wife is continually to be on the defensive and the husband accusatory and never the reverse. It is important to note that the couple cannot avoid establishing these rules: whenever they complete a transaction, a rule is being established. Even if they should set out to behave entirely spontaneously, they would be establishing the rule that they are to behave in that way.

The couple must not only set rules, but they must also reach agreement on which of them is to be the one to set the rules in each area of their marriage. The process of working out a particular rule always occurs within a context of resolving who is setting the rule. For example, a wife might not object if her husband has an evening out—unless he insists upon it; then she might object but her objection would be at a different level. Similarly, a husband might not protest if his wife wishes to send her mother money, but if the wife implies that he has no say in the matter he might then announce objections. In the early days of a marriage each spouse might graciously let the other be labeled as the one in charge of the various areas of the relationship, but ultimately a struggle will set in over this problem.

As a part of the struggle to reach agreement on rules for living with each other, a couple is inevitably establishing another set of rules—those rules to be followed to resolve disagreements. The process of working out conflict over rules becomes a set of metarules, or rules for making rules. For example, two people might establish the rule that they will only resolve a difference after the husband has made an issue of the matter. When the wife has tested his concern by provoking him until he treats the matter as important, then they will resolve it. Or a couple might establish the metarule that they will never fully reach agreement on any rule and so they maintain a state of indecision. Similarly, the act of avoiding certain areas of discussion is an establishing of metarules about how to deal with those areas.

If a marital relationship could be worked out by the application of agreement on rules, who is to make them, and how to make them, a marriage would be quite a rational affair. Obviously it is not. Couples find themselves struggling with great intensity of feeling over minor matters in a most irrational way. This intensity of feeling about who is to set rules in the marriage would seem to have several sources. A major cause is the fact that any marital partner was raised in a family and so given long and thorough training in implicit and explicit rules for how people should deal with each other. When a person gets married, he attempts to deal with a spouse who was given training in a different institution. The couple must reconcile long-term expectations which have all the emotional force of laws of life. The wife raised in a family where an open show of emotion was forbidden will become disturbed when her husband expresses his feelings strongly, even though she might have married him because she wished to move in that direction. The husband whose mother made an issue of being an excellent housekeeper may find it difficult to tolerate a wife who is not, and he may take her inability as a personal comment on him rather than mere inefficiency. It is sometimes difficult to realize how subtle are the patterns we learn in our families where we are exposed to millions of messages over time. For example, the "proper" distance one should stand from another person while talking to him will vary from family to family. A person may feel uneasy because the other person is too close or too far away without ever realizing that there is a disagreement in how far apart they should stand. The transition to a person's own family from a previous one requires considerable compromise with inevitable conflict.

Describing marriage in terms of working out rules for living together is another way of describing marriage as a process of definining relationships. Any rule established by a couple defines a certain type of relationship. A rule that a husband is to comfort his wife when she is in distress defines a relationship as *complementary*. Similarly, an agreement that the wife is to have equal say about the budget is a mutual definition of a *symmetrical* relationship in that area. In a reasonably successful marriage a couple is capable of establishing both complementary and symmetrical relationships in various areas of their marriage. The husband can take care of his wife and she can accept this, the wife can take care of husband and he can accept it, and they are able to exchange the same kind of behavior. When a couple is unable to form one of these types of relationships, the marriage is restricted. If a marital partner has had unfortunate experiences with certain types of relationships in the past, he or she might be unable to permit this type in a marriage. For example, if a wife has been disappointed in complementary relationships with her parents, she will respond to her husband's attempts to take care of her in a way that indicates she would prefer a symmetrical type of relationship. A wife might be unable to follow any directions given by her husband if following directions in her past cost her too much. Once when a wife was asked why she did not do what her husband told her, she said, "Why, I'd just disappear. I'd have no identity." Similarly, a husband might be unable to take direction from his wife or even let her take care of him when he is ill (and so retires only to a sick bed when he has collapsed). He may indicate that he wants her to be an equal, but does not want her to "mother" him. An inability to accept a range of types of relationships creates a marriage which is to some extent a depriving situation for both spouses.

CONFLICT IN MARRIAGE

Marital conflict centers in (a) disagreements about the rules for living together, (b) disagreements about who is to set those rules, and (c) attempts to enforce rules which are incompatible with each other.

For a honeymoon period after marriage each spouse is willing to overlook the disagreements which develop. When the husband is treated by his wife in a way he does not like, he avoids mentioning it for fear of hurting her feelings. When the wife discovers some aspect of her husband which irritates her, she does not bring the matter up because she wishes to avoid conflict. After a period of time the couple have a rousing fight in which they express their opinions. After such a quarrel, there are changes made and each is willing to compromise. Often they overcompensate by going too far as they give in to each other and this overcompensation provides the need for the next conflict.

If a couple is unable to have a fight and so bring up what is on their minds, they are dealing with each other by withdrawal techniques and avoiding any discussion of certain areas of their relationship. With each avoidance, the area that cannot be discussed grows larger until ultimately they may have nothing they can safely talk about. One of the functions of a marriage therapist might be to provoke a couple to fight and say what is on their minds so they do not continue to punish each other indirectly for crimes which have never been brought up as accusations. When a couple cannot fight, all issues which require defining an area of the relationship are avoided. The couple will then eat together and watch television side by side, but their life has little shared intimacy. At the other extreme a couple may stabilize into a relationship which requires constant fighting. They repeatedly share demonstrations of strong feeling for each other, but they cannot reach amiable agreement on who is to control what in the marriage.

The more easily resolved conflicts in a marriage are those involving which rules the couple will follow. The two people may disagree about an aspect of living together or about how they should deal with each other, but they can reach a compromise which resolves the matter. Sharing the work about the house, agreeing on friends or types of social life, and problems of consideration for each other in various areas of living can lead to disagreement which is reasonably easy to resolve.

Although disagreements tend to be about which rules to follow, emotional fights tend to be about *who* is to make the rules and this problem is not so easily solved by compromise. For example, a wife could insist that her husband hang up his clothes so that she does not have to pick up after him like a servant. The husband might agree with his wife that she should not be his servant, and so agree to the definition of the relationship, but he still might not agree that *she* should be the one to give him orders on what to do about his clothes. What rule to follow is more easily discussable than who is to make the rules to follow. The process of defining who is to make the rules in the marriage will inevitably consist of a struggle between any couple. The tactics in this struggle are those of any power struggle: threats, violent assault, withdrawal, sabotage, passive resistance, and helplessness or physical inability to do what the other wants. The struggle is by no means pathological; it only becomes pathological if one or the other spouse attempts to circumscribe the mate's behavior while indicating that he or she cannot help it. This type of labeling requires symptomatic behavior and is a product of pathological relationships.

When the issue between two people centers on who is to make the rules, they will behave as if basic rights are being violated. Similarly, the internal burning which goes on within spouses who have withdrawn from each other and are not speaking will center in conflict over who is to define what kind of relationship they will have. Typically the two spouses will be silent but busy rehearsing conversation in their heads; this conversation will include lines such as, "Who does he think he is," and "If she thinks I'll put up with that she has another think coming." The question of rights involves a complicated labeling procedure in any discussion. A wife might not mind being advised by her husband, and so be cooperating in a complementary relationship, if he offers the advice in just the right way or if she has asked for it. However, she may stoutly oppose such a relationship if her husband has initiated it or insisted upon it. Similarly, a husband might be quite willing to treat his wife as an equal in a certain area, but if she demands that he do so he may lose his willingness. The physical violence which can occur over minor matters is generated by a struggle at this control level of marriage. Whether to go to one movie or another may lead to threats of divorce when the conflict centers on who is to tell who what to do in the marriage.

If marital partners communicated only a single level message, conflicts would be more easily resolvable because cycles of conflict would not be generated. For example, if a husband bids only for a complementary relationship and the wife responds with only an acceptance or with a counteroffer for a symmetrical relationship, then the issue can be resolved between them. However, people do not communicate only on a single level so they offer each other messages which define one type of relationship at one level and an incompatible type of relationship at another. The conflict produced cannot easily be resolved and, in fact, usually provokes a response which perpetuates the conflict. For example, if a wife *orders* her husband to *dominate* her, the couple is caught in a network of incompatible definitions of the relationship. If the husband dominates her at her insistence, he is being dominated. To put this another way, if he accepts the secondary end of a complementary relationship by doing what she says, he is faced with a paradox if what she says is that he must tell her what to do. This is like the paradox involved in the statement "disobey me." If the respondent disobeys, he is obeying and if he obeys he is disobeying. A similar situation occurs if a husband orders his wife to supervise or take care of him. Similarly, the paradox occurs if a wife insists that her husband assert himself in relation to his mother and not be a "mama's boy" by letting himself be dominated by a woman. The more he is forced by his wife to assert himself with mother, the more he is accepting being dominated. Two incompatible types of relationships are simultaneously being imposed. Sometimes a wife will quite explicitly say that she wants her husband to dominate her in the way she tells him to—without realizing the incompatibility of her requests.

The communication of bids for two incompatible types of relationhips can occur whenever there is an incompatibility between (a) the rule defining a relationship, and (b) the type of relationship implicit in *who* is defining the relationship. For example, if a wife tells her husband to pick up his clothes she is indicating that their relationship should be symmetrical; each person should pick up his own clothes. However, *when she tells him to do this* she is defining the relationship as complementary—she orders and he is to follow the orders. The husband is then faced with two different definitions of the relationship so that which-ever way he responds he cannot satisfy both requests. If he picks up his clothes, accepting the symmetrical definition, he is following her direc-tions and so accepting a complementary definition. He cannot accept one definition without the other unless he comments on the situation in a way that redefines it. More likely he will erupt in indignation while uncertain what he is indignant about and his wife will similarly be in-dignant because he erupts over this simple request.

A further area of conflict for a couple occurs if there is an incompati-bility between (a) the metarules they establish for resolving disagree-ments about rules, and (b) the rules themselves. For example, a couple might reach an agreement that whenever they are in conflict about the rules for dealing with each other, the husband will make the final deci-sion and set the rules. However, the final decision he might make could be that he and his wife are to be equals, or in a symmetrical relationship. If they are equals, he cannot be the rule setter, yet that is the rule he sets. Similarly, a couple may establish the rule that they will resolve all disagreements in a mutually satisfactory way—by discussion and com-promise. However, when the wife attempts to express her opinion on a particular issue the husband may point out that getting emotional does not solve anything and since she will not listen to him he will withdraw from the field. His behavior defining the relationship as complementary on a particular issue is incompatible with their agreement to handle issues symmetrically, and the result is mutual dissatisfaction and indig-nation.

In summary, conflict between a married couple can arise in several areas: (a) conflict over what kind of rules to follow in dealing with each other and so what type of relationship to have, (b) conflict over who is to set the rules with the types of relationships defined by the ways this conflict is worked out, and (c) a conflict over the incompatibility be-tween these two levels; a relationship defined in one way on the first level conflicts with the relationship defined another way on the other level. Besides these conflicts, another may be generated by (d) an in-compatibility between the process of working out conflicts and the con-flicts themselves, so that what will be resolved at one level is incompatible with what can be resolved at another.

Almost any marital conflict which occurs can be described within this formal scheme, even though the description is confined to two levels instead of the multiple levels of communication which occur in human relations. Presumably too, this scheme would apply to marriages in different cultures since it is not a description of which rules a couple follows, which would be culture-bound, but a description at a more formal level. A couple in any culture must deal with what rules to follow, who is to enact them, and what rules to follow to resolve disagreements. In a changing culture there will inevitably be more conflict, as there will be in cross cultural marriages. The shift in the status of women in America has produced a breakdown in many of the elaborate ways of defining relationships between men and women which were once taken for granted as courtesy procedures. As a result a man is often faced with a wife who insists that she be treated as an equal while simultaneously insisting that he take charge of her in a complementary relationship.

If one describes marital relationships in terms of conflicting levels of communication, the description is complex, but any less complex description is too oversimplified to be useful. For example, to describe a marriage as one where there is "a dominating wife and a dependent husband" does not include the idea that the husband might be provoking his wife to be dominating so that actually he is "dominating" what type of relationship they have. Similarly, the "submissive" wife can actually be the one who, by helpless maneuvers, is managing whatever happens in the relationship.

The realm of sexual relations can be used to illustrate typical patterns of conflict in a marital relationship. The inhibitory processes in sex are based not only upon guilts which are brought into the marriage, but also are a product of a struggle by the two people over the definition of their relationship. The physical enjoyment of sexual relations by both partners requires a rather intricate coinciding of appropriate physical responses occurring in the individuals and appropriate behavioral responses to each other provoking those physical respones. When there is a conflict over what kind of relationship the sexual act implies, or over who is defining what kind it is, the appropriate responses are not forthcoming.

The procedure for initiating sexual relations can be described to illustrate the types of conflicts which arise. One couple may reach the implicit agreement that the man is to initiate sexual relations and the woman is to respond when he does. The relationship is complementary on this issue—he offers and she receives, although she may indirectly and covertly stimulate him to do the initiating. Another couple might adopt the reverse arrangement and find it equally satisfactory for the wife to be the one who initiates sex. Other couples might define the relationship as symmetrical on this issue and both spouses could initiate sexual relations.

Conflict can occur under several circumstances. The spouses are in conflict over the rules if the husband indicates that he should initiate sexual relations and the wife indicates that such an arrangement places her at his beck and call with no rights of her own, thereby defining the relationship in a more symmetrical way. Or a wife may indicate that only the husband should make overtures, and the husband could be dissatisfied with this arrangement because he preferred a more symmetrical one. These types of conflict over what kind of relationship to have tend to be resolved in the ongoing interaction of a marriage.

However, the conflict at the next level—who is to define what kind of relationship they will have, is less easily resolved. For example, if a wife turns her back on her husband in bed, assuming that if he is interested in sexual relations he will turn her over, the husband might assume from her behavior that she is not interested in sexual relations and so he does not turn her over. Both spouses can then feel that the other is disinterested, and both can feel righteously indignant. If this conflict is at the level of what kind of relationship to have, it can be resolved as a misunderstanding. Discussion and correction of the signals involved will lead to more amiable relations. However, if the couple is in a struggle over who is to define the type of relationship, discussion of the situation will not necessarily relieve the problem. After discussion, the wife may still feel that it is a law of life that only the man initiates sexual relations, and she will not let him impose a different relationship upon her. The husband may continue to feel that he will not impose himself upon his wife until she has expressed some interest, and she is not going to tell him how to conduct himself. In this struggle he might label her as frigid and she might label him as unmanly.

When a couple is in a struggle over who is in control of the relationship, the pleasure of sexual relations becomes a peripheral matter, if it is there at all. Sexual relations become merely a way of working out the conflict over the relationship. For example, if a wife feels that she is placed in a secondary position when her husband initiates sexual relations because he is dominating her, she may follow several tactics; she may refuse him, she may be unresponsive to him, or she may initiate sexual relations herself. If she refuses him, the husband may respond as if his rights have been violated and make no more overtures for a period, laying the groundwork for future problems. If she is unresponsive, he may withdraw, he may become more tentative in future approaches to indicate that sexual relations will be really on her terms, or he may confine himself to only responding if she makes overtures. If angry enough, he may be unresponsive when she initiates sexual relations as a retaliation for her previous unresponsiveness.

The process of working out a sexual problem is part of the larger problem of defining a relationship in a mutually satisfactory way. The subtle maneuvers which take place between a married couple as a pre-liminary to the sexual act are formally similar to other procedures in their lives together. The wife who cannot say "no" to her husband and therefore often cooperates in sex reluctantly will behave in a similar way in other areas of their life together. The wife who "tests" her hus-band by showing reluctance "to see if he is really interested," will tend to follow a similar pattern in sexual relations or on the question of going out to dinner together. A husband who is tentative in his advances in sex and overalert to his wife's moods will tend to deal with her in a simi-lar way in the joint task of purchasing something for the house. The explicit sexual aspects of a marriage need not necessarily be dealt with in marriage therapy: as the couple work out their relationships in other areas, the sexual area becomes less conflictual.

The existence of symptomatic behavior in a spouse handicaps any working out of a sexual relationship. The woman who frequently de-velops low back pain, dizziness when she lies down, or anxiety spells at appropriate times can prevent sexual relations from occurring except precisely on her own terms in her own time. The husband cannot im-pose upon her on his terms without appearing a cad. However, the problem is difficult to work out because attempts to improve the situation meet the problem that a symptom by definition is something the person "cannot help." If a wife should indicate to her husband, "approach me differently and I'll be more responsive," he can do so or argue the point. If she indicates, "I have this terrible headache" at a time when he is making overtures to her, he can only withdraw in exasperation but be unable to blame her or resolve the problem. Similarly, impotence or ejaculatio praecox in the male places the wife in the position of con-stantly risking disappointment if she attempts to arrange sexual relations. She must let sexual relations occur on her husband's terms, and yet she cannot blame him for something he cannot help. The spouse of a patient with symptoms is faced with incompatible messages: his behavior is circumscribed by his mate, but at the same time it is not circumscribed by the mate because the mate's behavior is labeled as "involuntary."

When paradoxical communication occurs in a marriage, the conflicts are the most difficult type for a couple to resolve on their own. Such sit-uations not only occur with symptoms, but with any incompatible set of messages. For example, a paradox occurs when a husband indicates that his wife should show an interest in sex and initiate the activity, but when she does he behaves unresponsively because she is being demanding and managing. If a husband receives his wife's advances as too demand-ing and her absence of advances as prudishness, the wife is wrong whatever she does. Similarly, a wife may encourage her husband to initiate sexual relations but when he does she may indicate that he is imposing on her, yet if he does not, that he is disinterested in her.

When these paradoxes occur in the sexual area they represent themes which appear throughout the marriage as incompatible definitions of the relationship. A husband is defining the relationship as symmetrical when he encourages his wife to initiate sexual relations, and if he also indicates she should not do so, he defines the relationship as complementary. These two incompatible definitions in this area place the wife in a paradoxical situation: whichever way she responds, agreeing to his definition of the relationship, will be opposed by him as a wrong definition. The wife might find a solution by posing incompatible definitions of the relationship in return. She might do this in "normal" ways or by developing symptoms. As an example of a "normal" way to offer an incompatible definition of the relationship in response, the wife might talk about initiating sex, and so define the relationship as symmetrical, but leave all such initiating up to her husband, and so define the relationship as complementary. Or she might indicate an interest in sexual relations and then appear indifferent so that her husband must pursue her; she has then initiated sexual relations, but she also has not since the major move resides with him.

Symptoms can be seen as a product of, or a way of handling, a relationship in which there are incompatible definitions of the relationship. It is easy to assume that a wife's symptoms which interfere with sexual relations are only expressions of her guilts and fears about sex, but she might be demanding less of her husband in this involuntary way because he has indicated that she should (in such a way that she cannot accuse him of doing so). If a husband asks his wife to show an interest in sexual relations and opposes her when she does, the wife can become unable to because of symptomatic distress. Similarly, a wife who cannot tolerate "surrendering" to her husband in a complementary relationship but insists that he take charge in the relationship, can produce impotency in the husband as a convenience to them both. If one is asked to do something and not do it at the same time, a possible response is to be unable to do it—which means indicating that one's behavior is involuntary. The physiology of the human being seems to cooperate in this situation even to the point of producing somatic symptoms.

RESISTANCE TO CHANGE

A married couple in difficulty cannot be rational about the matter. Both husband and wife might know perfectly well how they could treat each other to relieve their distress, despite an appearance of misunderstanding, but they continue to provoke discomfort in themselves and each other. When a therapist tries to bring about a change, he finds two central problems that inhibit a shift in the relationship.

One problem in the way of change is a couple's persistence in protecting each other. Although they could be making wild attacks upon one another, or be appearing to tear each other down constantly, a little probing usually reveals that they are protecting each other in a variety of ways, thus keeping the system stable. For example, a wife who was the manager in a marriage would insult her husband for his drinking, lack of consideration, bad behavior, and general boorishness. Alone with the therapist one day she said the real problem was the fact that her husband was just a big baby and she was tired of mothering him. When the therapist asked why she had not brought this up in a session with her husband present, the woman was shocked at the idea of hurting his feelings in that way. Yet she was consistently indicating that he was a baby in her eyes without ever making the accusation explicit so the husband could deal with it.

One of the functions of an angry quarrel in a marriage would seem to be to give the participants permission to stop protecting each other temporarily. Typically a wife and husband will let each other know what areas are too sensitive for discussion. When one of these areas is touched upon, they will respond in an anxious or angry way so that further discussion will not occur. When a spouse finds one of these undiscussable areas to be a central problem in their relationship, he or she often will not discuss it because of the other person's sensitivity there. Yet often a change can occur only if there is discussion, not necessarily because understanding is brought about, but because a change is being made in the rules for who is to talk about what. That is, if a wife has established the implicit rule that something is not to be discussed and then the husband discusses it, his act of discussing it signifies a change in the relationship quite independent of whatever enlightenment may occur because of the discussion.

Although it might be considered a natural aspect of marriage that the couple protect each other, there are aspects of protectiveness which are not so amiable. If a wife does not discuss something because she feels her husband cannot tolerate it, she will be exhibiting a lack of respect for him which may be unjustified and which he will feel as patronizing. The problem in the marriage can center more in her lack of respect for her husband than it does in the content of the sensitive area. Similarly, if a wife restrains her own abilities and accomplishments so that she will not outshine her husband, she is not necessarily doing him a favor. For example, a wife decided not to continue in school and get a higher degree because she would then have had a higher academic status than her husband. When a wife decides to restrain herself for such a purpose, not only will she be patronizing her husband, but she may be using this protection as an excuse when there are a number of other reasons why she would not seek a higher degree. Usually if one mate is protective of another, there are unexpressed needs being served. For example, there may be a bargain involved. If a man protects his wife on a certain issue, it is often with the implicit agreement that she will therefore protect him on another issue. This may be all right unless the marriage is in distress. Such a state usually indicates that one or the other is getting the poorer part of the bargain. Should one cease such protection, the other does also and changes can occur. A further aspect of protection is the confusion that occurs over who is protecting whom. Rather typically, if a spouse prefers not to discuss something to protect the other spouse, there is self-deceit involved. For example, a husband might indicate that his wife cannot tolerate a discussion of sex when, in fact, he is the one who becomes uncomfortable in such a discussion, but his wife will accept the label as the sensitive one.

One of the more severe forms of resistance to change in a marriage occurs with the development of symptoms in one or both of the partners. The symptom is then used by the couple, as a disturbed child is used in a family, to avoid defining their relationship and so avoid dealing with the marital distress. Typically the couple will say they would be perfectly happy if it were not for the husband's headaches or if it were not for the wife's anxiety attacks. However, as the symptom is alleviated, they do not evidence this happiness; in fact their conflict might increase to the point where the disappearance of the symptom may mean separation or divorce. Psychotherapists who see only individuals are likely to miss discovering how a relationship with an intimate family member profoundly effects the patient's rate of improvement.

Typically, symptoms not only protect the individual as an intrapsychic defense, but they also protect the marital partner and the marriage itself. A woman with a variety of hysterical symptoms was treated by interviews with husband and wife together. The husband was reluctant to enter therapy because he insisted the problems resided in his wife, not in himself, or the marriage. The wife too indicated that she could not see the relevance of her husband to the physical distress she was experiencing. As her symptoms improved, the couple began to fight more openly. The wife's dissatisfactions became more easily expressed. In the process of treatment, the woman revealed almost accidently that for many years she had also suffered from claustrophobia. Since she could not ride in an elevator, the couple could not go for a drink at a popular bar on the top of a tall building. As the woman was encouraged in the interview toward planning a drink at the top of that building, both she and her husband became rather anxious. The woman said her symptom was not at all an inconvenience and she would prefer to retain it. Further inquiry revealed that the husband suffered from a fear of heights. However, no issue was ever made of this fear because of the "agreement" between the two of them that she had problems and he did not. Should this woman overcome her fear of enclosed places and ride an elevator, she would expose her husband's inability to go with her. Such an admission would require a revision of a basic premise that their marriage was a complementary relationship with the husband the strong one and the wife the one with symptoms and difficulties.

One finds, if he explores a symptomatic marriage, that one spouse characteristically has symptoms which are integrated with the symptoms of the other spouse. For example, a husband who feared he was going to die at any moment from heart failure could be seen as a classic heart phobia case if he was seen alone. If his wife was seen briefly, it would be noted that she was doing her best in a difficult situation. However, treating wife and husband together a different picture appears. In this case it became apparent that the wife regularly evidenced withdrawal and depression. It was at those moments when the wife was depressed and withdrawn that the husband began to make an issue of his heart by taking his pulse and asking her to call the doctor. The wife then became angry and upset, reassuring him that his heart was all right, but she would come out of the depression. When the husband felt all right, the wife would begin to be withdrawn and depressed again. Although the wife's depression was related to having a husband with a heart phobia, his phobia was also related to her depression. Improvement in one of the spouses can be a severe threat to the other or to the marriage.

Actually it is impossible for one spouse to have severe symptoms without the other being integrated into the situation, but sometimes the cooperative aspects of a symptom may not be immediately apparent. For example, a wife can seem to be inadequate and helpless because of her emotional problems, but exploration reveals an even more helpless and inadequate husband who is constantly required by his wife's difficulties to maintain the fiction that he is taking care of *her*. Often in such cases, despite the wife's helpless incapacity, one finds that she handles the budget, organizes the family activities, deals with the outside world, and generally manages the home. The credit for strength in the family, however, is handed to the man by man by mutual agreement.

In this type of marriage the wife will often have symptoms when the husband is so shaken by something in his life that he is threatened with a breakdown or the development of symptoms. At that moment the wife has her problems and the man must pull himself together to help her. Occasionally the wife can have symptoms at the time the husband takes a step forward and begins to assert himself with more self-confidence in the marriage. As he makes more demands upon her, the wife will gain control of the relationship by becoming too "ill" to meet the demands. Sometimes these two circumstances occur simultaneously; the husband experiences some success in his field of endeavor which causes him to assert himself more at home and at the same time shakes him because of his uneasiness about added responsibilities. As he oscillates between breaking down under the threat of greater success and becoming more self-assertive, he offers his wife incompatible definitions of the relationship and she cooperates by developing symptoms which stabilize the situation.

An example of this type of situation is the graduate student who receives his degree and begins his first job. Threatened with a change in his relationship to the world because he must go out and deal with people as an equal adult after years as a student, he, in this time of success, enters a crisis. In the case of a particular student, the wife, who had been supporting him through college, was the one who collapsed. She was suddenly faced with a shift in their relationship as he went to work and started supporting her. He became both more assertive at home and more shaken by his new responsibilities in life. At the moment he was expressing his uncertainty about leaving his new job and going back to school, the wife had anxiety attacks. She was unable to continue work because of these anxiety attacks, or even to leave the house alone, and so he was required to continue in his new job and support her. When the wife moved in the direction of getting on her feet, the husband indicated he might collapse. Yet when the husband attempted to take more charge of the marriage, which the wife indicated she wished, she would become uncooperative but indicated she "could not help it." Whenever the couple began to deal with their conflicts with each other, the wife would indicate that she would respond to her husband differently if it were not for her anxiety. The husband would indicate that the problem was not between them but centered in her internal anxiety. As long as the couple maintained an emphasis upon the wife's symptoms when threatened with change, the marital relationship could not be worked out in a more satisfying way.

THERAPEUTIC INTERVENTION

The typical marriage therapist brings a couple together and tells them he wants them to talk and correct the misunderstandings which have arisen, to express their feelings, and to gain some insight into their difficulties. However, merely because this procedure for change is outlined to the married couple does not necessarily mean that therapeutic change is brought about by self-expression, correcting misunderstandings, or gaining insight into difficulties. The explanation to a patient of what will bring about change need not be confused with what actually brings about a change.

The argument that insight and self-understanding is the primary factor in producing change cannot be sufficiently supported. Some couples will undergo a change from following directives without insight. Other couples will evidence considerable understanding, particularly of their unconscious motivations and the effects of the past on their present behavior, and yet they will continue to behave in distressing ways. More important, understanding and self-expression cannot be separated from the effects of the therapeutic context in which they occur. Shifts in relationships with the therapist can effect a change which appears as a shift in understanding. For example, a wife can "discover" that she is unwilling to let her husband be the authority in the home because of the inadequacies of her father in the past. However, when she makes this discovery in the therapeutic context, she will be presenting the idea to the therapist and so accepting him as the authority on the point she is making. What change occurs may not be brought about by her self-understanding but by her acceptance of the therapist as an authority when she has never allowed anyone to be in that position with her.

THE EFFECT OF THE THIRD PERSON

When a couple comes to a marriage therapist, changes can occur in their relationship because of the mere existence of the therapeutic triangle. The marital partners may have various motivations for entering therapy, including a determination to prove that the other is the villain in the marriage. The ways spouses attempt to use third parties are often what needs to be changed about their relationship. Most couples have managed to use in-laws, intimate friends, or children against each other. A marriage therapist, by dealing fairly with each spouse, deals differently with them than others have. By not letting himself be provoked into condemning either marital partner, the therapist disarms a couple and prevents many of their usual maneuvers. (Actually on the basis of his fee alone the therapist is involved in a different way with a couple than family members can be.)

The mere presence of the therapist, as a fair participant, requires the spouses to deal with each other differently. Each spouse must respond to both therapist and mate instead of merely to mate. For example, a husband who handles his wife by withdrawing into silence will find that he cannot easily continue with this maneuver in the therapy setting. Instead of being incapacitated by his silence, the wife can discuss it with the therapist and use it to prove her point. The husband must change his tactics to deal with both people. Many maneuvers a spouse habitually uses to provoke a response in his partner can lose their effectiveness when used against two people at once, particularly if the third party is not easily provoked.

Although it is not possible for a marriage therapist to be "objective" with a couple since he rapidly becomes a participant in the interaction, it is possible for him to side with one spouse and then with another and so be fair. It is convenient for some therapists to argue that they do not take sides in a marital struggle but merely "reflect" back to the couple what they are expressing. Such an argument requires considerable naiveté. If a therapist listens to a wife's complaints and then turns to her husband and says, "How do you feel about that?" he cannot make his classic statement without his inquiry being in some sense directive. A therapist cannot make a neutral comment; his voice, his expression, the context, or the mere act of choosing a particular statement to inquire about introduces directiveness into the situation. When the therapist is being directive, coalition patterns are being defined and redefined, and a crucial aspect of this type of therapy is continually changing coalition patterns between therapist and each spouse. The wife who drags her husband into marriage therapy soon finds that the therapist does not join her in condemnation of the fellow, and the dragged-in husband discovers with some relief that the focus also shifts to how difficult his wife can be.

A further effect of the presence of the therapist is the change brought about by each spouse when he has the opportunity to observe the other dealing with the therapist. For example, a man who had paid little attention to his wife's protests must sit and observe an authority figure treat her in a symmetrical way by paying careful attention to what she says and encouraging her to say more. Not only do questions of coalition arise in such circumstances, but a model is being set for the spouse. Similarly, a therapist can prevent a wife or husband from dealing with him the way he or she has habitually provoked the marriage partner. For example, by commenting on how he is being handled the therapist can set a model for dealing with such provocations.

The difficulty a couple have in accepting a complementary relationship with each other is profoundly affected by the fact that they place themselves individually and collectively in a complementary relationship with a marriage therapist by asking for his services. When the therapist cooperates in such a relationship by taking charge, as most marriage therapists tend to do, he is accepting this type of relationship. Although such a therapist is not necessarily overtly authoritarian, in fact that may not be wise or possible except in special circumstances, he is willing to listen and explore the problems and offer directives like the expert he is expected to be. If a couple is to pay attention to him, he must be an authority figure, although not so omnipotent that it is necessary for the couple to topple him. Their acceptance of an authority figure, and therefore the acceptance of a complementary relationship, becomes a part of the process of working out types of relationships with each other.

DEFINING THE RULES

Besides intervening in a marriage merely by being present, a marriage therapist will actively intervene by relabeling or redefining, the activity of the two people with each other. In the early stages of treatment his comments and directives tend to be permissive as he encourages the couple to express themselves in a context where each will have a fair hearing. Accusations and protests are nurtured so that as much as possible is made explicit. One way of encouraging a more free discussion is to define the consultation room as a special place, a "no man's land," where the rules are different from ordinary situations. In this special place it is appropriate to bring up matters which they have on their minds but have avoided discussing. Although this framing of the therapy situation appears a mild directive, couples will often accept the idea that they can protect each other less in that room. Sometimes a therapist may forbid the couple to discuss certain topics between sessions so that only in that special place are they discussed.

As a couple express themselves, the therapist comments upon what they say. His comments tend to be the following: those comments which emphasize the positive side of their interaction together, and those comments which redefine the situation as different from, if not opposite to, the way they are defining it.

An emphasis upon the positive typically occurs when the therapist redefines the couple's motives or goals. For example, if a husband is protesting his wife's constant nagging, the therapist might comment that the wife seems to be trying to reach her husband and achieve more closeness with him. If the wife protests that her husband constantly withdraws from her, the husband might be defined as one who wants to avoid discord and seeks an amiable relationship. Particularly savage maneuvers will not be minimized but may be labeled as responses to disappointment (rather than the behavior of a cad). In general, whenever it can be done, the therapist defines the couple as attempting to bring about an amiable closeness but going about it wrongly, being misunderstood, or being driven by forces beyond their control. The way the couple characterize each other may also be redefined in a positive way. If a husband is objecting to his wife as an irresponsible and disorganized person, the therapist might define these characteristics as feminine. If the husband is passive and inactive, he can be defined as stable and enduring. When the therapist relabels a spouse in a positive way, he is not only providing support, but he is making it difficult for the couple to continue their usual classification. In addition, when the therapist redefines a spouse, he is labeling himself as the one who classifies the couple. By emphasizing the positive, he does his classifying in such a way that they cannot easily oppose him.

The other type of comments by the therapist emphasize the opposite of what the couple is emphasizing. If both husband and wife are protesting that they remain married only because they must, for religious reasons or for the children's sake, the therapist focuses upon the voluntary aspects of their relationship. Emphasizing how they chose each other and have remained together for many years, he minimizes the compulsion in the relationship. When husband and wife are protesting that their relationship is strictly voluntary and they can separate at any time, the therapist indicates that they have remained together so long despite their difficulties and they obviously have a deep unwillingness to end their association.

The therapist also relabels the type of relationship of a couple. If a wife protests that she is the responsible one in the family and must supervise her husband, the therapist not only commiserates with her for depriving herself by cooperating in this arrangement, but he also points out the husband's supervision and responsible acts. In addition, he might suggest to the wife that the husband is arranging that she be the responsible one, thereby raising the question who is supervising whom. Similarly, if a husband labels his wife as the helpless one, the therapist points them in the direction of discovering who gets her own way. By subtly focusing upon the opposite, or a different, aspect of a relationship, the therapist undermines the couple's typical ways of labeling the relationship and they must define it in a different way and so undergo a change.

A further product of encouraging a couple to talk about each other is to make explicit many of the implicit or covert, marital rules. When they are explicit, they are more difficult to follow. For example, if an implicit agreement between a couple is that they will visit his in-laws but not hers, the therapist might inquire whether they both prefer this arrangement. If they have not discussed the matter explicitly, an issue is then raised where a decision can be made. Similarly, there may be an implicit agreement that the wife never lets her husband speak. When the therapist points out that the wife seems to be interrupting her husband before he has a chance to say what is on his mind, the wife will be less able to do so, even though the therapist is not suggesting a change but "merely" commenting on what is happening. A comment can also make mutual protection less effective. By suggesting to a husband that his wife seems to be treating him like a sensitive plant, the therapist can provoke a more straightforward discussion. Conflicts about what rules to follow can be resolved by encouraging a couple to discuss their lives together and to work out compromises with a therapist emphasizing the positive. However, conflicts about who is to set the rules require more active direction from a therapist.

RESOLVING PROBLEMS OF WHO IS TO SET THE RULES

Although the major conflicts in a marriage center in the problem of who is to tell whom what to do under what circumstances, the therapist might never discuss this conflict explicitly with the couple. If a husband says that he gets angry because his wife always gets her own way and is constantly supervising him, the therapist will not emphasize the struggle for control but will emphasize the strong feelings in the situation. Explicitly talking about the control problem can solidify it. However, specific directives given by the therapist are most effective when they are designed to resolve the struggle over who is to set the rules for the relationship.

Any comment by a therapist has directive aspects, if only to indicate "pay attention to this," but the marriage therapist often specifically directs a marital couple to behave in certain ways. These directives can but classed for convenience into two types: the suggestions that the couple behave differently, and the suggestions that they continue to behave as they have been.

A marriage therapist will direct a spouse to behave differently only in those cases where the conflict is minor or where it is likely that the spouse will behave that way anyhow and is only looking for an excuse. That is, a husband who never takes his wife out may be advised to take her out to dinner, but usually only if the husband is moving in that direction. Such a suggestion permits a couple an evening out without either spouse having to admit they wish it. Mere advice to a couple to treat each other in more reasonable ways is rarely followed or goes badly if it is followed. A couple, like an individual patient, can only be diverted into more productive directions and cannot be forced to reverse themselves. To tell a husband and wife that they should treat each other more amiably does not provide them with new information or give them an opportunity to follow the directive. More important, if a therapist directs a couple to behave differently, he has often been led into this directive by the couple and so is responding to their directive. A couple in distress have provoked many people to advise them to behave more sensibly; such advice proves only to the couple that the other person does not understand them and they continue in their distress. In general, when a therapist is provoked into giving advice, the advice will be on the terms of the person doing the provoking and therefore will perpetuate the distress. For example, if a wife says to the therapist, "Don't you think my husband should stay home nights instead of going out every night of the week," if the therapist agrees he is being led down the garden path. If instead of agreeing and so offering such advice the therapist says, "I think it's important to understand what this is about," the therapist is not only encouraging understanding but making it clear that he offers advice on his own terms only, not when provoked into it. However, this does not mean that the therapist should not offer advice or directives on his own terms. The psychoanalytic approach to couples is to merely listen and such a procedure avoids being led into directives by the couple. Although there may be theoretical rationales for remaining silent, such as developing deeper layers of the intrapsychic conflicts, the main function of silence is to avoid behaving on the patient's terms. However, a therapist who remains silent also avoids taking those actions which would move a couple in the direction of a more satisfactory relationship. To be silent when provoked by the couple may be necessary; to remain silent when directives which would produce change could be given on the therapist's terms is wasting time.

A couple can be instructed to behave differently if the request is small enough so that the implications of it are not immediately apparent. For example, if a husband says he always gives in and lets his wife have her own way, he may be asked to say "no" to his wife on some issue once during the week. When this is said in the wife's presence, the groundwork is laid for the suggestion to be more easily followed. Further, the suggestion is more likely followed if a rationale is provided, such as saying that any wife should feel free to do what she pleases with confidence that her husband will say "no" to her if she goes too far. Given such a directive, the couple may at first treat the "no" lightly. However, if it is on a major issue, or if the instruction is followed for several weeks, there will be repercussions in their relationship. The more rigid the previous "agreement" that the wife will always have her own way, the greater the response in both of them if he says "no" and thereby defines the relationship differently. The fact that he is doing so under direction, and so still accepting a complementary relationship, will ease the situation. But since the message comes from him, the wife will react. Similarly, an overly responsible wife may be asked to do some small irresponsible act during the week, perhaps buy something she does not need that costs a dollar or two. If the previous agreement was that she was the responsible one and her husband the irresponsible one, a small request of this kind undermines this definition of the relationship. Even though the wife is being irresponsible under therapeutic direction, and so doing her duty by doing what the therapist says, she is still spending money for something she does not need and so behaving irresponsibly. However, in general whenever a directive is given for a husband or wife to behave differently, and so break the marital rules they have established, the request must be so small that it appears trivial.

Actually it is extremely difficult to devise a directive which is a request for marital partners to behave differently from their usual ways when their usual ways of behaving are conflictual. That is, a wife who insists she is the responsible one in the marriage is usually irresponsible at another level. For example, she may be so responsible about the budget that she is irresponsible because she is overemphasizing money at a cost to her husband and children. To ask to her to do something irresponsible is not necessarily to ask something new of her. Similarly, a husband who never says "no" to his wife directly, is usually a man who is constantly saying "no" by passive resistance. To tell him to say "no" is only partly asking for different behavior. Even if one should suggest that a husband who is treating his wife coldly be more considerate of his wife, this may not be a request for a change in behavior because treating her coldly may be considerate of this type of woman. In fact, if her husband treated her more amiably she might feel great demands were being placed upon her or become so overwhelmed with guilt that sudden amiable behavior on his part would actually be inconsiderate.

Often a directive can appear to be a request for different behavior when actually it is not. For example, a husband had spent some years crusading to have his wife enjoy a sexual orgasm. He had made such an issue of the matter, and become so angry and exasperated with her, that the issue had become a grim one between husband and wife. The wife was told, in the husband's presence, that one of these days she might enjoy some sexual pleasure and when she did she was to tell her husband that she did not enjoy it. If her husband insisted on her saying whether she had really not enjoyed it or was just following this directive, she should say she had really not enjoyed it. This directive had various purposes, including the purpose of introducing uncertainty into the situation and freeing the man from his overconcern about his wife's pleasure (he suffered from ejaculatio praecox). However, from what had been said, there was some indication that the wife was enjoying sex while denying it and so the directive actually was an encouragement of her usual behavior.

Encouraging a couple to behave in their usual way is paradoxically one of the most rapid ways to bring about a change. Such a directive can be calculated or it can occur as a natural result of encouraging a couple to express themselves. A wife can say that her husband should stop being so ineffectual, and the therapist might respond that perhaps he needs to behave in that way at times and they should try to understand his reasons for it. When the therapist makes such a statement, he is permitting—if not encouraging—the husband to continue to be ineffectual. Most procedures which ostensibly emphasize bringing about understanding can be seen as subtle encouragement of usual behavior. Note that this procedure is quite different from the way the spouse typically handles the problem: a spouse usually tells the other to stop certain behavior and the result is a continuation of it. When the therapist permits and encourages usual behavior, the person tends to discontinue it.

When a therapist "accepts" the way a couple is behaving he begins to gain some control of that behavior. He is placed immediately in the center of their problem: Who is to lay down the rules for the relationship? Although a couple cannot easily oppose the kind of relationship the therapist is prescribing if they are already interacting that way, they can still respond to the idea of someone else defining their relationship for them and this response will produce a shift. For example, if a wife is managing her husband by being self-sacrificing and labeling all her behavior as for the good of others, the husband cannot easily oppose her, even though he may not wish to be in a secondary position in a complementary relationship with her. Such a woman will tend to handle the therapist in a similar way. However, if the therapist encourages her to be self-sacrificing, the woman is placed in a difficult position. She cannot manage him by this method when it is at his request. If she continues to behave that way, she is conceding that she is managed by the therapist. If she does not, then she must shift to a different type of relationship. If the therapist goes further and encourages the wife to be self-sacrificing and the husband to attempt to oppose her and fail, then the couple must shift their relationship with each other to deal with being managed by the therapist.

As an example of a typical problem, a couple can be continually fighting, and if the therapist directs them to go home and keep the peace this will doubtfully happen. However, if he directs the couple to go home and have a fight, the fight will be a different kind when it happens. This difference may reside only in the fact that they are now fighting at the direction of someone else, or the therapist may have relabeled their fighting in such a way that it is a different kind. For example, a husband might say that they fight continually because his wife constantly nags. The wife might say they fight because the husband does not understand her and never does what she asks. The therapist can relabel or redefine their fighting in a variety of ways: he might suggest that they are not fighting effectively because they are not expressing what is really on their minds, he can suggest that their fighting is a way of gaining an emotional response from each other and they both need that response, he might say that when they begin to feel closer to each other they panic and have a fight, or he can suggest they fight because inside themselves is the feeling that they do not deserve a happy marriage. With a new label upon their fighting, and directed to go home and have a fight, the couple will find their conflict redefined in such a way that it is difficult for them to continue in their usual pattern. They are particularly tempted toward more peace at home if the therapist says they *must* fight and that they must for certain reasons which they do not like. The couple can only disprove him by fighting less.

As a marriage therapist encourages a couple to behave in their usual ways he gains some control of their behavior because what occurs is being defined as occurring under his direction. At this point he can shift his direction to bring about a change. The change he brings about may be an expansion of the limits of the type of relationship of a couple, or a shift to a different type of relationship.

An example of extending the limits of a type of relationship is a classic case reported by Milton Erickson. A woman came to him and said that she and her husband were finally going to purchase a home, as they had hoped to all their married life. However, her husband was a tyrant and would not permit her any part in the choice of home or in the choice of furnishings for it. Her husband insisted that everything connected with the new house would be entirely his choice and she would have no voice in the matter. The woman was quite unhappy because of this extreme version of a complementary relationship. Erickson told the woman that he wished to see her husband. When the old gentleman came in, Erickson emphasized the fact that a husband should be absolute boss in the home. The husband fully agreed with him. Both of them also enjoyed a full agreement that the man of the house should have complete say in the choice of a house to buy and the choice of furnishings for it. After a period of discussion, Erickson shifted to talking about the type of man who was *really* the boss in the house. When the old gentleman expressed a curiosity about what type of man was really the boss, Erickson indicated that the real boss was the type of man who was so fully in charge that he could allow his underlings a say in minor matters. Such a boss kept full control of everything, but he could *permit* certain decisions to be made by those beneath him. Using this line of approach, Erickson persuaded the tyrannical old gentleman to lay out 20 plans of houses and 20 plans of house furnishings. Then the husband permitted his wife to choose among *his* plans. She chose a house she liked and the furnishings she liked. In this way the husband was still fully in charge of all aspects of the house purchase, but the wife could choose what she wanted. The limits of a complementary relationship were extended to satisfy both partners' needs.

Accepting what a couple offers, or encouraging them to behave in their usual ways and later suggesting a change can also provoke a shift in the type of relationship. For example, a wife was protesting that her husband avoided her, and that he would leave the dinner table when the family was eating to sit in the living room alone and later make himself some dinner. Although the husband at first indicated he did not know why he behaved this way, he also indicated that his wife spent the time at the dinner table nagging the kids and nagging at him. At the first suggestion that she was behaving in this way at the table, the wife said that she had to correct the children at the table because he never did. The husband said that when he attempted to, she interrupted, and it was not worth a battle.

The wife was instructed to correct the children at the table during the coming week, and to observe the effect of this upon her husband. Her husband was instructed to observe the way his wife dealt with the children, and if he strongly disagreed with it he was to get up and leave the table. Actually the instruction was merely to continue to behave as they had been. However, when they were instructed to do so, the couple found it difficult to behave in their usual ways because the behavior became both deliberate and occurred under duress. After a week of this procedure, the couple was instructed to shift their behavior: for a week the wife was to be relieved of all responsibility for discipline at the table and could just enjoy her meal, and the husband was to fully take charge at the dinner table. The wife was not even to point at one of the children to indicate that her husband should take some action. Since their behavior was defined as occurring at the instigation of the therapist, rather than originating within each other, the couple could tolerate this shift in their relationship at the table with a consequent carryover into other aspects of their lives together.

Similar encouragement of typical behavior occurs if the therapist instructs a distant couple to maintain a certain distance from each other and not risk becoming too close for a period of time, if he instructs a nonfighting couple to avoid a fight but to rehearse in their minds what they would like to say to each other, if he instructs a spouse who always gives in to give in for a period of time, and so on. This procedure not only gives the therapist some control of what the couple is doing and lays the groundwork for a later shift, but it also utilizes whatever rebellious forces are latent within the couple.

Often an instruction to one spouse in the presence of the other has its effects on them both. For example, a couple who are constantly fighting and the wife is flaunting her extramarital affairs before her husband will see their struggle from a particular point of view. They will usually see what they do to each other in terms of revenge. If the therapist, from his vantage point of an expert, advises the wife that she is protecting her husband by her dalliances with other men because he is uneasy about sex, the wife is faced with a different point of view. To label her behavior as protective, when she sees it as vengeful, makes it more difficult for her to continue it, particularly if the therapist suggests that it may be necessary for her to continue to help her husband in this way. When such a comment is made in the husband's presence, he is almost obligated to prove that he does not need such protection by attempting a closer relationship with his wife. Naturally the couple will disagree with such a comment, but the idea will continue to work upon them. If there is sufficient disagreement, the therapist may suggest they should experiment; if they manage a closer relationship, they will find that they panic. To disprove this, they must manage a closer relationship. If they become upset as they become closer, they are accepting the therapist's interpretation of the situation and so accepting him as someone who can arrange a change. If they do not become upset, they have a closer relationship which is the therapist's goal.

When a therapist provides a framework which is to bring about a change, and within that framework he encourages a couple to continue in their usual ways, the couple is faced with a situation which is difficult to deal with without undergoing change. If, in addition, the therapist makes it an ordeal for them to continue in their usual ways, the problem is compounded for the couple. Relabeling what they do in a different way often makes it more of an ordeal for the couple to continue their usual patterns. This "different way" might be a relabeling of negative behavior as something positive; it can also be the reverse. The therapist can suggest that certain behavior by one of the spouses, which they consider positive is really negative. For example, the therapist might define protectiveness as really selfishness because of the protecting person's needs being satisfied. Another procedure is to raise the question with the marital partners how they usually punish each other. Typically they say they do not, but when the punishment is defined as that behavior which the other spouse feels as punishing then they become more loquacious. Couples will then discuss such behavior as withdrawing, complaining, arguing, refusing to do what the other asks, and so on. Such a discussion makes explicit many of the maneuvers a couple use against each other, and also leads to a relabeling of those maneuvers. It is possible to lead up to the idea of symptomatic behavior as punishing. Since symptoms in one spouse are always hard on the other, one can suggest that a symptom is a way of punishing the other. A spouse with an obesity problem, headaches, hysterical symptoms, or compulsions usually prefers to define the symptom as something occurring independent of the spouse. To call such a symptom a way of punishing makes it more difficult to exist. At times a spouse can be asked to inquire of the other, "Why are you punishing me," when the other complains of a symptom. Such an inquiry provokes a denial but also provokes an inhibition of the symptomatic experience. This procedure is similar to other relabeling of symptoms so that they are characterized differently and thus a change is induced. For example, one can ask a spouse, in the presence of the other spouse, to choose a time when the symptom is better that week and announce that it is worse. Such an instruction increases the uncertainty of the severity of the symptom and lays the groundwork for change.

The idea of a therapist encouraging a couple to behave in their usual ways can be varied by a therapist directing a spouse to encourage the other spouse to exhibit symptomatic behavior. Typically the mate of a spouse with symptoms opposes the symptomatic behavior but also encourages it. If a marriage therapist directs a mate only to encourage symptomatic behavior in the spouse, there is often a rather drastic response. For example, a wife became anxious whenever she tried to leave the house alone. When she attempted to go out, she suffered anxiety feelings and a terrible pain in the eyes. She had suffered this problem for years and her husband was constantly assuring her that she should go out alone and that it was perfectly safe. However, he was also fully cooperating in her staying at home by doing all the shopping, escorting her where she needed to go, and indicating some uneasiness whenever she started to go out alone. After several sessions of marriage therapy, the husband was asked, in the presence of the wife, to do something he might think was silly. He was asked to tell the wife each day as he left for work that she was to stay home that day and not go out alone. He could say this seriously, or as a joke, or as he pleased. The husband agreed to follow this procedure. On the third day that he told her to stay at home the wife went out to the store alone for the first time in 8 years. However, the next interview was devoted to the husband's expressions of concern about what his wife might do if she went out alone, where she might go, whom she might meet, and would she even get a job and become so independent that she would leave him.

This directive to the husband to tell his wife to stay at home was actually a double encouragement of usual behavior: the husband was directed to encourage his wife to stay at home, as he had been covertly doing, and the wife was being encouraged by the husband to stay at home, as she had been doing. The product of such a directive is a shift in type of relationship. Although the wife had been behaving like the helpless one, *she was in charge* of being the helpless one by insisting on staying at home. When her husband directed her to stay at home, the question of *who* was laying down the rules for their relationship was called in question. The wife responded by a symmetrical move, leaving the house, which was her only way of taking charge in this situation. Although it seems a mild directive when a therapist directs a spouse to encourage the other spouse to behave as usual, there is inevitably a marital upheaval because such a directive centers on the crucial problem in a marriage; who is to define what kind of relationship the two people will have.

CHANGING THE STABILITY OF A SYSTEM—SUMMARY

A marital couple in difficulty tend to perpetuate their distress by attempting to resolve conflict in such a way that it continues. The goal of a marriage therapist is not only to shift, or to expand, the types of relationships of a couple, but also to provoke a change in the ways the couple keep the marital system stable. Such a change requires influencing the corrective variables in the system so the system itself can undergo a change.

The appearance at the door of a marriage therapist is essentially an attempt by a couple to find a more satisfying means of perpetuating their relationship. The therapist provides an opportunity for change in a variety of ways: he encourages discussion to resolve conflict rather than previous methods, such as withdrawal and silence; he provides a reasonably impartial advisor and judge; he encourages a couple to examine motivations which they might have outside awareness; he makes many maneuvers explicit and therefore more difficult to follow; and he engenders habits of dealing with sensitive topics. Granting that discussion, encouragement of understanding, and new points of view are offered in the marriage therapy context, there is another source of change which has been emphasized here—the paradoxical position a couple is placed in if they continue distressing behavior when undergoing marriage therapy. The paradoxical strategies of a marriage therapist are formally similar to those used by therapists of individuals.

A couple is faced with a paradox, or a conflict of messages at different levels, when the therapist offers benevolent help to a couple and within that framework he requires them to go through an ordeal which they can feel as punishing. It is not easy for a couple to expose their problems and petty conflicts, and the situations the couple are most sensitive about are often those most explored. Still another dimension of paradox occurs when the therapist encourages them to continue in their distress, while communicating to them at another level that he is helping them over that distress. Similarly, he assumes the posture of an expert and often declines to directly advise the couple as an expert would.

The question why paradoxical situations are evident in therapy is related to the question of how change is brought about and how difficult it is for a couple to undergo change without assistance. It would seem reasonable that if a couple is obviously compounding their difficulties by their behavior they would cease such behavior, particularly if offered sensible advice to do so. However, such advice is not usually offered in therapy and if offered it is not usually followed. It is possible to postulate deeply rooted psychodynamic causes to explain why change in a marital relationship is difficult, but it is also possible to approach the problem from a relationship rather than an individual point of view. People in a relationship tend to govern each other's range of behavior, and when one of them indicates a change the other tends to react against that change even when it might lead to less subjective distress. As it is sometimes said, if a wife wishes her husband to remain unchanged, she should set out to reform him.

A couple, like an individual, tends to react to the relationship with a therapist in a similar way. Direct indications for change are responded to with a persistence of unchanged behavior. The various tactics of a therapist to avoid indicating a change makes paradoxes evident in the therapeutic setting since he must find ways of inducing change without asking for it to occur. In fact, when he paradoxically encourages an increase in distressing behavior, within a framework of alleviating it, he is most likely to bring about change.

Although a marriage therapist typically emphasizes to a couple the need for self-understanding, there is little evidence that achieving understanding causes a change in a marital relationship. More apparently, marriage therapy offers a context where couples can learn alternative ways of behaving while being forced to abandon those past procedures which induced distress. By advice, counsel, and example the therapist offers methods of resolving conflict. By imposing therapeutic paradoxes, the therapist both forces and frees the couple to develop new ways of relating to one another.

CHAPTER VII

Family Conflicts and their Resolution

WITH THE SHIFT in orientation in psychiatry from the individual to the relationship between people, it would follow that inevitably the focus of treatment would shift to the family. Although some therapists who treat individuals have been family-oriented in the past, the procedure of regularly interviewing the entire family together as a group would appear to be only a decade old. This idea that all members of a family should be observed and treated simultaneously has certain consequences which are only beginning to be recognized and which lead psychiatry, and the social sciences in general, over roads never before travelled.

Two premises are typically offered as reasons for bringing in all family members when one member is exhibiting symptoms. These reasons apply to treating couples when one spouse has symptoms or to treating the whole family when one child or one parent is in distress. It is said that the person with symptoms is serving some family function by experiencing the psychopathology; he is satisfying the needs of relationships in the family by serving a scapegoat function, he is holding the family together, he is providing a focus for family discontent, and so on. It is also said that when the family member with the presenting problem improves, other family members exhibit distress, symptoms, or the dissolution of the family unit is threatened.

Granting these premises, a clinical portrait appears which constitutes a discontinuous change from the ideas about psychopathology of traditional psychiatry. The family therapist is suggesting that psychopathology in the individual is a product of the ways he deals with intimate relations, the ways they deal with him, and the ways other family members involve him in their relationships with one another. Further, it is suggested that the appearance of symptomatic behavior serves a function in perpetuating a particular family system. Consequently, changes in the individual will not only have effects upon intimates, but such changes can occur only if the total family system changes with resistance to change centering in the relationships with other family members.

This clinical portrait is revolutionary when contrasted with past psychological points of view. According to the traditional approach, which reached an extreme in psychoanalysis, symptoms and resistance to change center in the internal processes of the individual. The function of symptoms is to maintain an intrapsychic balance and family relations are secondary, if not peripheral, to the problems which psychotherapy must resolve. To suggest that symptoms maintain the balance of the family system rather than the balance of intrapsychic forces is to request a major change in psychiatric thinking.

It might be possible to have the broad, flexible viewpoint and say that both the individual and the family points of view are true, but such innocent tolerance confuses the theoretical and descriptive problems. Those who attempt to think in that way find themselves talking about unconscious forces in family relationships and family relationships inside the individual. Such metaphors may be entertaining, but they will not lead to scientific rigor. What is evident is the fact that *the description of the "individual" is going to change when his relationships are included in the description.* If the individual descriptions offered in the past are used, the family context must be ignored. What a person does, why he does it, and how he can be changed will appear different if the description shifts from *only* him to the context in which he is functioning. It is this new vantage point which is the focus of family work.

Among the difficulties in shifting to this new point of view is the assumption that it is not new but merely an adjunct to previous ways of looking at human beings. Instead, it would appear to be a discontinuous change so that what we know about the "individual" must be either cast aside or cast in a totally different light. An analogy might be helpful. It was once thought that everyone fully understood what was up and what was down. Standing upon the earth one could point up and one could point down with absolute confidence in his conception of the nature of upness and downness. When it was discovered that the earth was round, a revolution in thinking had to take place. The person who pointed "down" was pointing in the same direction as someone on the other side of the earth who was pointing "up." A change in vantage point required a major change in thinking about a descriptive problem. Similarly, those who now *know* what an individual *is*, or who insist that the individual's "inner condition" is the place to begin a description, are being asked to change their vantage point and include a larger context. With that change must come a new concept of the "individual."

DESCRIBING A FAMILY

The transition to the family point of view has been gradual both in theory and therapeutic practice. Confusion still exists over whether a family should be conceived of and treated as a collection of individuals or a system in itself. One area where the change to a family orientation has been most evident is the field of schizophrenia. At first the schizophrenic was described as an isolated individual whose problems were independent of his relationships because he was "withdrawn from reality." If his parents were noticed at all, it was assumed that any distress or deviance they might evidence was the result of having such an unfortunate child. Then the suggestion began to be made that the mother of the schizophrenic was relevant to his psychopathology and the term "schizophrenogenic mother" was coined in the 1940's. From being only a love object in the Freudian scheme, mother began to fall from grace. It was said that the schizophrenic's apparent fixation at an oral period was related to his mother's depriving him in infancy. At first her immediate influence on him was ignored, so that theoretically and practically schizophrenia continued to be an individual problem. However, it began to be said that the mother of the schizophrenic was *currently* influencing him to be schizophrenic as an expression of her own needs. To document this idea, it would be necessary to describe and contrast two mother-child relationships (rather than two individuals). At this point the field of psychiatry started to undergo a major change. The immediate influence of family members needed to be considered in the therapeutic picture, and the problem of psychiatric description shifted from classifying and differentiating individuals into clinical types to classifying and differentiating relationships. With the later discovery that fathers make a contribution to schizophrenia in the offspring, the descriptive field was expanded to include whole families.

This changing explanation of schizophrenia has been paralleled by changes in the description of other types of psychopathology. The disturbed child was once described as an individual phenomenon, then it was suggested his parents might have influenced him in infancy, and, finally, it was thought that current parental influence was "causing" the disturbance of the child. Inevitably a transition in treatment methods took place from interviewing only the child to also requiring individual therapy for each parent to finally bringing in child and parents and treating them as a family.

Because of the influence of past tradition, the first attempts to describe families were investigations of whether or not the individuals in one family were different from the individuals in another. The results of this individual testing were inconclusive, particularly in schizophrenia (e.g. cf [2]), but this was not considered sufficient evidence that the parents were unrelated to the child's psychopathology. It was argued that parental behavior *with the child* was the relevant factor, not the personality and character of the parents as expressed in individual responses to testers. That is, the suspicion had developed that the "individual" is different in his family and in other contexts. At this point it was necessary to bring in families as groups for examination of their relationships with each other, just as it was thought necessary to bring in the whole family for treatment.

The advance in the practical problem of how best to gather data on interaction in families has not been paralleled by success in conceptualizing those data in new ways. Investigators continue to use concepts of the individual when attempting to describe family relationships. As a result, a number of pseudo-relationship studies and tests have been published. For example, individual family members are tested to discover how each perceives the relationships in his family. This is apparently a study of relationships, but essentially it is merely a study of individual perception. Similarly, studies will focus upon the shared individual delusions or thought disorders of family members, the conflicts between individual value systems, the feelings of inadequacy in each member, their frustrated expectations of each other, and so on. These descriptions are confined to the individual in the sense that the terms apply to a single person rather than the relationship between two or more people.

Today there is still no adequate theoretical concept which describes the interlocking relationships in families in terms of a system. Inevitably, the therapeutic approach to families has suffered from this same lag so that the goals of family therapy as well as therapeutic tactics are typically phrased in terms of individual family members.

CONFLICT: A PARALLEL BETWEEN INDIVIDUAL AND FAMILY DESCRIPTIONS

The nature of any description will be determined by its purpose. If one is describing a family as a social institution, the description will be of quite a different kind than if one is describing a family to indicate how to change the patterns in that family. Just as one might not be interested, for purposes of psychotherapy, in classifying individuals in terms of hair color, so one is not interested in describing many of the multitudinous aspects of family life if the emphasis is upon treatment. These data which can be derived from observation of any one family are so rich that books could be written about single moments or single aspects of a family's daily living. The focus of description offered here is geared to emphasizing those aspects of cyclical family patterns which induce distress and which are relevant to bringing about change. Such a clinical emphasis must produce a description which is only partially relevant to the more abstract problems of classifying families into types or describing them as systems for other purposes. In particular, the emphasis here upon conflict and struggle does not imply that this is the most important aspect of family life or that all families are continually in conflict or that a family obviously in conflict is always that way. At certain times in families, and most of the time in "disturbed" families, the members find themselves caught up in a power struggle which is central to the distress of the individual family members. It is this struggle which is the focus of the description here, and the therapeutic tactics are defined as attempts to resolve it. When resolved, the struggle is peripheral to more important aspects of family living, such as the enjoyment of group or private enterprises.

From the beginning, psychopathology in the individual has typically been conceived of in terms of conflict. The metaphors used for portraying intrapsychic life are about forces in opposition to one another with the human psyche divided into elements which are given names. Psychopathology is said to be a product of a power struggle between these elements. As portrayed, the individual is said: to have instincts or drives which are in conflict with societal forces internalized in his superego; to have Id impulses in conflict with inhibitory forces within him; to have unconscious ideas striving toward awareness which conflict with repressing forces; to have memories of the past conflicting with present perception; to have an ego which is overwhelmed by the forces of the Id in psychoses; to have ideas in a dream conflicting with repressing forces and producing disguised symbolic content; to have desires struggle against fears; to have defenses opposing certain ideas; and to have fantasies which reflect this war within him as man struggles against himself. The idea of conflict is sufficiently accepted in the study of neurosis and psychosis that when neurosis is supposedly experimentally induced this is done by placing a subject in a situation which results in conflicting fears or desires. The central notion of Freudianism, the Oedipal conflict, represents a point of view which is typical of the individual approach—the child has sexual impulses toward his mother which conflict with his fear that his father will castrate him, resulting in a repression of ideas about these impulses and a continuing conflict between these impulses and the defenses against them. Throughout individual psychiatric description there is a formal theme centering upon a power struggle within the person with consequent neurotic and psychotic symptoms.

The family point of view does not refute the typical portrait of intrapsychic conflict. Such a refutation is, perhaps, impossible. If one looks at the data the way Freud did, the Oedipal conflict is apparent in the individual's statements and in the fiction and drama he creates. Similarly, if one records what a patient says and interprets those statements as symbolic expressions of a struggle between instinctual drives and repressing forces, the metaphors of intrapsychic conflict are appropriate. What the family point of view adds is a *different* way of looking at the same data as well as an emphasis upon collecting new kinds of data. A similar formal theme runs through psychiatric descriptions of families, although the data are interpreted differently. It is said that: family members are in conflict with one another; dominating mothers are in a struggle with passive fathers; children are used as scapegoats in parental conflict; the nuclear family is split by coalitions with the extended family, the in-laws; family members withdraw and attack and sabotage as they participate in mutual aggression; dissension arises when an individual in the family changes his behavior; there is said to be conflict between family needs and the stresses of environmental influences such as job changes, depressions, wars, and the societal expectations when children mature; and it is said that the conflicts can be overt or concealed with tactics ranging from physical assault to helpless incapacity. The consequence of these conflicts within the family is a member who manifests neurotic and psychotic symptoms.

Although the family point of view also emphasizes conflict and the struggle between opposing forces, the area of conflict is shifted outside the person to the context of his actual relationships. That is, psychopathology is a product of a power struggle between persons rather than between internal forces. This shift from conflict within to conflict without requires a major rethinking of psychiatric theory. From the family point of view, the statements of an individual can be interpreted as metaphoric expressions describing his *actual* relationships. It is in the nature of metaphor that the two points of view reach their opposite extremes. To the individually-oriented, a symbolic statement is not only a metaphor about internal conflicts, but conflicts in relationships are said to be metaphoric expressions, or "acting out" of an internal drama. Quite the reverse is true of the family point of view; external conflicts induce inner ones which reflect them.

As an example, let us suppose that a young man says he became uneasy at home on a certain evening and had to leave the house. The psychiatrist notes that the young man was home alone in the house with his mother that evening. When the patient has said the same thing several times, the psychiatrist would begin to take his statement as a metaphor about a conflict. If individually-oriented, he might interpret the statement to be an expression of an Oedipal conflict. The patient feels sexual impulses when alone with his mother and responds with anxiety. Faced with the threat of his unconscious desires, he must defend himself against these unconscious wishes by leaving the house.

The family-oriented psychiatrist, observing ,the same young man, would see the matter differently. His premise would be that there was an actual danger present for the young man. If interested in the sexual aspects of the situation, he would want to know whether the mother behaved seductively with the young man when alone with him. (Recently the psychoanalytic position has shifted to a concern about whether or not some mothers behave more seductively with their children than others, which is a move toward the relationship point of view). He would also be interested in the coalition problem at home: when alone with her son, does the mother attempt to ally with him against father? Is there a consequence the next day in the father-son relationship, or in sibling relationships, if mother and son have had an evening alone together? That is, a family orientation would assume that the young man's leaving the house was a response to a real situation rather than to a fantasy.

The question of the Oedipal conflict has always been a problem in psychoanalysis. Whether every male child experiences it or not has been questioned, and if every male child does the question has been asked, particularly by Otto Rank, whether the conflict can be etiologically significant for a particular psychiatric malady. To say that one male has "more" Oedipal conflict than another is to raise peculiar problems of quantities or amounts. When described as a fantasy, the concept is necessarily simplified so that variations are few: the child has the unconscious wish and not much more can be said except to add that it might be "weaker" or "stronger," again raising a problem of quantity.

However, if the Oedipal conflict is taken to be a description of an actual family triangle, then a classification of variations is immediately apparent. Any male child with two parents is inevitably going to face a problem of coalition; he cannot avoid it. This coalition problem can be handled in various ways just as it can vary in different circumstances and at different times. For example, if it is a coalition with mother against father, several possibilities are apparent; the child may instigate it, or the mother, or even father if he wishes to provoke a coalition against himself. Similarly, the response can vary; mother may instigate it and child decline, so that a pattern of mother-child conflict appears. Or child may instigate it and mother decline, and so on. That is, the permutations of such a triangle when seen as an *actual* situation are many, and the child raised in one kind of habitual triangular pattern will presumably learn to behave differently from one raised in a different one, even though the problem of such a triangle is universal.

A major hope in choosing the family point of view is that psychiatry can ultimately be based upon observable data and so have a chance to become a a science. If one interprets a patient's statements as symbolic expressions whose referents are inferred objects or forces within the individual, then verification can only come from further statements of the patient interpreted as symbolic expressions whose referents are the same inferred objects. There can be no verification of hypotheses in terms of some observable actuality. If a patient's statements are interpreted in terms of referents in his actual living situation, one can observe and verify. For example, if a patient implies that his mother is behaving seductively with him and this is interpreted as a projection of his unconscious impulses toward her, the interpretation can be supported only by interpretations of other similar statements. In contrast, if his statement is taken as an expression about his actuality, his interaction with his mother can be observed to test the interpretations of his statements. However, such verification will require ways of describing and classifying behavior in relationships.

THE DESCRIPTION OF CONFLICT

When one shifts to the family point of view and sets out to describe the interaction between people and to contrast types of relationships, it becomes immediately apparent that we lack the most rudimentary terminology for such a task. To shift from an intrapsychic emphasis to an emphasis upon the behavior of a person is difficult enough, but to shift further and attempt to describe two or more people in a relationship means facing complex descriptive problems. Past psychological and psychiatric descriptions are not helpful and can be a handicap, even if one attempts to use only past behavioral descriptions instead of inferred internal processes. For example, to describe a person as "infantile" or to describe a wife as dominating and a husband as passive is a long way from making a description of types of relationships. Simple dichotomous descriptive ideas are not adequate for family descriptions because they do not take into account interactive processes or communication on several levels.

It would appear that we need, at the very least, three classes of terms if we are to describe the repetitive exchanges people make in relationship with one another. We need terms for (a) the tactics, or behavior, of the single individual, (b) the exchange of tactics between people so that we can label the product of a set of tactics as a particular class of relationship, and (c) the total system which any set of relationships produces and therefore terms for classes of family systems.

To illustrate the descriptive problem, let us examine the following sequence which a family presented in a repetitive way during family interviews. The child would misbehave in some way, for example, by leaning down and looking under the table. The father would speak to the child and tell him to straighten up. Mother would then speak to father and tell him he should not have chastised the child at that time or in that way. Father would say he was merely reprimanding the boy because it seemed necessary, and mother would look exasperated with him.

To describe such a sequence in terms of its formal pattern—the pattern which occurs with various types of contents—we need terms for the behavior of each individual, for the type of relationship being perpetuated by boy and father, father and mother, and mother and boy, and terms for the type of system in which these relationships occur and which they define. The system description would also include the function of this particular sequence; for example, the sequence itself might occur at those moments in the family interchange when a relationship, or the system, is threatened with change. That is, such sequences can be seen as part of a system at one level, and a homeostatic mechanism functioning as a governor of the system at another level.

To construct terms for a sequence of this kind, the categories must fit together in some conceptual scheme. This theoretical framework must include a way of describing the behavior interchanged so that it can be shown to be a product of, and producing similar sequences so that repetitive cyclical patterns are revealed.

It would seem evident that the "cause" of any particular behavior in such a sequence is best sought after making a description of the total system. To say that the boy provoked dissension between mother and father is inadequate. The boy's misbehavior can be seen as a product of a previous sequence, and if the sequence is to be repeated father must cooperate by reprimanding him and mother by reprimanding father. The most useful conceptualization must be one which includes all the individuals as participants in keeping the system going. To devise therapeutic tactics for changing this sequence, it would seem one must attempt not merely to change one person's behavior but also the other people's responses. If one merely persuades the child not to misbehave, the system does not change, for father is then likely to say to the child "Why are you so quiet," and mother will respond with "He can be quiet if he wants, leave him alone," and father will say, "I was only wondering," and mother will look exasperated. That is, a change in one individual can lead only to an adjustment, perhaps a relabeling of his behavior, so that the system continues unchanged.

A FAMILY MODEL

As one observes that the behavior of one individual in a family exerts influence upon the others in the family, and as one further notes that a change in one person's behavior provokes responses in other family members, it becomes apparent that the theoretical conception being proposed is a cybernetic one. It follows that people associating together during long periods of time will not put up with any and all kinds of behavior from each other; they will set limits upon one another. Insofar as family members set limits for one another, it is possible to describe their interaction in terms of the self-corrective processes in the total system. The family members respond in an error-activated way when any individual exceeds a certain limit. This process of mutually responsive behavior defines the "rules" of the family system. In this sense the family is a system which contains a governing process. However, there is not just a single governor for the system; each member functions as a governor of the others and thus the system is maintained.

In a self-corrective governed system, such as the thermostatic system in heating a house, it is possible to see the thermostat as the governor of the system since it controls the heat from the furnace and so the temperature of the room. However, it is also possible to see all the elements in the system as part of the governing process. The furnace responds to the signal from the thermostat, but the thermostat responds to the temperature of the room which responds to the heat from the furnace. No single element can be "blamed" because each serves a function in the total system. To produce a change if the room temperature is too high, it is not sufficient merely to open the windows and try to influence the room temperature, one element in the system. The introduction of cold air will lower the room temperature but simultaneously it will impel the thermostat to cause the furnace to burn more fiercely and so raise the temperature of the room. The only way to make a change in the range of any element of the system is to change at least two elements simultaneously, or the "setting" of the system.

The model of a simple homeostatic system, such as a household thermostat, is not adequate to describe a family. In such a system the elements respond in error-activated ways to changes in range, but the setting of the range is made by a metagovernor; someone outside the system. A human being in the house sets the thermostat at, for example, 70 degrees and the system fluctuates around that setting. The elements in the system influence the setting, but only through a different feedback loop; the total system influences the person who sets the range of the system. In the family no outsider sets the limits of family behavior, although the culture might be said to partially function in that way. The limits of the family system are set by the members of the family as they influence each other. Therefore in describing a family two levels of governing process must be included: (a) the error-activated response by a member if any member exceeds a certain range of behavior, and (b) the attempt by family members to be the metagovernor, i.e., the one who sets the limits of that range. It is at this metagoverning level that the control problem enters the picture because the governing process at this level will manifest itself as a struggle by each family member to be the one who determines the limits of the behavior of the others. An additional complexity is the existence of subsystems within the family which govern one another; the in-law subsystem has its influence upon the nuclear family, the sibling subsystem has its influence upon the parental relationship, and so on. The addition of a family therapist is not a mere metagovernor of a single system but of the interlocking subsystems, each of which has a reciprocal influence with the therapist.

These two levels of governing process, the error-activated governing response and the metagoverning, typically occur in a single exchange of behavior. For example, if a husband says he has a headache and asks his wife to bring him an aspirin and his wife does not do so or brings the aspirin resentfully, two levels of governing are implicit. By not bringing the aspirin or by responding resentfully, the wife is indicating that her husband has exceeded a certain range of "permitted" behavior. However, she is also indicating that *she* is governing what kind of behavior he should offer, and therefore what kind of relationship they should have. With one response she both reports that he has made an error and she attempts to "set" what kind of behavior he should present. That is, she indicates a broken rule and also establishes herself as the one who sets the rules. Her unwilling response can be provoked by the *way* the husband makes his request, or it can be a response to the level of *who* is going to determine whether they have an "asking and receiving" relationship. It is at this metagoverning level, "which person is to determine the type of relationship," that the tactics of a power struggle become relevant for describing families.

The dictionary defines "power" as "the possession of sway or controlling influence over others." If one is struggling for power, he is struggling to be the one who possesses this controlling influence. Conceiving a disturbed family in this way, one is faced with the problem of how to devise therapeutic tactics for resolving power struggles. If there were in existence an adequate description of tactics in power struggles, the problem would be simplified. However, there seems to have been an almost studied avoidance of the tactical nature of such struggles by social scientists and philosophers, despite the history of man's struggle with man. We do not have a taxonomy of power tactics so that we can say this family uses this class of tactics and this family uses another. The terms for, and hierarchical classification of, such tactics must ultimately be devised.

If we approach a family in terms of the tactics family members use in their struggles with one another, and if we see these tactics fitting together so that a change in the tactics of one family member causes a self-corrective response in the others, the problem of inducing change appears to be no simple matter. When individuals in "groups with a history" are interlocked in complex ways each governing the responses of the others, and when we have not even the terminology to describe their interactive behavior, it is apparent that procedures for inducing change cannot easily be laid out in a systematic manner. However, we do know in theory and from empirical observation of families that *by definition the function of governors is to diminish change* and therefore that *if one is attempting to induce change in a governed system one must expect a continuing process of resistance.*

If a family therapist were wise enough to see how the members of a family should change and advise them to do so, they would not be able to follow that advice and change. There are two major factors which inhibit family change: the complications which develop in a self-corrective system when one element behaves differently, and the fact that when a therapist becomes included in the family system he will be dealt with at the level on which family members are struggling with each other—the level of who is going to govern the behavior of whom.

RESISTANCE TO CHANGE: CONFLICT OF LEVELS

If one accepts the idea that a family can be described as a cybernetic system, he is accepting a number of premises one of which is paradoxical in nature. To say that family members respond in error-activated ways to one another so that the family system is kept stable is to suggest that the reinforcements which keep the system stable are produced by the attempts of members to bring about change. That is, the more one individual attempts to change the system, the more he is activating the processes which maintain the system unchanged. It would follow too that the more "discontented" the family members the more they would attempt to bring about change and so reinforce the perpetuation of the system as it is. This is the tragedy of the "disturbed" family.

Approaching the family in terms of levels of governing process, one can see how complex the system is and how easily conflict can be generated. Parents are faced with difficult problems in rearing a child. If they overemphasize taking care of him and so impose only a complementary relationship with him, they are not providing a learning context where he can experience behaving as an equal with them. If they overemphasize equality and so impose only a symmetrical relationship, the child is not only incapable of dealing with such a relationship in the realistic setting of being taking care of by them, but he is not learning to experience being cared for. Rather typically in the disturbed family the parents go to either extreme or attempt to define both types of relationships at once for the child and so face him with a paradoxical relationship. For example, they ask his permission—thus defining the relationship as symmetrical—to tell him what to do—thus defining the relationship as complementary. Whatever the child does then can be wrong. If he merely does what he is told, he is not responding symmetrically, and if he denies permission, he is not accepting a complementary relationship. This kind of situation occurs whenever the parents seek to make either directives or punishment agreeable to the child; they are asking an equal to accept being treated as an unequal and so posing a paradox. As one mother stated, "It's simple to get a child to do something, you say, 'Do you want to do it? Do it.'" The fact that her child was disturbed and did not do what she said could be related to her lack of simplicity, since to ask him if he wants to do something and also to tell him to do it is to pose incongruent definitions of the relationship. Often such mothers will be unable to be simply directive with the child because if they assume this "authoritarian" position with the children there are repercussions in their relationships with their husbands. Some mothers will behave helplessly in order to induce the father to take charge more, but at the same time they cannot cope with the children by helpless behavior and so they attempt to be both helpless and firm simultaneously.

When a child is reared in a family where there is a constant power struggle, all of his actions become significant to other family members because they are responded to at a level of who is to govern whom, the metagoverning level. If a disturbed child merely takes a walk, this act can be taken as an expression of independence and so an act which is determining what kind of relationship he is to have with his parents. In terms of content, the walk may be taken as a criticism of, or an indirect comment on, the home rather than a desire to take a walk. Because what he does is given such significance, the child is given power in a disturbed home—particularly being in distress gives him power—which other children do not have so that a patient's seemingly omnipotent expressions will have some actual basis. A particular type of power he is typically given is the power to divide his parents and set them against one another. The more the parents are struggling with each other at a metagoverning level, the more the child's symptomatic behavior perpetuates their particular struggle.

If a therapist attempts to induce a change in a homeostatic system by influencing only one member, he finds that the problems of levels of communication inhibit the change. For example, a rebellious child can be blamed for family difficulties because he does not do what he is told but acts in such a way that he is telling his parents what to do, if only by inducing their exasperated responses on his terms. His parents respond with angry helplessness, irritated with him but unable to enforce a complementary relationship. If the therapist should succeed in influencing the child to attempt to change this relationship so that the child indicates he will henceforth do what he is told, there will be repercussions throughout the family. The parents must then be willing to tell him what to do and might have to change their relationship with each other to deal with the child in this new way. They might also have to shift their relationship with the child's siblings to adapt to treating this child differently. Besides these consequences, there is a paradox which the parents can face when a child indicates a change of this kind. Placed in crude terms, if the child says, "All right, tell me what to do from now on and I'll do it," he is not merely accepting this type of relationship, he is governing what kind of relationship there will be. The fact that he is instigating the change can be taken to mean that he is directing the parents to direct him. If they comply with his demand, they are continuing to do what the child tells them. To "demand" to be told what to do is to pose a paradox which is similar to the problem posed when a wife "orders" her husband to dominate her. If he dominates her, he is being dominated because it is at her request. When the rebellious child attempts to initiate more compliant behavior, his parents can respond as if he is governing them and so react with angry helplessness as they always have to his demands. Naturally, the child is then encouraged to revert to being an angry and rebellious child again. (A naive therapist might then blame the parents for not accepting the child's willingness to be directed without seeing the paradoxical position in which they are placed; if they direct the child, they are following his directives as they always have.)

Although it is difficult for any family member to induce a change in a homeostatic system, sometimes this can occur if the changed behavior is labeled as instigated by the therapist. Family members can more easily accept one member governing the type of relationship if his behavior is labeled as instigated by the therapist. However, they can have a similar response to the therapist governing them, and there is the additional complication that change within the system has not taken place unless the family members are labeled as initiating new behavior themselves. At some point the therapist must emphasize that the changed behavior of a family member was *really* not because of his influence but initiated independently. When a therapist indicates this, he is following the fundamental rule of all psychotherapy; he is indicating the therapeutic paradox, "I am influencing you, but the change which occurs is spontaneous." Before dealing further with the peculiarly paradoxical messages presented by a therapist, a further resistance to family change should be discussed.

RESISTANCE TO CHANGE: RESISTING THE THERAPIST

If there were no control problem in human relationships and it was a mere matter of lack of information or incorrect understanding, a therapist could direct family members to behave more sensibly and reasonably with each other, correct their misunderstandings, fill in missing information, and the system would change. However, family members do not respond to this approach. If the therapist has become important enough to a family to influence them, he has been included in the family system (and if he has not become that important they will ignore him). This means the family members will struggle with his governing them just as they struggle with each other over this. Should he offer them advice to behave more sensibly, they will respond at the metagoverning level of who is going to "set" or circumscribe, their range of behavior. To avoid conceding that he is governing them, they must not follow the advice or see that the result goes badly. In fact, if the family can *provoke* the therapist to offer good advice, they have succeeded in governing how he is to behave. When the family members set the terms for the therapist's behavior, he will be joining them in perpetuating the system unchanged.

When a therapist gains some control, or metagoverning function, with a family it is only over certain settings of the relationships in the system. There are definite limits to his influence on many aspects of family life, as there should be, since the ideology of families will be so diverse. One family might function quite satisfactorily with one way of life and another with quite a different one. In this sense a therapist does not change a family, he produces only a shift in the power struggle which is incapacitating the family members.

THERAPEUTIC INTERVENTION

Now that the methods of family therapy are being added to the many existing methods of individual therapy, an opportunity arises to examine common factors in the hope of discovering the "causes" of therapeutic change. The general argument will be offered here that family therapy is formally similar to the individual methods which have been discussed, insofar as therapists offer families an educational factor to help them behave differently and therapeutic paradoxes to force them to do so.

As with other methods of psychotherapy, the published literature on family therapy contains more discussion of the nature of the problems than of the tactics for dealing with them. The description of some of the family methods presented here includes references to publications but also includes the author's observations of family therapists at work.

Family therapy differs more in its setting than most other methods of therapy. Although it is common to bring the family group to the office and have joint discussions with them, this is not the only procedure used. Some therapists see the family members individually, with only an occasional joint conference, but the focus is upon bringing about a change in the family system.[17] Other therapists prefer to see the parents first and then bring in the children later.[8] One therapist uses a unique setting. He brings the family to his office where he has two rooms with a one-way mirror arrangement. The family talks together in one room while the therapist observes from the other, and he enters regularly to make comments and interpretations.[26] One group of family therapists sees the family in the home,[21] and another group sees the family intensively for 2 or 3 full days and then has long recesses.[42] Several methods involve the use of two or more therapists and one extreme method included hospitalizing the entire family for observation and treatment.[10]

Although there is not yet a "conservative" way to treat families, it is generally assumed that the best procedure is to bring the family members all together and have the therapist explore the family problems with them. The method of exploration will vary with the style of the therapist. There are three general approaches, or therapeutic styles, commonly used. In the *one-to-one* style, the therapist treats individual family members in the presence of the others. For example, he will talk to the father and explore with him his past and present while other family members observe. Then he will switch to another family member and proceed similarly. What he says to the individual is said with full recognition that the other family members are part of the setting.

Another procedure is the *therapist as a funnel* style. All family members are included in the conversation, but each speaks to the therapist rather than to each other. Such a therapist typically interprets and clarifies what one person is saying and then switches to another person to ask for a comment which he then interprets and clarifies.

In contrast, there is the *enforced family conversation* style, where the therapist encourages the family members to talk to each other rather than to him. Should a husband begin to defend himself to the therapist, he will be diverted towards talking to his wife. The therapist will summarize or make comments, or he will prevent family arguments from getting out of hand, but he typically serves a function of instigating family members to talk with each other.

Any particular therapist may use all three styles depending upon the circumstances, but some will confine themselves quite rigidly to one of them. Besides variations in setting and style, therapists also vary in their orientation to the problem: some will emphasize the effects of the past on present behavior, others will focus upon the clarification of messages, and others will emphasize misunderstandings and interpret whatever happens as positively as possible. All of them try to shift the focus from the identified patient to the family group.

Many of the tactics of family therapy are formally similar to those discussed under Marriage Therapy, and these will not be repeated here. Often when the focus shifts from a disturbed child to the conflict between the parents, the children may drop out of the therapy while the parents continue. Some therapists, however, will require all family members to be present from the beginning to the end of therapy. What will be emphasized here are the similarities between family and individual therapy with the general argument that they are not as different as they appear. One of the most obvious similarities is the typical approach to the symptom in both methods: in individual therapy the therapist usually indicates to the patient that the symptom is only a manifestation, not the real problem, and they must work upon what is behind it —the "roots" of the disturbance. In family therapy, the identified patient, usually a child, is offered as the problem and the therapist typically tells the family that the child is only a manifestation of the real problem and they must deal with what is behind it—the "roots" in the family disturbance.

FAMILY AND INDIVIDUAL THERAPY: SIMILARITIES

If individual and family therapy are examined in terms of theory, they are decidedly different. If they are looked upon in terms of practice, the differences are few. In the past there has been little description of therapeutic practice—what the therapist of an individual actually does with a patient. For example, descriptions of the psychoanalytic method are typically about a theoretical process rather than what therapist and patient actually do in relation to one another, even among writers who have attempted to focus upon practice.[44] Particular emphasis is placed upon the transference and upon uncovering ideas out of awareness. From the theory point of view, it is important that the transference relationship not be disturbed by the intrusion of other people—certainly not by the relatives of the patient, as Freud pointed out. The careful handling of defenses is another way of looking at individual therapy through a theoretical set of glasses. The process of interaction between therapist and patient is seen as a careful uncovering of ideas within the patient in the face of the patient's resistance to these ideas. Assuming that the transference and dealing with internal resistance are crucial to change in individual therapy, the various ways of treating whole families are not only different but could be called antitherapeutic. The transference relationship is thoroughly confused by the presence of other family members, and defenses cannot be dealt with in an orderly fashion when family members are flinging accusations about, including accusations about incestuous desires and acts.

However, individual therapy need not be seen only through the narrow focus of past theories, particularly when they are not based upon a description of what happens but upon conjecture about what must be happening given certain theoretical ideas. If we merely note the obvious fact that individual therapy is a conversation between two people, not only does the procedure look different from past descriptions but similarities with types of family therapy begin to appear. At a descriptive level, the difference between the two methods centers largely in the presence or absence of other family members in the room. Other differences are difficult to find, and apparent differences become similarities upon closer examination. For example, ostensibly individual therapy could be described as a two-person system and family therapy as a three or more person system. Related to this difference is the way the family therapist becomes included in the family group and is used by members in their dealings with each other. Yet individual therapy is not essentially a two-person system, even if the therapist attempts such a restriction physically. The patient's family is in the room in his discussions, his wife is inquiring at home what he says in therapy, and he reports to his family the ideas he gains in therapy and so uses the therapist at home. The therapist rapidly becomes a part of the power struggle in the family group, although the other family members have all information about him funneled through the patient. The difference, again, resides in the physical absence of other family members during interviews, even though they may be present in the discourse or as indirect supervisors of what is to be said in the room.

It would be possible to argue that individual and family therapy are similar because some therapists in both situations encourage patients to understand themselves better and to express their feelings. Even if one accepted this implicit premise that self-understanding and the expression of feelings are the source of therapeutic change, it is apparent that different kinds of understanding are focussed upon in different procedures, and it is even more obvious that the results are going to be different in individual and family therapy. If a husband expresses his feelings while alone with an individual therapist, the therapist might not take his statements personally. Yet a wife will have such a response when she is also present in the interview because she will think herself responsible for how her husband feels (as a therapist might after some years with the patient).

TRAINING IN METACOMMUNICATION

It is the point of view of family therapy that the individual can change only when his family system changes, and so logically it would follow that individual therapy must somehow lead to a change in a family system which permits the patient to undergo change. From the family point of view, individual therapy is a way of working with one person and using him as a lever to produce change in his family. An important question is what the patient learns in individual therapy that can be used by him to influence his family system.

If one looks for an understanding of what occurs in individual therapy that is comparable to family therapy, a major factor appears. Individual therapy is a training institution for verbalizing about one's relations with other people. The constant emphasis is placed upon talking about oneself and others, including the therapist, with a premise that if a patient talks sufficiently he is less likely to act out or somatize. Inevitably the individual patient will carry into his family a newly learned way of commenting upon what is going on. For example, when a patient with headaches comments on her husband's behavior instead of exhibiting distress and withdrawing, she is requiring him to deal with her differently than he has in the past and so both of them are changing their behavior. By communicating verbally about a family member's communicative behavior, the patient is inducing a change in the family system.

The encouragement of verbal metacommunication is a common factor in various types of individual therapy, and the basic procedure in family therapy is to sit family members down together and have them talk about their relationships with each other. As they talk together and are pressed to comment on each other's communicative behavior, they are using verbal comments rather than previous tactics and consequently the system must undergo a change.

COALITIONS: THE THERAPIST AS A MODEL

Although we have no taxonomy of the tactics people use in power struggles, we know that an absolutely essential aspect of such struggles is the problem of coalition. Most of the usual tactics, such as threats, promises, sabotage, passive resistance and physical assault are used to maintain or to change coalition patterns. When a family member exhibits symptoms, the power struggle has usually settled into a stable set of coalitions, but a set which is in some sense threatened or family members would not seek outside assistance. Since in power relationships an advantage gained can lead to further advantages, the family can be threatened with an imbalance of power so that one faction will call upon the services of an outsider, such as the state, to restore stability. In this sense, the hospitalization of a family member does not mean the member is expelled from the system. Usually the family stabilizes its set of patterns by using the hospital as a threat or as a means of maintaining the system unchanged by the use of hospital forces. A family therapist will also find himself considerably under pressure to use his support to maintain the family system unchanged.

When a therapist enters the power struggle in a family, the most immediate question will be this: Where will he fit into the coalition patterns? Each warring faction will attempt to bring him on their side. If the therapist accepts a particular side, such as joining the parents in the idea that the child is the problem, or if he even accepts the idea that sides must be taken, he is likely to end in the morass which the family is in and be caught up in their struggle. The way he handles his entrance onto the field initially can have considerable effect upon the course of the therapy.

The mere act of talking together in the presence of an outside authority will have influence on a family but will doubtfully induce basic changes, even though many families who enter therapy find an hour's conversation together a unique experience. The addition of a therapist who is not merely an outsider but who is a participant provides a different context for the family if he behaves differently from the habitual behavior of family members.

A therapist behaves differently from family members in various ways. For example, he is behaving differently when he proceeds in the usual family therapy style of encouraging the democratic virtues; each person is to have a fair turn, minority views are to be expressed, and everyone is encouraged to make compromises for the good of the group. This emphasis alone effects the current power relationships in the family and makes it clear that the therapist is not siding with a particular faction. Therapists of all schools particularly emphasize being fair and not taking sides with any one family member. This usually means the therapist shifts coalitions so that he is on one side at one moment and another later, sometimes announcing in advance that he will do this. Ideally, the therapist sides with all at once by finding a level where he is placing all factions within a single class. For example, he might side with the parents because the child is misbehaving but also side with the child because he is being provoked into misbehaving. When the therapist does not join the family in insisting that one member is the problem and asks them to consider the entire family as a problem, he has stepped to a higher level where he can coalesce with all members in a common cause.

The therapist provides the family a model, either implicitly or explicitly, for handling disciplinary problems. Typically the disturbed family is an inconsistent family. Extreme behavior is permitted and then opposed and permitted again. Both overprotection and harsh punishment can alternate, and the problem member usually has few consistent restraints upon him. By his advice, and by the ways he handles the family in the room, the therapist exhibits ways for family members to deal with each other more consistently.

Related to both restraints and metacommunicative training is the way the therapist sets himself as a model by not letting himself be provoked by family members. He particularly does not let himself be provoked into coalitions which are being instigated by symptomatic behavior or distress in a family member. For example, the father in the family might always be provoked to apology, or to exasperation, by pained looks or weeping from his wife, but the therapist does not let her distress engineer either an antagonism or a coalition. Similarly, a child who looks pitifully unhappy can provoke the parents but not the therapist, just as a husband can induce condemnation from his wife by behaving irresponsibly but he finds the therapist does not condemn him as expected. Regularly the therapist is likely to set an example of metacommunication by commenting on the way he is being handled rather than by merely responding on the other person's terms and so being caught up in the system.

By not responding on the patient's terms when the patient is exhibiting symptomatic or distressful behavior, the therapist requires the patient to deal with him in other ways, in both individual and family therapy. A difference lies in the fact that in family therapy the other members can observe, and utilize for themselves, the ways the therapist handles provocation. In individual therapy only the patient can do this by observing how he himself is handled. He might then carry the therapist's techniques into his family, as people report who have lived with family members undergoing psychotherapy.

COALITION: THE CONTROL ASPECT

In previous chapters there has been a discussion of the ways a therapist gains control of the relationship with individual patients in various forms of psychotherapy and a discussion of his strategies with married couples. A similar process takes place in family therapy with the additional problem that the therapist is dealing with more than two people at once.

The family therapist takes charge by laying down the general rules of the game for the family, and within this framework he places the family in charge of what is to happen in the room. Placing the emphasis upon the family's initiative in solving their own problems, he sometimes even points out that they are the best therapists for each other. By doing this the therapist takes a metagoverning position while denying it, and the family is placed in a position where their usual methods of taking charge of a relationship are being encouraged and requested by the person in charge. When the therapist uses passive silence, the paradox faced by the family is essentially the one set up by the psychoanalytic procedure. More active therapists first set the framework of being the expert in charge and then proceed with a constant disinvolvement from responsibility so that the family members are consistently encouraged to be in charge. For example, if mother asks what she is to do with a recalcitrant daughter, the therapist does not tell her. He might ask her what she feels like doing, he might suggest more discussion to clarify the situation, he might point out that she seems to feel helpless in this situation, he might raise a question why it is such a problem to her, and so on. As he shifts the responsibility for what to do with the daughter to her, the mother is being placed in charge by him and so cannot take charge of him. Similarly, the daughter cannot engage him in a power struggle on this issue because he is confining the responsibility within the family. Some family therapists will directly tell a family what to do, but then the directive usually places the initiative upon the family.

As one might expect in a power struggle, the problem of control for the therapist centers in the attempts by family members to initiate coalitions with him. Typically the therapist arranges the situation so that the coalitions which occur are on his terms. Attempts by family members include provoking him to side with others or inducing him to side with them and such maneuvers can be active or passive. Mother might say, "Don't you think my husband should go to work?" thus inviting a coalition against her husband, or she might just appear helpless and anxious and apparently needing support, thereby inviting a coalition against the family members who are distressing her. If the therapist does accept the coalition, he manages to side with both. For example, he might say, "Naturally you would want your husband to work, but perhaps he doesn't feel ready to yet," thereby siding with the wife but also with the husband in the sense that he has rights about going to work. Faced with helplessness or distress as an invitation for coalition, the therapist might say, "Have you noticed how the others in the family become uneasy when you're upset?" indicating he is on the side of all. Sometimes coalitions are difficult to avoid. For example, some mothers of schizophrenics will act as a kind of chorus for the therapist. Each thing he says they will say "That's right, yes, that's right," so that the therapist continually has mother on his side even if he would rather not. His problem is to prevent such support from her without letting her antagonize him and force him into a coalition with someone else.

Most of the tactics of family therapy are essentially similar to those of marriage therapy once the emphasis has shifted from the ostensible patient to the family as a group or the parental conflict. However, the shift of focus from the identified patient is not an easy one to make and requires bringing about a change in the system. Because of the power given to the patient by his symptomatic behavior, as well as because of the use of him in factional struggles, the patient can be the center of attention. A child who refuses to talk, such as a mute schizophrenic, can carry more weight in a family conversation than the most loquacious parent. Typically such a child is only mute verbally; if the conversation goes in certain directions, he will move restlessly, thereby suddenly calling the attention of the whole family to himself. Similarly, a child can set off in psychotic verbiage, or threaten some act, at those moments a change is threatened in other relationships in the family, including a change to someone else as the focus of attention. Usually the child can provoke people to respond to him in conflicting ways: they are sorry for him and so wish to side with him, but also they are antagonized by him and so wish to side against him. The problem for the therapist is to respond in such a way that what he does is not at the instigation of the child or his response will be conflicting.

If the child does not behave in a provoking way when change is threatened, the parents are likely to turn to him or refer to him at those moments. For example, if mother and father begin to exhibit more open conflict with each other, and so are breaking a rule of the system, one or both of them will choose that moment to say, "Well, if it wasn't for our son's difficulties everything would be all right."

Although therapists usually handle the emphasis upon the child by pointing it out when it occurs, such comments do not usually produce a change. Ways to deal with the problem have by no means been solved. Typically the family therapist will take charge of the situation himself when he sees this sequence occurring. He might use one of several tactics: he can say that something is distressing the child and suggest examining what is being said to see if touching on a sensitive family problem has provoked the misbehavior from the child. Or he might go further and say to the child that it would be helpful in the future if he exhibited some distress whenever the parents are talking about something they are too sensitive about (thus defining the patient explicitly as a thermometer of parental tensions). Or the therapist might stop the conversation and deal with the interruption and return precisely to the point where the conversation left off so the interruption loses its function. Some therapists will define the child's behavior as an attempt to divide the parents, and so encourage them to form a coalition against his provocations, while others will occasionally see the parents without the child so that they are not distracted from sensitive subjects by him.

The behavior of the problem member of a family, usually a child in family therapy, is gross enough to observe a reaction in him when there is a shift in relationships in the family. However, similar reactions occur in father and mother. If father and child threaten a change in their coalition, mother will react in such a way that change is inhibited, and if mother and child are shifting their relationship, the father will respond.

Since the problem of being engineered into coalitions in the family power struggle is central to family therapy, one would expect that the different methods which have developed would focus around this problem. Whether or not therapists deliberately set out to cope with coalitions as part of their method, it would appear they have done so. For example, Bell[8] will begin therapy by seeing the parents alone together, thereby apparently siding with them, and then ask them to remain silent in the next session while he talks with the child about the family. The parents must then sit quietly and listen to the child's side being elicited by a sympathetic therapist. In this way Bell sets up a framework of siding with the parents and within that framework he sides with the child, the ultimate result being an actual coalition with neither faction but with the family as a whole. By using two rooms, Fullweiler[26] prevents the family members pulling him into coalitions because he is not in the room with them to be pulled in. He makes his entrances and exits on his own terms, and confining the family alone in a room emphasizes the family as a problem rather than a particular faction. The use of multiple therapists, as in the Galveston school[42] where not only is each family member given a therapist but they are then exchanged, makes it difficult for family members to engineer coalitions. Other schools using two therapists experience the extent of the family power struggle as the therapists find themselves under pressure to break up their own coalition and side with different family factions.

GOVERNING THE GOVERNORS

If a therapist is going to change the "setting" of a family system, he must become a metagovernor of the system, and the procedures for succeeding in this task have by no means been fully developed. The process of disentangling himself from coalitions and commenting upon how he is being handled as he declines to respond to provocation will help a therapist avoid being governed by the family members. However, the process of change requires more than avoidance behavior by him; he must also do some governing. Yet any direct governing he does will be met by resistance and, in fact, activate the very system he is trying to change. The more the therapist attempts direct reform in a disturbed family, the more likely he is to induce the self-corrective processes in the system and so achieve only greater rigidity. It would appear that to successfully govern the family, as with the individual, the therapist must permit and encourage typical behavior in such a way that the behavior is changed.

There are three major tactics typically used by family therapists. The first is that class of directives to the family which are phrased in such a way that they cannot be resisted because of their ambiguity. For example, if one directs someone by saying, "Put your feet up on that desk," the other person can easily resist if he chooses. However, if someone directs another to "express your feelings," there is no way to avoid following the directive. Whatever the person replies can be taken as an expression of feelings. It is in this aspect of therapy that the ambiguity in psychiatric concepts becomes important, but clearly for tactical reasons. When open conflict has reached a certain point in a family, the therapist is likely to say something like, "Now it's important that we get at the real feelings behind this situation, so let's try to get them expressed." Such a directive is irresistible since even declining it will involve the expression of real feelings. Similarly, a therapist will say, "All right, today let's try to get some understanding of what happened in that crisis over the weekend." Since any crisis is extremely complex and mirrors many aspects of family life, any discussion will be following the directive. Should the family overtly refuse to talk about the weekend and only discuss something else, the therapist is likely to say at the end of the session, "Apparently that crisis was a little too much for you to tolerate discussing at this time, but I think in these other things we're talking about we've really been talking about what happened this weekend." The use of ambiguous terminology involving the language of emotions, the language of meaning, the idea of achieving understanding or reaching each other as well as those ideas about behavior outside of awareness may all be impossible language if one is attempting to achieve scientific rigor in description, but when manipulating a family in such a way they cannot resist, such language is most effective.

A second major tactic in family therapy is the emphasis upon the positive. If a therapist should merely agree with a family that everyone is behaving badly and life is miserable, he is likely to find his therapeutic result confirming such a point of view. Typically the therapist looks for positive aspects in the family's dealings and redefines the negative behavior as positive strivings whenever possible. Such an emphasis upon the positive makes the therapist difficult to oppose. When the therapist asks the family to undergo a painful ordeal, such as a discussion of something they would rather not discuss, he will define this request as having the positive goal of being good for each family member. Faced with such benevolence, the family members find it difficult to resist without appearing recalcitrant malcontents. When the therapist emphasizes that he is siding with the whole family and that he has the good of the whole family in mind whatever he is doing, splinter groups within the family find it difficult to oppose him without appearing selfish and disloyal. The therapist introduces uncertainty into a deadlocked struggle by redefining negative behavior of a family member as an attempt to reach other family members or as misunderstood attempts to be helpful. In one family where father took after mother with an axe and almost caught her, the therapist succeeded in defining the situation as *really* an attempt by father to bring about a closer relationship with his wife and reach her emotionally.

The third major tactic is the one which has been emphasized throughout this work—the encouragement of usual behavior so that resistance can only manifest itself as change. When one conceives of a disturbed family as one where the conflict centers in who is to govern whom, it would follow that a tactic to govern this system would be to step to a higher level by encouraging the family members to continue in their usual ways. Faced with this approach, the family members could only resist by behaving differently. The general permissiveness of family therapists functions in this way, and more active therapists will directly encourage usual behavior. For example, a therapist will, in treating a family in which mother insists upon being the group leader, ask her to take charge in the family, either in general, or in a session, or for a particular task. She can attempt only to govern the therapist when he has directed her in this way by permitting other family members to govern her. (One can observe such a mother's response easily. When she is speaking for the group, if the therapist asks her to speak for the group that day, she expresses immediate reluctance.)

The encouragement of usual behavior is implicit in many of the instructions by therapists about ways to gain understanding. A family therapist will say, "I want you to talk together so we can discover what the problems are." He is asking the family to demonstrate its system and so encouraging usual behavior.

The resistance of families to being governed by a therapist can pro-

vide problems when the identified patient's condition begins to improve
in treatment. If only the child changes, it can be because the therapist
has replaced the child in the family system. Drawing the parental focus
upon himself, the therapist can liberate the child from parental coalition
pressures and so free the child to manifest change and clinical improvement. However, if the therapist then removes himself from the picture
without further resolution of the family conflicts, the child can be
brought back into the position he formerly occupied and so manifest a
relapse. Improvement in the child can also be used tactically by the
other family members in relation to each other. A mother can say that
such improvement indicates that father was always inadequate; if he
had dealt with the family as the therapist has, the family would have
been happier. Similarly, the father can define the successful intrusion
of the therapist as an indication that mother was inadequately mothering the family previously. Therefore improvement in one family member can sometimes provoke further family disturbance. Rather typically
therapists handle this problem by indicating that the improvement is
the result of parental activity or cooperation from the child and not a
result of their own influence. When credit for change is given to family
members, they more willingly accept the change.

In contrast to individual therapy, the problems of the family therapist
are multiplied by the additional relationships he must simultaneously
deal with. His influence on one member can induce repercussions in his
relationships with others. He is also unable to use some of the tactics of
individual therapy. For example, one can control a relationship with a
single patient largely by using silent permissiveness and the patient
must deal with the therapist no matter how frustrating his unresponsiveness might be. A family, however, can ignore a silent therapist and go
about its business of mutual destruction without dealing with the therapist. Silent tactics alone cannot induce change in severely disturbed
families; the therapist must participate. With that participation comes
all the complications which one meets if he steps into the center of a
power struggle.

The interventions of a family therapist are paradoxical in nature and
are, in fact, surprisingly similar to the tactics family members use with
one another. The family therapist who seeks a source for new techniques
will find them in the families he is treating. For example, therapists typically enter and withdraw from the interchange on their own terms, and
so do family members. Family members as well as therapists are often
slippery and ambiguous in their directives, and they often attempt to
form coalitions with opposing factions simultaneously rather than take
a firm position on either side. Just as a therapist declines responsibility

for expertly directing the family, so do parents in disturbed families decline to expertly direct the younger members or each other. Family members as well as therapists will often define what they are doing, particularly when providing ordeals, as having a benevolent and protective purpose. In addition, mothers of disturbed families, and often fathers, are busy being helpful and encouraging the others toward self-understanding, particularly of their faults. The therapeutic tactic of extinguishing resistance by encouraging it is commonly used by some family members. As one mother said when her schizophrenic child had gathered himself together to criticize. her, "You go right ahead and criticize me, dear, I'm perfectly willing to be hurt if it will help you."

The difference between the behavior of the therapist and family members would appear to reside in the outcome. The therapist is protective, but he also permits the family to work out problems independently. He will also encourage usual behavior, but in a framework which makes it difficult to continue it, and when the family members behave differently he accepts the change. Family members can be benevolent and helpful with each other, despite their conflict, but they typically oppose solutions independently arrived at and oppose change when it occurs. The family therapist may be approaching the family in terms of "like cures like," but the outcome is different, particularly in terms of the paradoxes posed. Family members can benevolently provide an ordeal for one another, thereby imposing a paradox, but if the victim attempts to escape from the impossible situation he is condemned for being unwilling to accept the benevolence. The therapist will provide a benevolent ordeal, but when it becomes intolerable and the family changes, the therapist accepts and rewards the change. The detachment of the therapist from the system, which is as necessary as his participation in it, gives him a position where he can function as a temporary intruder in the system and not a permanent element caught up in the resistance to change.

Whether a patient encounters a therapist when alone or when in company with his relatives, he finds himself involved in a relationship which contains multiple therapeutic paradoxes by its very nature, and to deal with these he must undergo change. The types of paradoxes, as they appear in all forms of psychotherapy, will be examined and summarized in the final chapter.

CHAPTER VIII

The Therapeutic Paradoxes

DEPENDING UPON the problem for which he sought relief, a person who changes in psychotherapy will undergo somatic changes, changes in emotional intensity, changes in his ideology or systems of belief, and changes in the ways he behaves in his organized relationships with other people. A variety of procedures have been developed in the last 50 years to bring about such changes in the individual, the married couple, and the family. Yet just how the various methods of psychotherapy "cause" a person to change has remained a mystery.

One causal assumption common to many psychotherapists is the idea that change is brought about by increasing the patient's understanding of himself and his difficulties. Different therapists who share this general point of view will emphasize different types of understanding, but basic in psychiatric tradition is the idea that a person changes as he gains more awareness of what he is doing and why. However, those who hold this view also say that mere understanding is not sufficient; there must be a relationship with a therapist, a working through of resistance to certain ideas, and something often called an emotional integration of the understanding. Besides the disagreement about what kind of understanding is best, many types of psychotherapy—such as the conditioning methods and some styles of hypnotic and directive therapy—do not include encouraging self-understanding at all. It would appear that the "cause" of psychotherapeutic change has not been explained to everyone's satisfaction. There is disagreement between therapists who treat neurotic individuals, and when therapists who treat psychotics, married couples, and whole families enter the discussion, the differences of opinion become even greater.

In this debate about the cause of change there are several possibilities. Perhaps only self-understanding will induce change, perhaps self-understanding as well as some other factor in nonawareness therapy will both induce change, or perhaps some factor which all types of psychotherapy have in common induces change. It has been the contention of this book that the "cause" of change resides in what all methods of therapy have in common—the therapeutic paradoxes which appear in the relationship between psychotherapist and patient.

With the description of psychotherapy recently broadened to include both the behavior of the therapist and the patient, factors which are relevant to change appear which were never evident when the patient

179

alone was described. With only one person in the picture, explanations must be confined to that person. For example, there are a number of people who attempt a self-analysis in the hope that they can bring about changes in themselves. A person might attempt to analyze his dreams and explore in reverie the influence of his childhood upon his present life. At a certain point he can feel relief and say that he has undergone a change. He would naturally believe this change was the result of his new self-understanding, as anyone would who described only him. Yet a more complete description could reveal other relevant factors. It is possible that his announcement of beginning a self-analysis could be described as part of his strategy in dealing with his wife. It is even possible that a fuller description would reveal that he analyzed a dream and discovered the "cause" of certain behavior and so abandoned it and felt relief at the moment his wife refused to put up with that behavior from him. Of course, the matter cannot be quite that simple, but whenever it is said that an increase in self-understanding produced a change it is reasonable to ask what shifts in relationship occurred in the person's life at the time of the change.

When a more full description of psychotherapy is made, one factor which is held in common by all types of psychotherapy is the way the psychotherapist poses paradoxes for the patient. Sometimes these paradoxes are obvious, and sometimes they are difficult to notice if a therapist takes certain procedures so for granted that he does not see the implications of what he is doing. A paradoxical situation is sometimes more apparent if it occurs outside the area of familiarity, and an example can be given here of a procedure for inducing change in Zen Buddhism. A Zen student who wishes to achieve *satori*, or a change in his conception of reality, seeks out a Zen Master. Typically the Master poses paradoxes for the student. These paradoxes can be in the form of *koans*, which are impossible questions, or they can occur more directly in the personal interaction of master and student. For example, a Zen Master will hold a stick over a student's head and say, "If you say this stick is real, I will hit you. If you say it is not real, I will hit you. If you don't say anything, I will hit you." The student is in an "impossible" situation if he attempts to solve it in ways he has previously solved problems. He is caught in a paradox; obviously a stick is either real or it is not real, and yet he can give neither answer. But he must answer or suffer the humiliation of being hit by his teacher.

From the Master's point of view, he has posed a paradox which can force the student to break free of his past ways of conceptualizing reality and meeting situations. The paradox posed the student is this: the master has defined the situation as one where he is going to change the student's conception of reality. Within that framework, the master encourages the student to continue with his conception of reality—his premises that things are either real or not real and one should always do what masters say. Simultaneously, the teacher provides a situation which makes it extremely painful for the student to continue with his usual conception of reality. The student can only resolve the problem by a shift in his classification system; he must discard the premises of the problem or discard his premises about his relationship with the Master which are implicit in the posing of the problem. He might do both by siezing the stick.

From the point of view of certain theories in Western psychiatry, particularly psychoanalysis, the Zen Master is not going about his business properly. If he wishes to induce change in a student, he should encourage the disciple to discuss his conception of reality and his feelings about his life situation. Then the Master should trace the development of the student's conception to the roots in childhood and relate this conception to his unconscious ideas. When the student has become sufficiently aware of the source of his ideas about reality, this self-understanding will permit him to correct himself and become enlightened.

However, if one examines this method of inducing change from the point of view of the *procedures* of Western psychiatry rather than *theory*, there are surprising similarities in the two methods. The Zen Master entraps the student in a paradoxical situation which is essentially the same one which has been traced through the various types of psychotherapy discussed in this book. The psychotherapist (a) sets up a benevolent framework defined as one where change is to take place, (b) he permits or encourages the patient to continue with unchanged behavior, and (c) he provides an ordeal which will continue as long as the patient continues with unchanged behavior.

THE CLASS OF CLASSES

The point of view presented in this work assumes that psychopathology occurs because man is a classifying animal and assumes that change occurs when a person must resolve paradoxes posed in terms of his classification system. Because we can classify the world as real or not real we pose problems of the nature of reality and so make Zen Masters necessary. Similarly, when we classify relationships as dominating or not, humiliating or not, voluntary or not, we are caught up in the classification problems which are central to psychiatric symptoms.

When a man divides the phenomena of the world, including himself, into classes, he faces the formidable problem of keeping different levels of classes straight. The act of classifying can immediately pose problems. To create a class of things means automatically creating another class which are not those things, and men can spend their lives pursuing a not-something, as busy philosophers demonstrate. The man who tries to avoid distress has divided the world into the distressful and the nondistressful. He cannot have one without the other because one class depends for its existence upon the other. Similarly, to postulate goodness is to create badness.

At more complex levels, the creation of a class poses problems about the relationship of a class to its members. What is an item in one class at one level can become the name of that class, or another, at a meta-level. We can find, for example, that a good thing might be done for a bad cause and our classification system on "good" and "bad" begins to be in difficulty. The problem of classification becomes particularly confusing as people communicate their classes to one another. Each message they exchange classifies some other message and is classified by it in turn so that paradox can arise whenever an item in a class also qualifies the class. If a man says, "I am lying," is he telling the truth? His statement is an item in a class of untruths, but it also defines the class so that if he is lying he is telling the truth.

When these classification paradoxes appear in the ways people deal with one another, the human dilemma becomes apparent. The woman who decides that she will not be a dominating woman is caught in a classification problem. The more helpless she becomes to place herself in the class of being nondominating, the more her helpless behavior will dominate others into taking care of her. In the reverse case, a man can decide that he is not dominating enough and so he will set out to dominate others and find himself helplessly dependent upon their cooperation in being dominated. Whenever a person offers to another a class of behavior which is incongruent with a qualifying class of behavior, a paradox is posed; the crusader who insists that everyone should be equal will *dictate* equality and so pose a paradox to everyone he attempts to raise to equal status with himself.

The extraordinary difficulties which men encounter when they attempt to communicate with one another center in the fact that each message communicated will classify and be classified by another message which will in turn classify the other two and so on in infinite regress. When these levels of message are incongruent with one another, confusion and distress must arise in a relationship. Certain areas of human life are most susceptible to classification problems; these are the focus of psychotherapy. Just as the Zen student's concern about problems of reality will be answered by paradoxes posing the nature of reality, so will areas of classification most relevant to psychopathology lead to paradoxes posed in those areas by psychotherapists. A summary is offered here of the paradoxes posed in common by all forms of psychotherapy which have been presented in greater detail in each chapter of this work.

THE VOLUNTARY AND THE COMPULSORY RELATIONSHIPS

Psychotherapy, with certain exceptions, is initially labeled as a voluntary relationship (as is the hypnotic and the master-student relationship in Zen). The patient is advised that he is seeking help of his own free will and the success of the treatment depends upon his willingness to cooperate and continue the relationship despite difficulties which might arise. Within that framework of a voluntary relationship, the therapist indicates that the relationship is compulsory by insisting that a patient not miss appointments and defining his attempts to end treatment as resistance to change. From the patient's point of view, he is being posed a paradoxical definition of the relationship: it is compulsory within a voluntary frame.

Those types of psychotherapy which are not voluntary pose the reverse situation. Certain types of patients, particularly psychotics, are sometimes brought into psychotherapy under duress. This duress labels the relationship as compulsory. Yet the therapist typically indicates that he is only forcing the patient to come to the interviews because the patient really wants to but cannot admit it. Within the compulsory framework, he defines the relationship as really voluntary, if only unconsciously so. At some point in this type of therapy the therapist usually tests the issue by pointing out to the patient that he does not really have to come for the interviews if he does not wish to. Often the patient accepts this voluntary label, and the relationship continues in a voluntary framework with the therapist opposing missed interviews or discontinuance. At other times the patient refuses to come. Then institutional pressure is brought to bear so that he is again brought in under duress until such time as the voluntary nature of the relationship is again tested. Whichever way the framework of the relationship is initially defined, within that framework it is defined as the opposite. This issue continues to be central as the patient is continually faced with it throughout treatment. The resolution of the problem is the end of treatment.

At the other end of the relationship, the patient is always somewhat uncertain whether the therapist is seeing him out of choice or as a paid duty—does he choose to see him or is it compulsory? Usually the therapist defines the relationship as one of the most intimate in human life and therefore the patient should reveal all to this man who is interested in all the details of his personality. Yet simultaneously the therapist indicates that when the interview ends he has no interest in seeing the patient outside the office. The interest and concern of the therapist appears within a framework of a lack of sharing any other aspect of social life together. The patient has difficulty clarifying the interest or disinterest of the therapist and so the voluntary or compulsory nature of the relationship.

If one wished to explore why a man is concerned about whether or not his relationship is compulsory or voluntary, one could do so in the history of the family. A major problem, particularly for psychiatric patients, is whether people associate with them because they wish to or because they must. From infancy to adulthood a human being can be raised in an atmosphere of uncertainty. Did his parents wish to have him or did they not? (This is the relationship birth trauma.) Do they continue to care for him out of choice or because they must? In this area resides the problems of dependency, threats of abandonment, and fears of separation. If the issue becomes a major one, a child might test the definition of the relationship by running away or by creating difficulties to see if his parents really want him. Often such actions confuse rather than clarify the situation. Similarly, parents can wonder if their child chooses to be with them or merely has no place else to go until he is of age. In certain types of family, such as the family with a schizophrenic child, there appears to be excessive concern over the child choosing to associate with people outside the home. The parents will oppose such association, yet if they do and the child remains at home the parents do not feel reassured because they feel he might only be staying with them because they insist. Therefore they often encourage him to associate with people outside the home while opposing his actions if he does.

When a person matures and leaves his family, he can continue to be faced with the same problem when he creates a new family. Is the marital relationship one of choice, or does the marriage continue because of legal sanctions or the presence of children or habit? The distress which centers in this uncertainty, particularly if the spouse simultaneously defines the relationship as both of choice and compulsory, can lead to distress in marriage and ultimately a relationship with a psychotherapist where this issue will be focused upon in that relationship.

THE BLAMED AND UNBLAMED

If a man is blamed for something he can accept the blame or deny it. If he is absolved of blame, he can appreciate it or protest his fault. In psychotherapy, the patient is faced with a relationship in which he is neither blamed nor absolved of blame but yet is presented with both messages simultaneously.

In general, a psychotherapist treats a patient as if the man cannot help behaving as he does. He is assumed to be driven by forces outside of his control and provoked by thoughts and fantasies of which he is unaware. Whatever distress he provides himself or others, it is clearly not his fault. Yet at the same time the framework of psychotherapy is based upon the premise that the patient can help behaving as he does— that is why he is there for treatment. While indicating the patient cannot help himself, the therapist will also make such statements as, "I wonder why you did that at that particular time," or "You must have felt very strongly about the matter to have that reaction," or "Let's try to get some understanding of why you would do such a thing." While absolving the patient of blame, the therapy focuses upon the patient's participation in bringing about his distress. This double level dealing with blame occurs in the ways the therapist handles the resistance of the patient. He cannot help resisting, yet he is expected to overcome the resistance.

The patient's willingness to blame others is also accepted in a paradoxical way. His parents are at fault by their mistreatment of him, and yet they are not at fault because they could not help themselves (they were driven by forces beyond them as he is). In Family Therapy, the blamed and unblamed of parents is particularly apparent. Typically the family therapist tells the parents of the disturbed child that they are not to be blamed for his difficulties. Yet they are also told that if they treat him differently he will not have difficulties.

DOMINATION BY THE UNDOMINATING

When a patient takes his problem to a therapist, he wishes to place himself in the hands of an expert who can and will help him. Yet his basic problem is usually the way he deals with people who try to help him. When he meets the psychotherapist, he faces an expert who takes charge by placing the patient in charge. The therapist assumes the posture of an expert, and within that framework he disinvolves himself from offering expert advice and places the initiative for what is to happen in the hands of the patient.

If one is openly directed by another person, one can deal with him. If one is not directed at all by another, the control problem does not arise. Yet if one's behavior is circumscribed by someone who is indicating he is not circumscribing it, a paradoxical situation has arisen. When a hypnotist tells a subject, "I can only hypnotize you by following your lead because you really hypnotize yourself," and then he proceeds to direct the subject and lead him, the subject is faced with an "impossible" situation and responds by undergoing a change in this behavior and his subjective sensations. This formal pattern of directing while denying direction is typical of psychotherapy. The patient cannot follow direction or refuse to follow it when he is faced with both messages simultaneously. Therefore the methods he has used to provoke direction or oppose it become impotent in the face of this therapeutic paradox.

In nondirective therapy this paradox is most obvious and becomes apparent the moment the patient attempts to control the therapist in his usual ways—by his symptomatic behavior. The therapist will use one or both of two tactics: he will encourage the patient to initiate whatever is to happen and say whatever comes to mind, thereby encouraging the patient to continue behaving in his usual ways. He will also suggest that the symptomatic complaint is not the point and they must deal with what is behind it. If the patient continues with an emphasis upon symptoms, the therapist is permissive. In both directive and nondirective therapy the attempts by the patient to control the therapist by symptomatic behavior are accepted in such a way that they cannot continue. When he is permitted or encouraged to control the therapist, the patient finds that he is being directed by the therapist to direct the therapist and he must abandon this type of behavior.

Should a patient attempt to use improvement or getting worse to gain control of a therapist, he meets the therapist's indication that the source of the change resides within the patient and not in the relationship. Yet this definition of change as "spontaneous" occurs within a framework of the therapist bringing about the change—that is what the patient is paying his money for.

It is in this area that the genius of Sigmund Freud is most evident. Faced with the typical psychiatric patient, Freud was dealing with someone who would resist directives or influence. In his method, Freud emphasized that as little influence as possible should be used with the patient. There should be no advice or directions and no analytic intrusion upon the patient's "spontaneous" behavior and productions. Yet by attempting to influence the patient as little as possible, within the framework of a relationship whose only purpose was to influence a patient, Freud posed the basic paradox of the method.

DEAD SERIOUS PLAY

One of our major tasks when we deal with people is to classify whether they are sincere or not, serious or not, playful or not, or whether they really mean what they say. The structure of psychotherapy is a peculiar mixture of play and dead seriousness. It is a kind of game in which the participants maneuver each other; yet it is defined as the very essence of real life. The interview is said to be a special place with different rules from ordinary life and so the patient can be more self-expressive. Yet within that framework the patient is to respond as one human being to another. In nondirective therapy the patient is asked to be spontaneous and responsive to a man who is unresponsive and unspontaneous; yet the therapist will suggest that the difficulty the patient has dealing with him is relevant to his difficulties in having satisfactory relationships with other people. The patient is taught that he must assume that the therapist will make comments which do not represent his true feelings because he is attempting to get over certain ideas to the patient. Yet at the same time if the patient indicates that the therapist is not sincere with him the therapist will wonder with him what could be the origin of such an idea. The relationship the patient faces is like no other in human life; but within that framework the therapist will "wonder" why the patient does not respond to him in ordinary ways.

THE BENEVOLENT ORDEAL

All forms of psychotherapy are designed to help the unfortunate who cannot help themselves, and so the basic framework of psychotherapy is benevolence. Within that framework, the patient is placed through a punishing ordeal which varies with the type of therapy. In general, he must expose all the sensitive areas of his life to a man who does not return the confidences, just as he must talk about all his inadequacies to a man who apparently has none. In directive therapy he can be asked to go through a specific self-punishing ordeal. In deconditioning therapy he is asked to focus upon the anxieties he has been attempting to avoid. In family therapy, the family must expose the details of their miserable existence to a man who is no doubt a successful family man and father. In the therapy of psychotics, the patient can have imposed upon him the company of a therapist he has not sought, he must be helped in a grim setting, and he might be offered for his benefit the rougher forms of treatment, such as shock treatment and lobotomy.

If a therapist was merely benevolent, the patient could deal with him. If he was merely a man who provides punishing ordeals, the patient could righteously seek the company of someone else. Yet when the therapist benevolently provides a punishing ordeal which will continue until the patient changes, the appropriate response for a patient is to undergo "spontaneous" change. When this change occurs, both therapist and patient can prefer to believe it is the result of the sincerity of their relationship and the greater self-understanding the patient has achieved.

RESISTANCE TO CHANGE

When one suggests that the "cause" of therapeutic change resides in paradoxical strategies within the therapeutic relationship, it is apparent that a new set of premises about the nature of change is being invoked. It is possible to resolve many of the paradoxes which have been discussed in this work, but only if one accepts the premises of this new point of view.

Traditional psychiatric theory has its own inner logic. If a patient is suffering distress, it would seem logical that advice and persuasion to change his way of life would lead to alleviation of that distress. If the patient does not change his way of life when offered such sensible advice and persuasion, it would also logically follow that he cannot because he is driven by internal forces which incapacitate his attempts at change. These forces might be phrased in terms of unconscious drives or repressed ideas or they might be placed in terms of past conditioning, depending upon one's theoretical orientation. But such explanations would seem to have been derived from the observation that patients resist changes which are in their best interests.

Today it appears that the logic of traditional psychiatric theory is dependent upon the focus being only upon the individual. With a shift of emphasis from the individual to his relationships, it becomes equally logical to explain the patient's resistance to change as a product of the network of ongoing relationships in which he is embedded, including the relationship with a therapist. This point of view, too, has a logic of its own, and from this viewpoint self-understanding is less relevant as an explanation of change than are paradoxical strategies.

When we shift from the focus upon the individual to the study of ongoing relationships, we note at least two kinds of patterns: those patterns which are confined to certain types of relationships, and those abstract patterns which appear to be inevitable by the very nature of forming and maintaining relationships. An example of the first kind is the difference between, say, a therapeutic relationship and a friendship. Presumably a friendship is a kind of relationship which will continue to remain the same. A therapeutic relationship is constructed upon the assumption that it will change: the patient seeking help from a helper will change to a person in an equal relationship with the other. In this sense the relationship begins as a complementary one with a built-in assumption that it will change toward symmetry. Questions about the nature of therapeutic change are imbedded in the nature of this shift in type of relationship.

It is at the abstract level of patterns which appear no matter what the type of relationship that we find a resolution, or explanation, of many of the paradoxes which have been described as existing in therapeutic relationships. It would appear possible that relationships are formed, perpetuated, and changed according to laws or rules over which the individual in the relationship has little or no control. The possibility of such laws would only become apparent with the study of ongoing relationships because they would be obscured with a focus upon the individual or the artificial group of unrelated people. One law which is pertinent to the question of paradox in psychotherapy can be stated in terms of its derivation.

Implicit in the point of view throughout this work has been the assumption that ongoing relationships between intimates can be described in terms of a cybernetic analogy—people function as "governors" in relation to each other by reacting in "error-activated" ways to each other's behavior. If a wife begins to exceed a certain range of behavior, her husband reacts in such a way as to re-establish the previous range of behavior. Granting that people in ongoing relationships function as "governors" in relation to one another, and granting that it is the function of a governor to diminish change, then the first law of relationships[32] follows: *When one person indicates a change in relation to another, the other will act upon the first so as to diminish and modify that change.* Granting the functioning of this law, a therapist must *avoid* making direct requests for change and bring change about while emphasizing some other aspect of the interchange, such as the gaining of self understanding. Yet by not asking for change, the therapist will have set up a paradoxical situation: in a framework designed to bring about change, he does not ask for change. It would also follow that a reasonable therapeutic tactic would be the encouragement of symptomatic behavior. When the therapist encourages an increase in symptomatic behavior, and the patient responds so as to diminish the change he is requesting, the patient will be moving in the direction of symptomatic change.

Postulating such a law in human relations explains many aspects of psychotherapy which are peculiar and paradoxical in nature. If people must follow such a law just as inevitably as they must follow the law of gravity, then relationships between couples and family members will be exceedingly stable. Each attempt by a family member to bring about change in the system will provoke the others to act to diminish that change and so reinforce the family system (even though a change might lead to less subjective distress in the members). Similarly, when a therapist establishes a helping relationship with a patient, if he then directly indicates that the relationship must change toward a relationship between equals, the patient must act to diminish that change. This does not mean that change is not possible, it merely means that resistance to change, because of the nature of relationships, must be taken into account and paradoxical strategies must be used to provide a context where change can occur.

Although the context of therapeutic change can be described, the nature of the change remains obscure. If one assumes that self-awareness causes change, then one can describe the changed patient easily—he is someone who is more self aware. Yet if the cause of change is a situation which forces a patient to respond differently, his after-change state is less easily described except to say that he responds differently, no longer exhibits symptomatic behavior, and relates to people in changed ways. The question of the nature of change and how it can be brought about has wider implications than the problems of psychiatry. One can assume that change in individuals will be better understood when we know more about the nature of revolutionary changes in societies. The patterns of organization learned by people in their families appear to reflect and influence the political structures of the culture they inhabit. Whether the formal patterns of a nation have changed after a revolutionary upheaval is a question related to the shifts in patterns of individuals and families after psychotherapy.

The change which occurs in psychotherapy would seem to be discontinuous; although a patient may improve gradually, he appears to change in discontinuous steps. At one moment he is in distress and in the next he feels relief. Typically he suddenly feels more casual about aspects of his life which were grimly serious to him. Often his involvement with the therapist changes from a tenacious struggle to one where he does not particularly care. The grim battle with intimates can shift to an attitude of amusement at the whole affair. An excessive concern with symptoms typically becomes a lack of interest in them and the development of other interests. Usually the patient shows a greater flexibility in his strategies with other people. Presumably the shifts in his organized relationships have induced a shift in his classification system.

The description of the context in which a patient changes has been broadened here to include the relationship with the therapist. If one describes only the patient, change can be described only in terms of what that person does. Enlarging the description reveals a therapist not only helping a patient toward self-understanding but also trapping him in a series of paradoxes which enforce a change. An even broader description might reveal additional causal factors which are not yet apparent. The influence of marriage and the family has been suggested here, but the environmental context which impels a patient into psychotherapy has not been fully described. Explanations of psychotherapeutic change might appear quite different when we have delineated the basic laws of human relationships and can describe the organized social systems in the society which produces people who want to change and people who want to change them.

In this work an attempt has been made to describe more precisely the strategies used in psychotherapy. Inevitably in such a presentation there is an oversimplification both of the nature of the problems and the techniques used to resolve them. Even if human beings were less complex and we could provide more exact procedures for a therapist to use with a particular patient, still the success of the process must depend upon many factors which cannot be taken into account and ultimately upon the individual therapist himself. The profession of psychotherapy is unique in that the therapist has only himself as the tool with which he works. He can bolster his position with office, desk, couch, theories and the counsel of his colleagues, but when alone with a patient he has only his voice, his manner, and his ideas. Whatever might be said about method, psychotherapy will remain an art.

REFERENCES

1. Ackerman, N.W.: *The Psychodynamics of Family Life.* New York, Basic Books, 1958.
2. Alanen, Y.: The mothers of schizophrenic patients. *Act. Psychiat. et Neurol. Scandinav.,* 33: suppl. 124, 1958.
3. Alexander, F.: *Psychoanalysis and Psychotherapy.* New York, Norton, 1956.
4. Bateson, G., and Ruesch, J.: *Communication: The Social Matrix of Psychiatry.* New York, Norton, 1951.
5. —, Jackson, D. D., Haley, J., and Weakland, J. H.: Toward a theory of schizophrenia. *Behav. Sc.,* 1: 251–264, 1956.
6. —, —, —, and —: A note on the double bind—1962. *Fam. Proc.,* 2: 154–161, 1963.
7. —: *Naven.* 2nd ed. with a new chapt. Stanford Univ. Press, 1958.
8. Bell, J. E.: *Family Group Therapy.* Pub. Health Mon. 64, U.S. Dept. Health Educ. Welfare, 1961.
9. Bernheim, H.: *Suggestive Therapeutics: A Treatise on the Nature and Use of Hypnotism.* New York and London, G. Putnam and the Knickerbocker Press, 1895.
10. Bowen, M.: Family psychotherapy. *Am. J. Orthopsychiat.,* 31: 40–60, 1961.
10a. Colby, K. M.: *A Primer for Psychotherapists.* New York, Ronald Press, 1951.
11. Cowles, E. S.: *The Conquest of Fatigue and Fear.* New York, Henry Holt, 1954.
12. Erickson, M. H.: A clinical note on indirect hypnotic therapy. *J. Clin. & Exper. Hyp.,* 2:171–174, 1954.
13. —: Special techniques of brief hypnotherapy. *J. Clin & Exper. Hyp.,* 2: 109–129, 1954.
14. —: Naturalistic techniques of hypnosis. *Am. J. Clin. Hyp.,* 1:3–8, 1958.
15. —, and Erickson, E. M.: Further considerations of time distortion: subjective time condensation as district from time expansion. *Am. J. Clin. Hyp.,* 1:83–88, 1958.
16. —: Further clinical techniques of hypnosis: utilization techniques. *Am. J. Clin. Hyp.,* 1:3–21, 1959.
17. —: The identification of a secure reality. *Fam. Proc.,* 1:294–303, 1962.
18. Ferenczi, S.: *Sex in Psychoanalysis.* New York, Robert Brunner, 1950.
19. Ferreira, A. J.: Psychotherapy with severely regressed schizophrenics. *Psychiat. Quart.,* 33:663–682, 1959.
19a. Frank, J. D.: *Persuasion and Healing.* Baltimore, Johns Hopkins Press, 1961.
20. Frankl, V.: Paradoxical intention: a logotherapeutic technique. *Am. J. Psychother.,* 14:520–535, 1960.
21. Friedman, A. S.: Family therapy as conducted in the home. *Fam. Proc.,* 1:132–140, 1962.
22. Freud, S.: *Collected Works,* Vol. 5. London, Hogarth, 1950.
23. —: *Inhibitions, Symptoms and Anxiety.* London, Hogarth, 1948.
24. Fromm-Reichmann, F.: *Principles of Intensive Psychotherapy.* Chicago, Univ. of Chicago Press, 1953.
25. Fry, W. F.: The marital context of an anxiety syndrome. *Fam. Proc.,* 1:235–252, 1962.
26. Fulweiler, C.: Personal communication.
27. Gerz, H. O.: The treatment of the phobic and the obsessive-compulsive patient using paradoxical intention sec. Viktor E. Frankl. *J. Neruopsychiat.,* 3:375–387, 1962.
28. Gill, M., and Brenman, M.: *Hypnosis and Related States: Psychoanalytic Studies in Regression.* New York, Int. Univ. Press, 1959.

28a. Goffman, E.: *Asylums*. New York, Doubleday, 1961.

29. Haley, J.: Paradoxes in play, fantasy and psychotherapy. *Psychiat. Res. Rep.*, 2:52–58, 1955.

30. —: The family of the schizophrenic: a model system. *Am. J. Nerv. & Ment. Dis.*, 129:357–374, 1959.

31. —: Wither family therapy? *Fam. Proc.*, 1:69–100, 1962.

32. —: Family experiments: a new type of experimentation. *Fam. Proc.*, 1:265–293, 1962

33. Jackson, D. D.: Countertransference and psychotherapy. In F. Fromm-Reichmann and J. L. Moreno (Eds.) *Progress in Psychotherapy*, Vol. 1. New York, Grune & Stratton, 1956, pp. 234–238.

34. —: The question of family homeostasis. *Psychiat. Quart. Suppl.*, 31:79–90, Part 1, 1957.

35. —: Family interaction, family homeostasis and some implications for conjoint family psychotherapy. In J. Masserman (Ed.) *Individual and Familial Dynamics*. New York, Grune & Stratton, 1959.

36. — (Ed.): *The Etiology of Schizophrenia*. New York, Basic Books, 1960.

37. —: The monad, the dyad, and the family therapy of schizophrenics. In A. Burton (Ed.) *Psychotherapy of the Psychoses*. New York, Basic Books, 1961.

38. —, and Satir, V.: Family diagnosis and family therapy. In N. Ackerman, F. Beatman and S. Sherman (Eds.) *Exploring the Base for Family Therapy*. New York, Family Service Assoc., 1961.

39. —, and Weakland. J. H.: Conjoint family therapy, some considerations on theory, technique, and results. *Psychiatry*, 24:30–45, 1961.

40. —, and Haley, J.: Transference revisited. *Am. J. Nerv. Ment. Dis.* In press.

41. Lindner, R.: *The Fifty Minute Hour*. New York, Rinehart, 1955.

42. MacGregor, R.: Multiple impact psychotherapy with families. *Fam. Proc.*, 1:15–29, 1962.

43. Masserman, J. H.: *The Principles of Dynamic Psychiatry*. Philadelphia, W. B. Saunders, 1955.

44. Menninger, K.: *Theory of Psychoanalytic Technique*. New York, Basic Books, 1958.

45. Noshpitz, J. D.: Opening phase in the psychotherapy of adolescents with character disorders. *Bull. Men. Clin.*, 21:154–164, 1957.

46. Rank, O.: *Beyond Psychology*. Published privately by friends and students of the author, 1941.

47. Rogers, C. R.: *Client-Centered Therapy*. Boston, Houghton Mifflin, 1951.

48. Rosen, J. N.: *Direct Analysis*. New York, Grune & Stratton, 1951.

49. —: Personal communication.

50. Scheflen, A. E.: *A Psychotherapy of Schizophrenia: Direct Analysis*. Springfield, Ill., Charles C Thomas, 1961.

51. Sullivan, H. S.: *Conceptions of Modern Psychiatry*. William Alanson White Psychiatric Fnd., 1947, p. 91.

52. Szasz, T. S.: *The Myth of Mental Illness, Foundation of a Theory of Personal Conduct*. New York, Hoeber-Harper, 1961.

53. Von Neuman, J., and Morgenstern, O.: *Theory of Games and Economic Behavior*. Princeton Univ. Press, 1944.

54. Watts, A. W.: *Psychotherapy East and West*. New York, Pantheon, 1961.

55. Weakland, J. H., and Jackson, D. D.: Patient and therapist observations on the circumstances of a schizophrenic episode. *Arch. Neural. & Psychiat.*, 79:554–574, 1958.

56. —, and Fry, W. F.: Letters of mothers of schizophrenics. Am. J. Orthopsychiat., 32:604–623, 1962.
57. Whitehead, A. N., and Russell, B.: *Principia Mathematica*. Cambridge Univ. Press, 1910.
58. Wittgenstein, L.: *Tractatus Logico-Philosophicus*. Routledge, London, 1960.
59. Wolberg, L. R.: *Medical Hypnosis*. New York, Grune & Stratton, 1948.
60. Wolpe, J.: *Psychotherapy by Reciprocal Inhibition*. Stanford Univ. Press, 1958.